DRAW
AMAZING
FACES

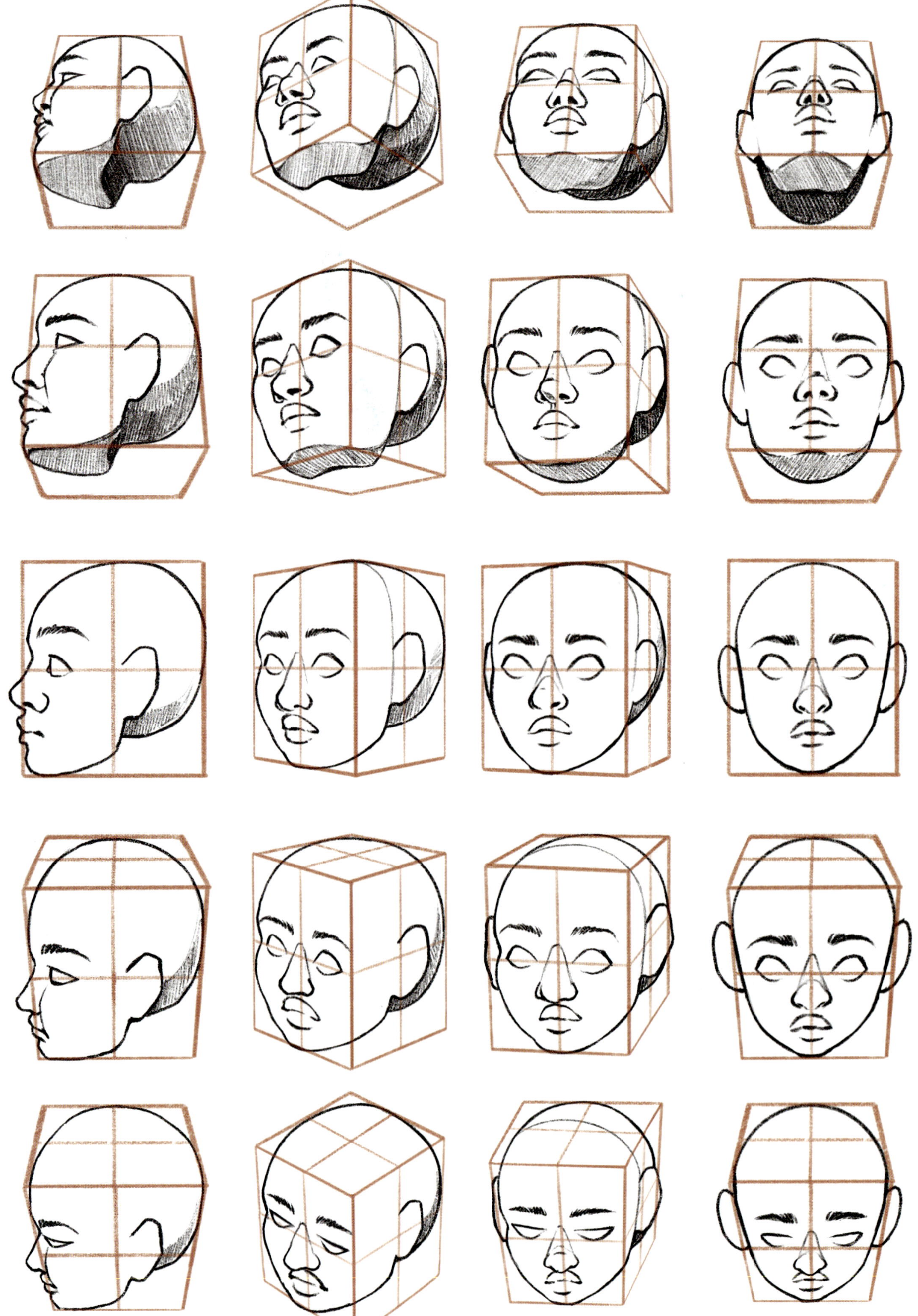

DRAW AMAZING FACES

LEARN THE BASICS AND DEVELOP YOUR OWN STYLE

PYPAH SANTOS

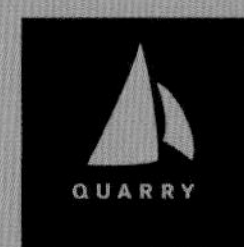

Quarto.com

© 2024 Quarto Publishing Group USA Inc.
Text, Photos, Illustrations © 2024 Pypah Santos, except photographs on pages
16–18, 24, 46–49, 60–61, 70–71, 84, 86, 112, 130, 133 © Shutterstock.

First Published in 2024 by Quarry Books,
an imprint of The Quarto Group,
100 Cummings Center, Suite 265-D, Beverly, MA 01915, USA.
T (978) 282-9590 F (978) 283-2742

EEA Representation, WTS Tax d.o.o.,
Žanova ulica 3, 4000 Kranj, Slovenia.
www.wts-tax.si

Quarry Books titles are also available at discount for retail, wholesale, promotional, and bulk
purchase. For details, contact the Special Sales Manager by email at specialsales@quarto.com
or by mail at The Quarto Group, Attn: Special Sales Manager, 100 Cummings Center, Suite 265-D,
Beverly, MA 01915, USA.

10 9 8 7 6 5

ISBN: 978-0-7603-8921-8

Digital edition published in 2024
eISBN: 978-0-7603-8922-5

Library of Congress Cataloging-in-Publication Data

Names: Santos, Pypah, 1998- author.
Title: Draw amazing faces : learn the basics and develop your own style /
    Pypah Santos.
Description: Beverly, MA : Quarry Books, 2024. | Includes index.
Identifiers: LCCN 2024019657 (print) | LCCN 2024019658 (ebook) | ISBN
    9780760389218 (trade paperback) | ISBN 9780760389225 (ebook)
Subjects: LCSH: Face in art. | Drawing--Technique.
Classification: LCC NC770 .S26 2024 (print) | LCC NC770 (ebook) | DDC
    743.4/2--dc23/eng/20240523
LC record available at https://lccn.loc.gov/2024019657
LC ebook record available at https://lccn.loc.gov/2024019658

Design: Megan Jones Design

Printed in Guangdong, China TT112025

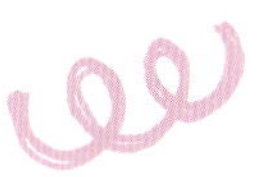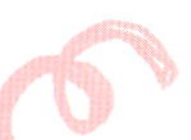

ACKNOWLEDGMENTS

Every artist has a reason why they create—because it's fun, because it's an escape, because it helps them process feelings, or maybe because it fuels them. Art, for me, has been a lifeline on many occasions and continues to be my oldest company and best friend. So first, I wanted to dedicate this book to my relationship with art and creativity for always being there in my best and worst moments.

To my family, who saw my love for creating as just a little artist, nurturing that passion and allowing it to blossom.

To my partner, who has been an incredibly supporting pillar in my life and who is my cheering squad through all my projects and creative endeavors.

To the Quarto team, who took an interest in an artist in a sea of creatives and gave her the opportunity of publishing her first book.

To everyone over the years who has supported me and my art, allowing me to continue creating for a living.

And of course to you, wonderful reader, for finding your way to this book and giving yourself the space to be creative and explore your love for drawing. I hope the advice and teachings of this book give you the guidance to fall in love with portraiture in the same way I did.

CONTENTS

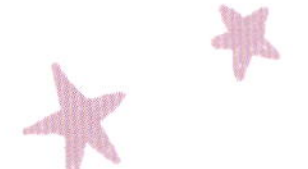

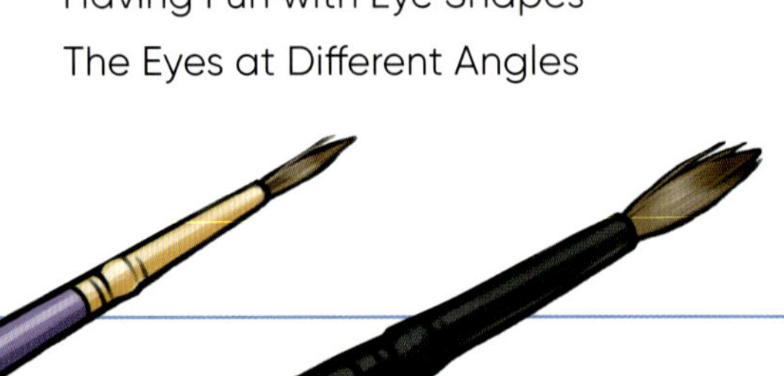

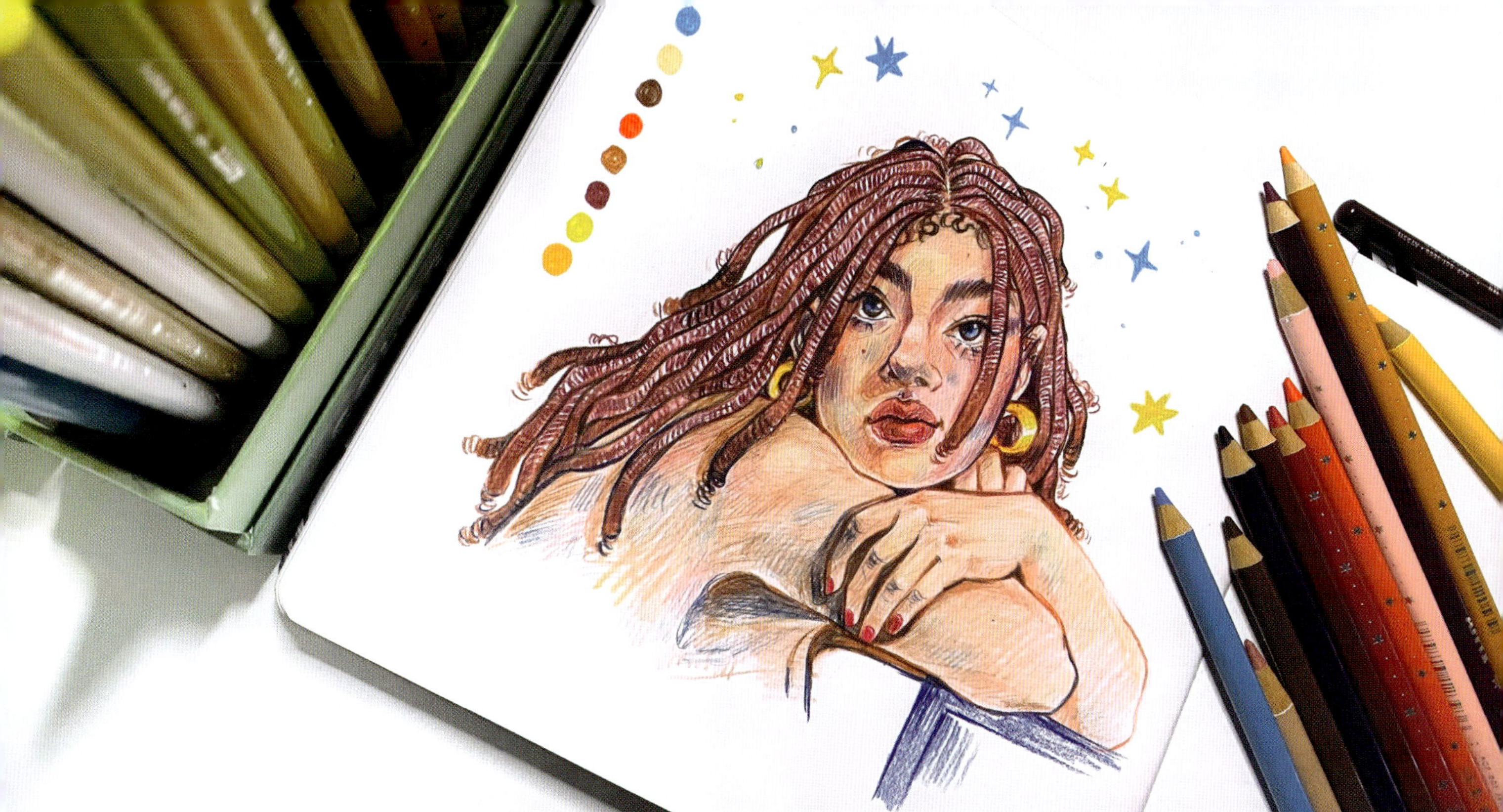

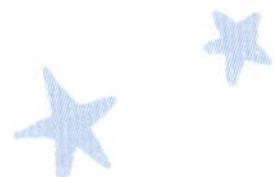
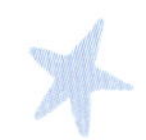

INTRODUCTION

Hello and welcome! I'm so glad you picked out this book and are on your way to learning more about drawing and improving your skills!

My name is Filipa "Pypah" Santos, and I am a Portuguese artist currently living in the UK. I grew up in Porto, Portugal, surrounded by the sea and delicious food! I then moved to England to study art and stuck around ever since. I actually studied animation at university, as I had a passion for illustration and animated films, and it seemed like animation would be the better career for me. But after doing freelance animation for a few years, I decided to finally go back to my true love—illustration.

I was always a quiet, creative child and could be kept busy for hours on end as long as I had some paper and pencils. I kept drawing and exploring my creative side my whole childhood and ended up taking my art into my adulthood, where I started my own small business as Pypah's Art: selling my artworks online, making content about my creations, and freelancing wherever I could.

I never expected much to come of it, but I always knew that art is what I was going to do for the rest of my life. The best part about it is that art is such a huge umbrella I doubt I will ever run out of new things to explore, mediums to try out, and art forms to marvel at.

During my early days of after-school art classes, one of the first things I was taught to draw was faces. I was asked to draw a bust of a Roman emperor over and over again, learning something new from every single drawing. And over time, I was able to draw a photorealistic portrait of this emperor. My teacher at the time taught me all the traditional mediums and techniques that I have been using ever since:

painting, pencil drawing, sculpture portraiture, etc. I learned so much from him. It's for this reason that I've always had a passion to help others improve their skills and feel comfortable enough with making mistakes in art in order to keep improving, and most importantly, to keep having fun with it.

This book is a hugely important project to me, as it's a culmination of all the love I have for art and drawing portraits and passing on all the advice and tips I've learned over the years. Hopefully this book deepens your love and passion for creating art as it did for me making it.

Love,

Pypah

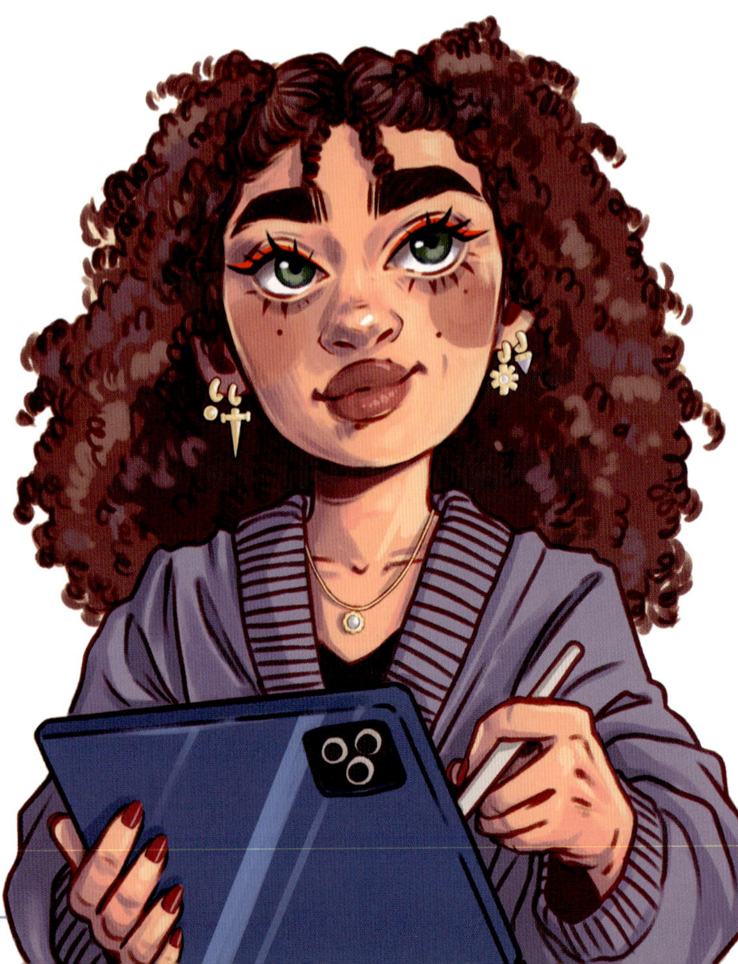

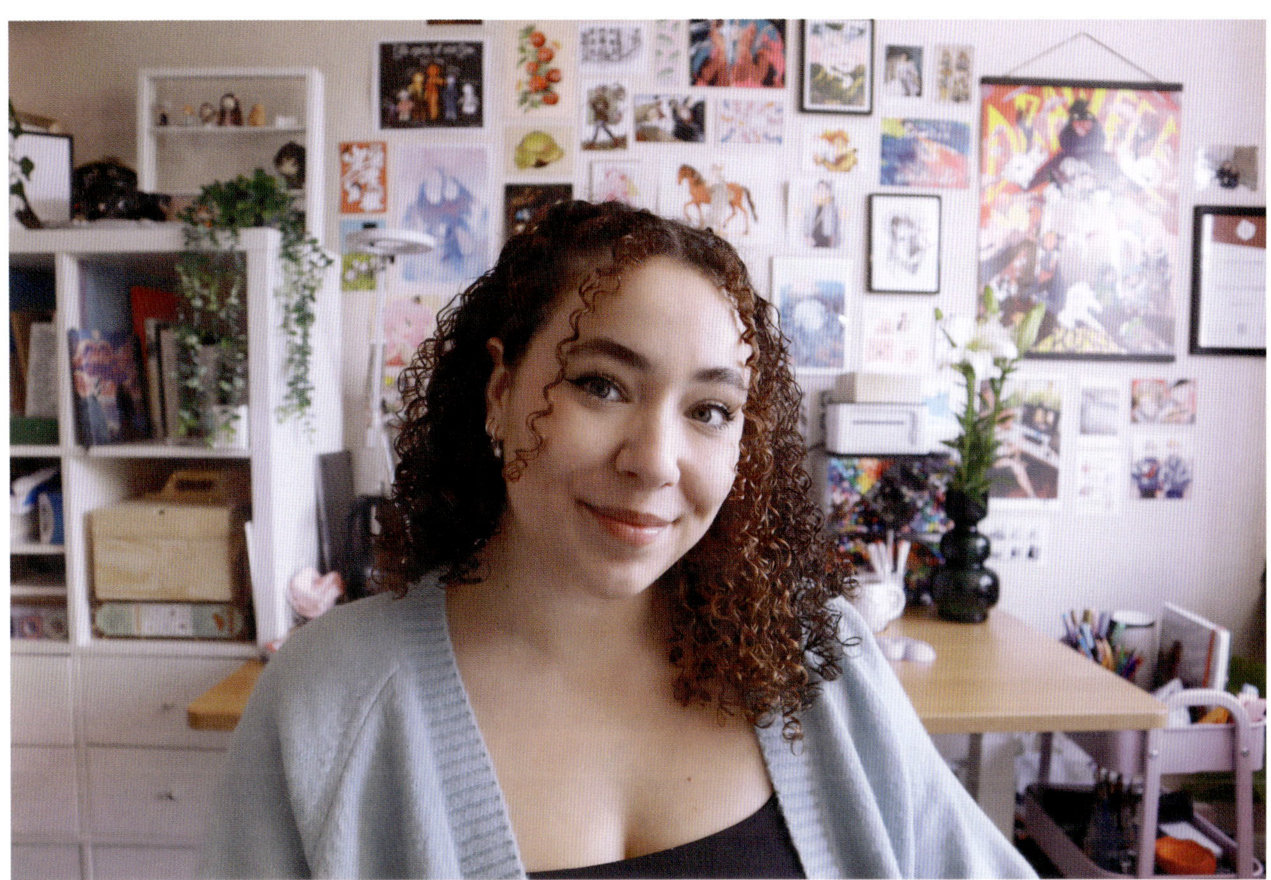

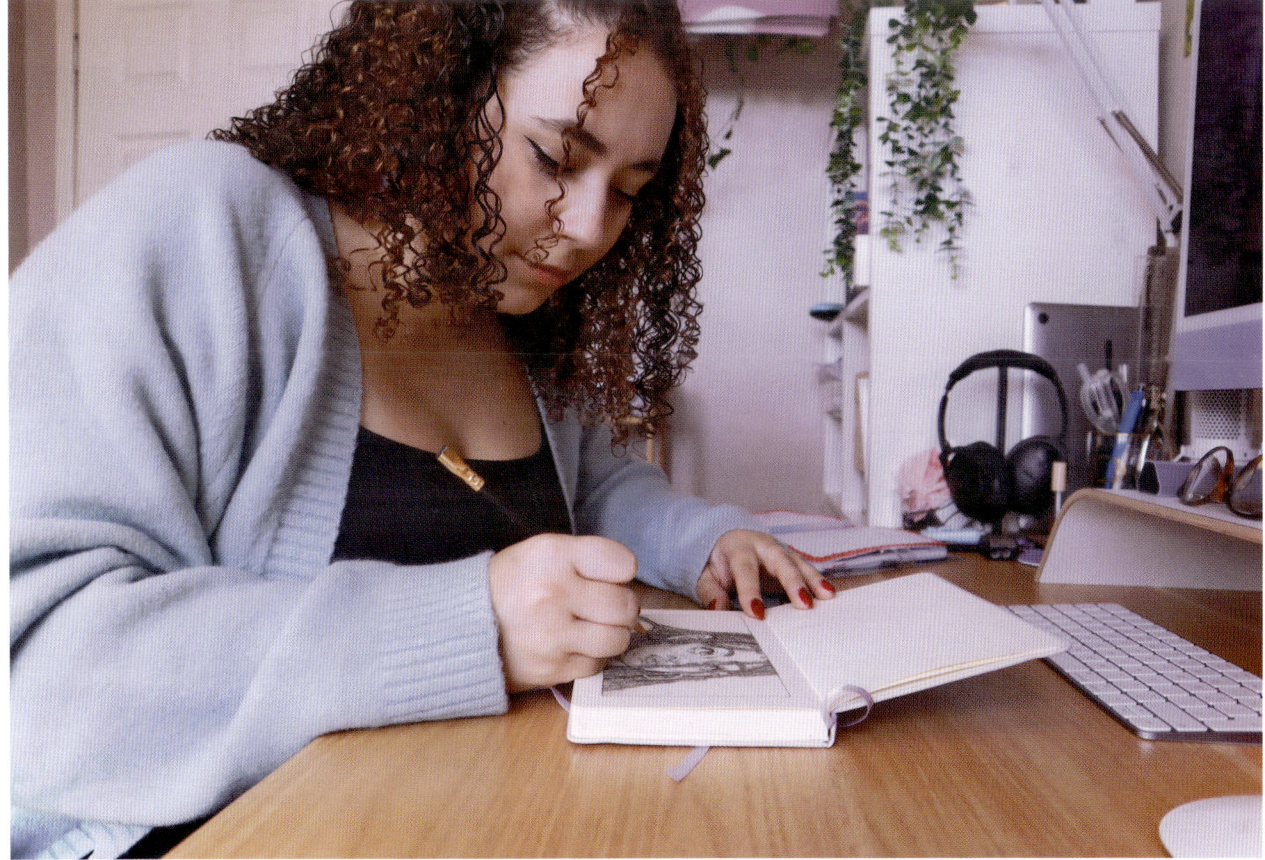

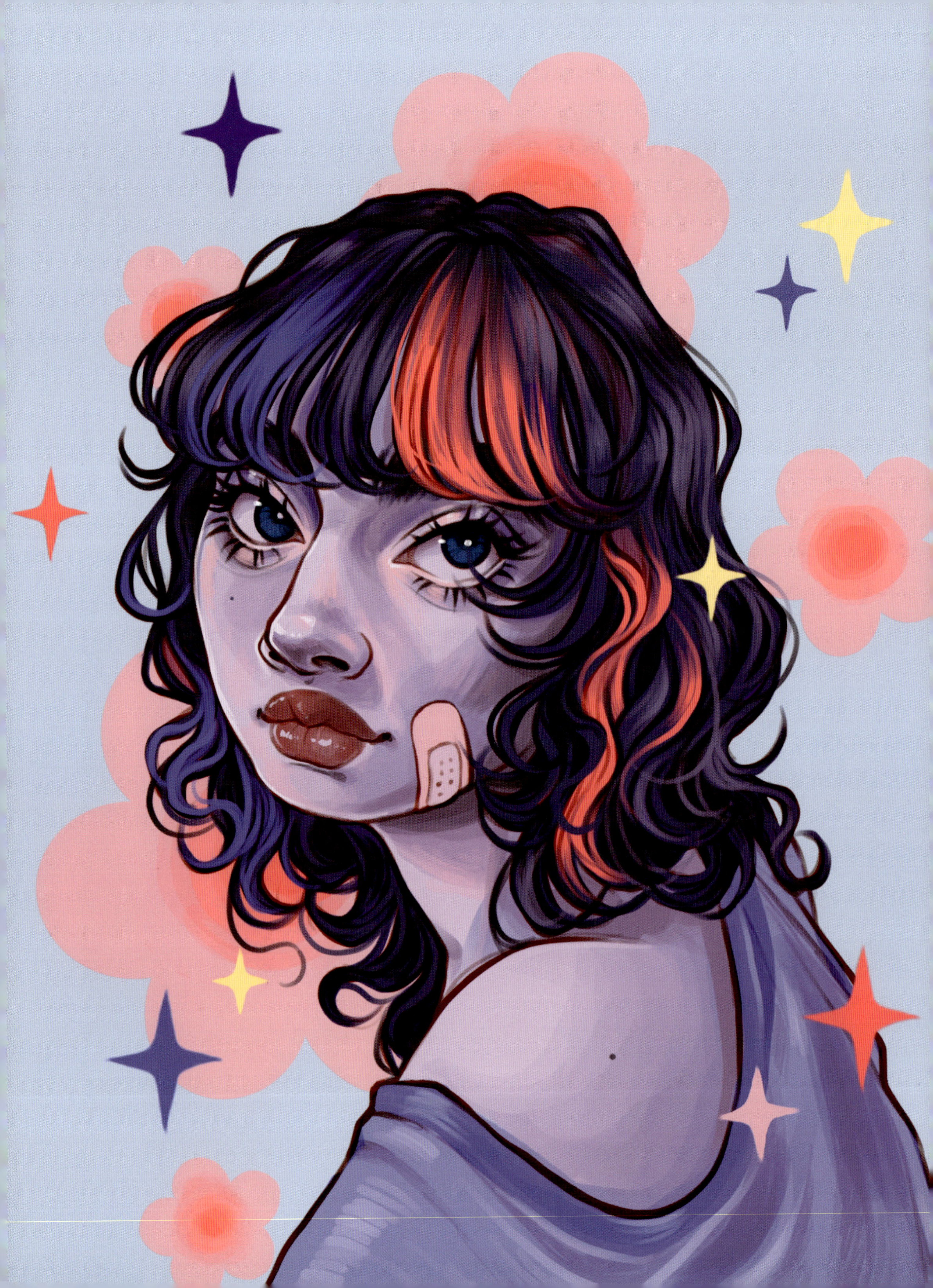

1

THE APPROACH

To me, drawing faces feels like completing a puzzle. It's up to everyone where they choose to start, but at the end of the day, once all the pieces are in the correct place, you get to take a look back and see an amazing face that you yourself have just created. It's an incredible feeling.

Although drawing faces feels like completing a puzzle, it doesn't have to be puzzling. I have been drawing faces and portraits for over a decade almost every single day and have picked up a few cool tips and tricks that will hopefully make it easier for anyone to learn how to draw them.

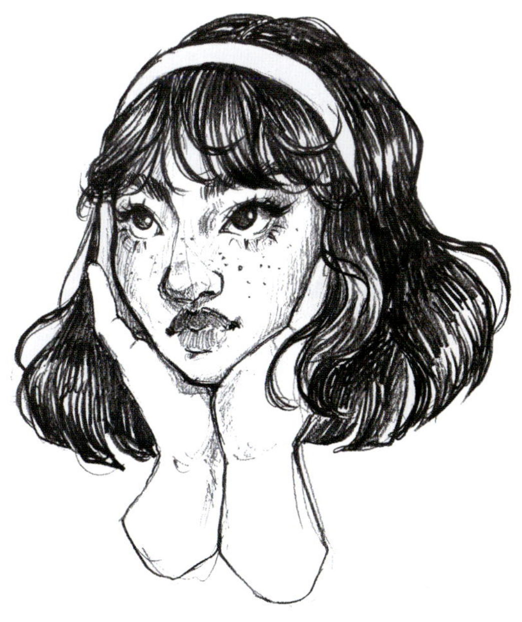

MY FAVORITE MATERIALS

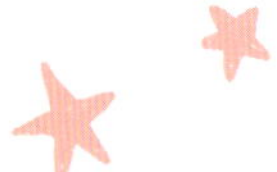

I'm of the school of thought that you don't need a bunch of fancy materials and supplies to create amazing art. Of course, good supplies can help, but they're merely tools to aid your creativity.

I love carrying around a sketchbook and a pencil case with all my essentials and favorite art supplies. I have been testing out all kinds of art materials, mediums, and supplies over the years and have found the items that work best for me and my workflow when creating art.

I like to make sure I have easy-to-use supplies so there is less fuss when using them and I can get right to creating—but there is also something so special about getting your first fancy set of colored pencils that will accompany you for years to come!

So even though it's a lot of fun to experiment with new art supplies (and shop for them), I'd like to keep things simple and show you some beginner-friendly supplies I recommend if you're getting into drawing.

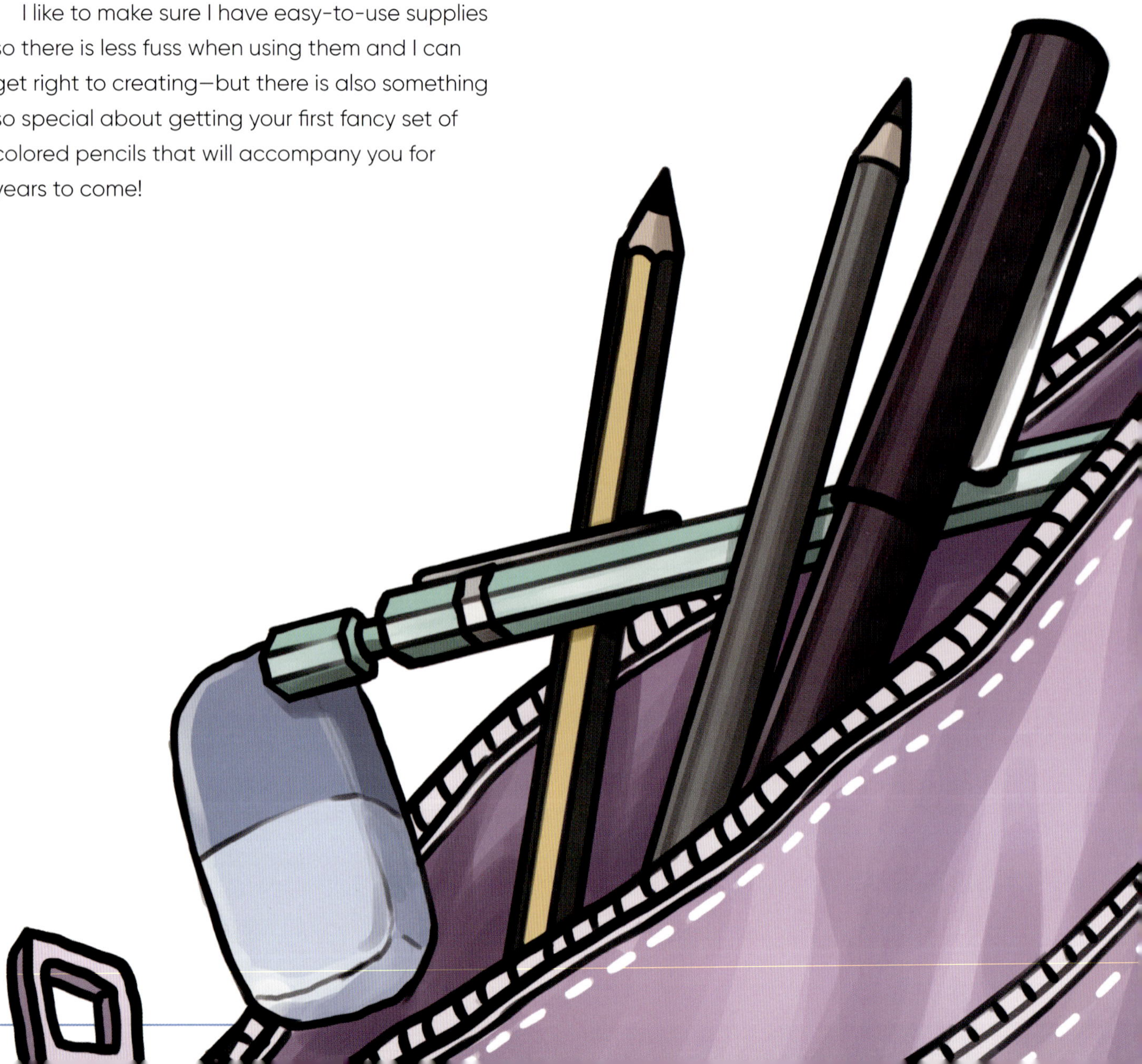

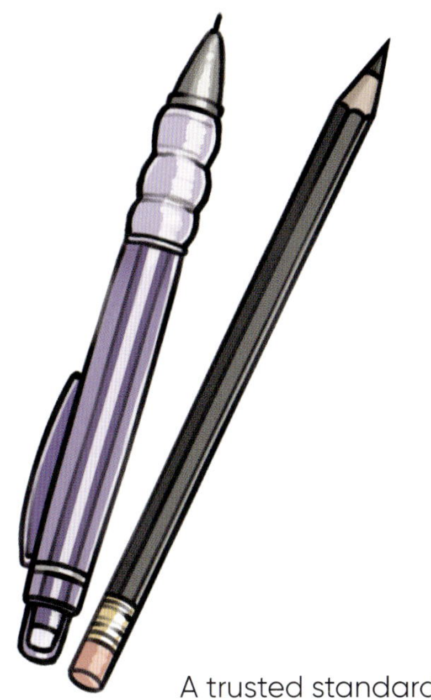

For starters, you'll need a pencil. A standard 2B pencil like the ones used in school is perfect for the job! A mechanical pencil is nice to have too, since you don't have to sharpen the lead.

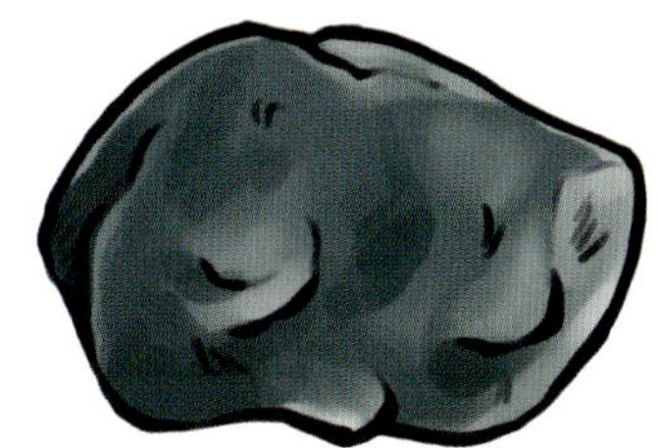

I recommend beginners try using a gummy "kneaded" eraser. It's a soft, doughlike putty that lifts graphite off the paper, allowing you to erase areas lightly. It's also a great way to add highlights to your drawings.

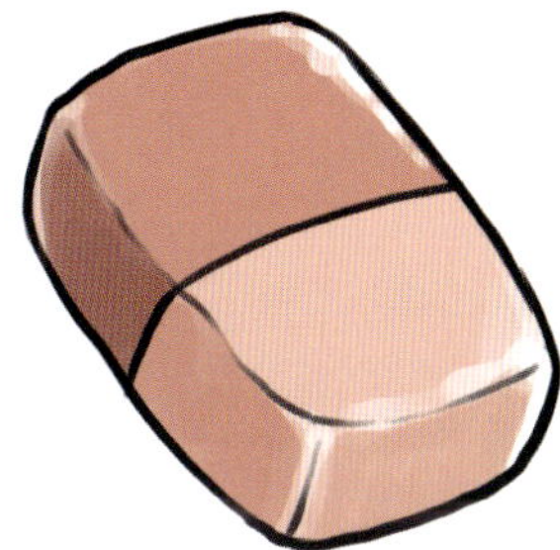

A trusted standard eraser is a must-have. (Making mistakes is super important if you want to improve!)

You might also need a standard pencil sharpener to keep your pencils sharp.

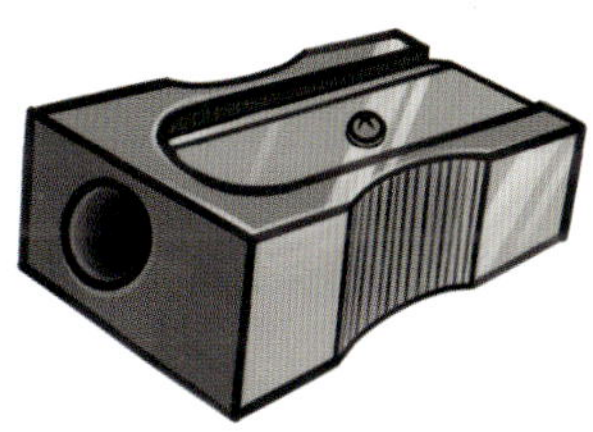

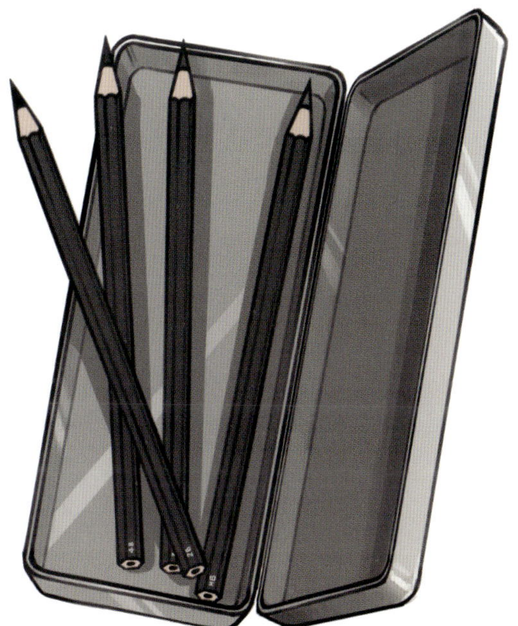

You can buy a set of drawing pencils to take your drawings to the next level. Having pencils with darker and lighter lead will help you to easily add shadows and different tones to your drawings.

Of course you'll need some paper to draw on. A pad of drawing paper is ideal, and a sketchbook is recommended to continue your practice even after you finish this book.

LET'S BREAK IT DOWN

It can be daunting to look at other people's art and see a fully rendered drawing, which is why I always like to share process videos and artwork breakdowns to show that with every drawing comes a process. Most of my drawings of faces start off as a simple collection of circles and lines. Without these basic structures, I wouldn't know where to place things or how big or small to make them.

In this book we will study the structure behind a face, each feature individually, proportions, and more. We will take things nice and slow, so before you know it, you'll be drawing a fully realized portrait.

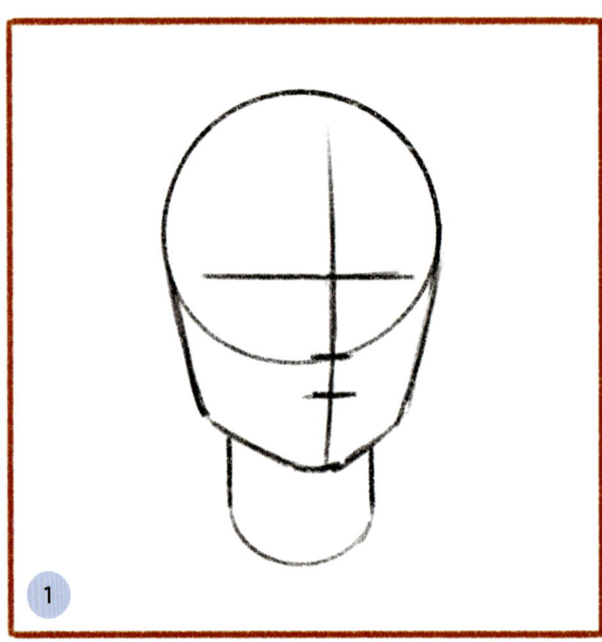

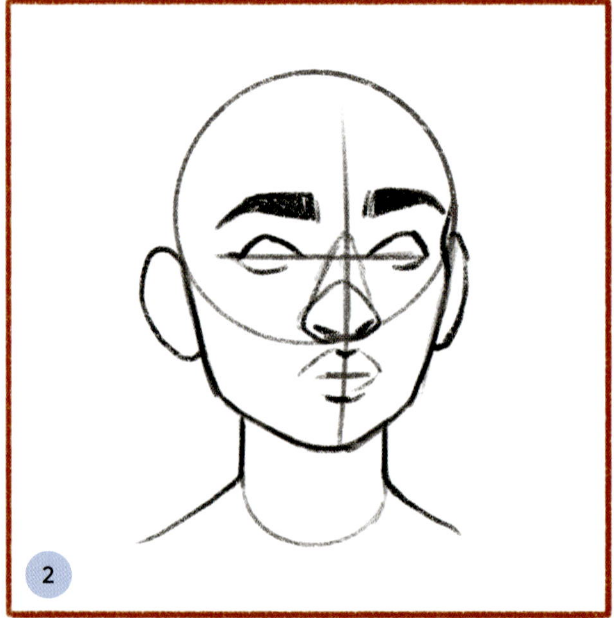

STEP 1. BASIC STRUCTURE

You should always start a drawing by blocking out the basic shapes. You need a head to put your face on, after all. These will be circles, lines, squares, and triangles—all very basic shapes you already know. Then you can add your guidelines for the proportions of the face. These will help you accurately place the facial features.

STEP 2. FACIAL FEATURES

Naturally, you can then place the facial features on the head using those guidelines. You can also play around with expressions and perspective to add emotion.

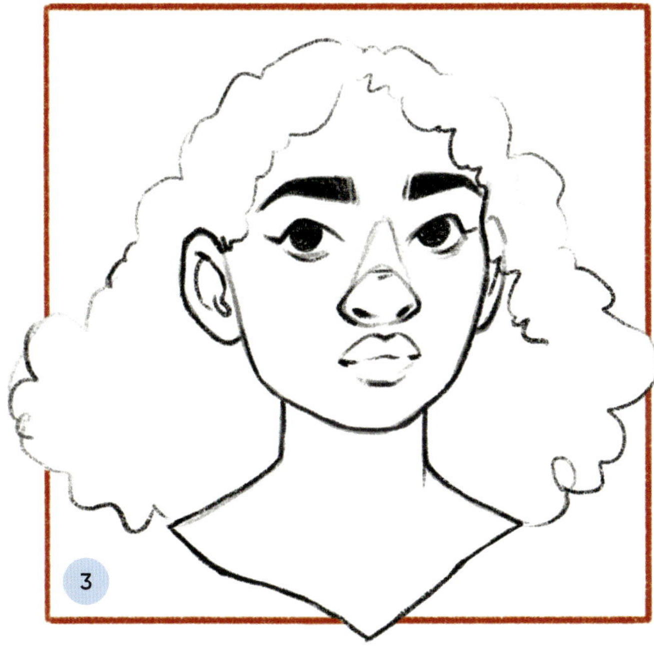

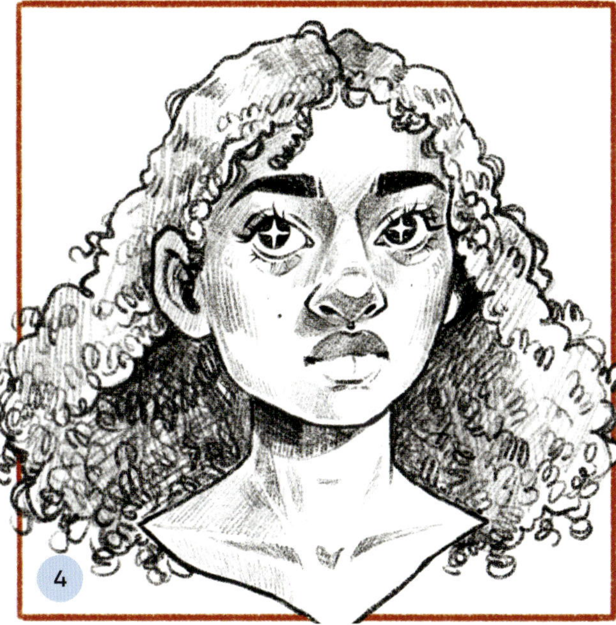

STEP 3. SKETCHING

After you sketch the basic facial features onto your face, you can start cleaning up what is now your sketch.

STEP 4. RENDERING

Finally you can start adding in more details to give your face some personality and even add shadows and highlights! You can really take this step as far as you want, adding your own flare to your portrait.

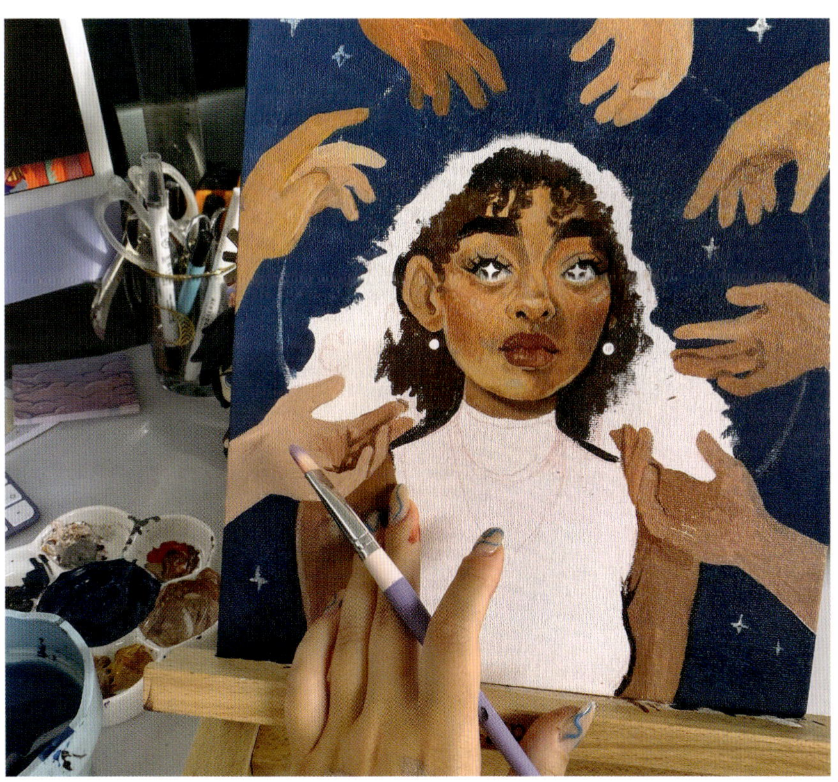

It seems a lot more manageable when it's broken down into just four steps, right? Making sure the first few building blocks are done properly will make your life a lot easier when you get to the rendering phases. After all, it can be pretty frustrating to get to the rendering step and realize that the eyes are in the wrong spot!

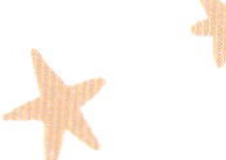

BASIC SHAPES OF THE HEAD & FACE

The easiest way to learn how to draw something is to first understand its structure by breaking it down into basic shapes. We will be doing that technique for most of the elements in this book.

FRONT VIEW

This person's face has been broken down into four main shapes and three guidelines.

- **Shape A:** the main circle that outlines the dome of the skull

- **Shape B:** the trapezoid/pentagonal shape for the jawline

- **Shape C:** a half-cylindrical shape for the neck

- **Shapes D:** the little semicircle shapes to dictate where the ears will go later

As you can see, a lot of these shapes and the guidelines converge and tangent with each other. These connections are very helpful in placing everything.

1. Draw the three main guidelines: the middle vertical line ① going all the way down the face and the two horizontal ones. The two horizontal lines should be equidistant from the true middle point of your face—which is where your vertical guideline crosses through the circle ②.

2. The top of the ears usually line up with where the jawline connects to the circle shape ⑤. The bottom of the ears should sit just above the jawline corner ④. This is where you will want to draw your second horizontal guideline ③.

3. Finally, the neck shape usually connects to the head about halfway along the jawline between the jaw corner and the chin ⑥.

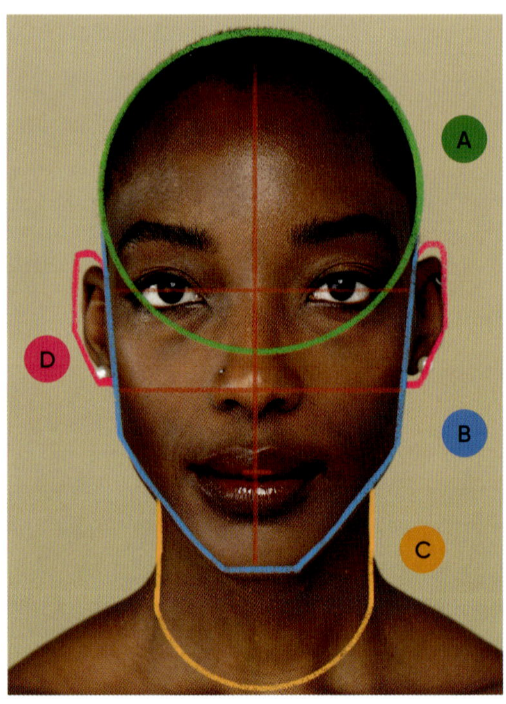

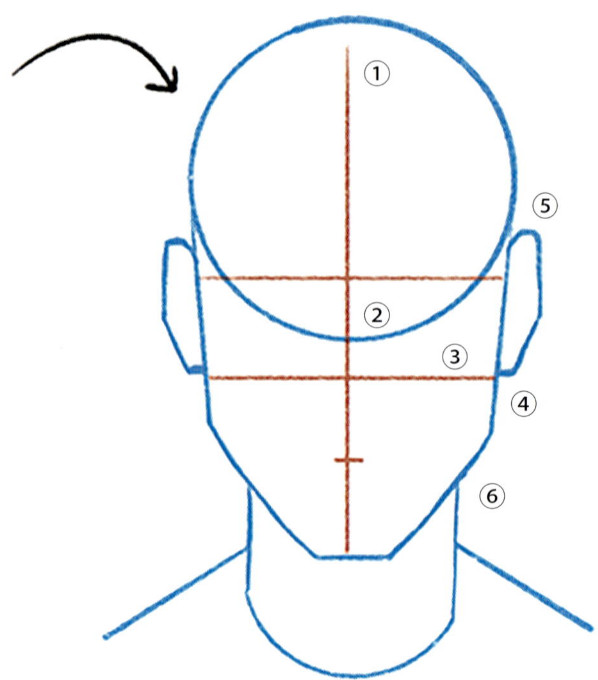

PROFILE

In profile, these shapes and guidelines can look a little different.

Shown here you can see there are now two circles making up the top of the skull. This is because the head is not round but oval, or bean-shaped.

For the jaw and front of the head, two lines are drawn down from where the two circles meet ② and dead center on the outside of the front circle ①. This shape should be a little pointier down toward the chin. The jawline should be almost parallel to the line tangenting the top of the two head circles ⑤.

The ear, again, goes right about where the jaw meets the head circle ②, following that jawline up into the head and into a semicircle.

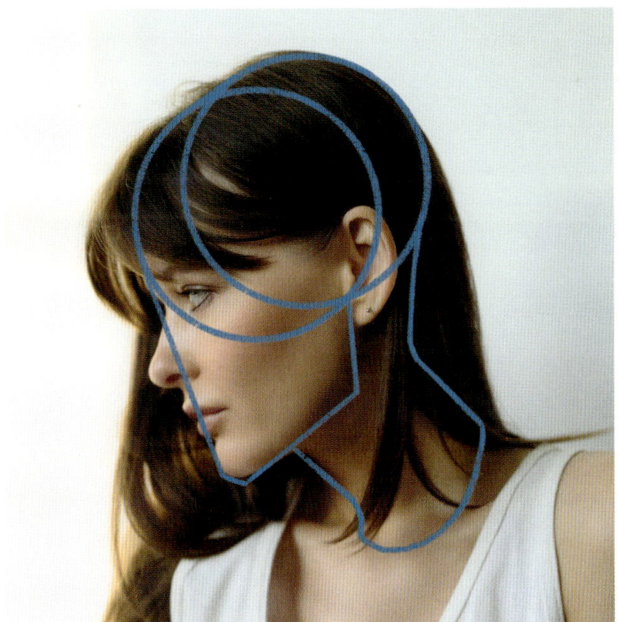

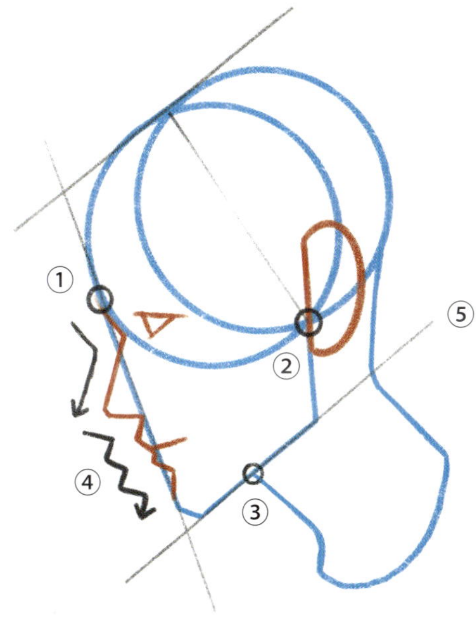

Depending on the position of your character, the neck position can differ, but as a rule of thumb, the neck connects to the outside of the back circle and, as before, connects back halfway between the jaw ③.

The eye should sit in the gap outside where the two circles meet and right in front of it (where the face line connects to the circles) is where you would start drawing the detailed curvature of the face in profile ④.

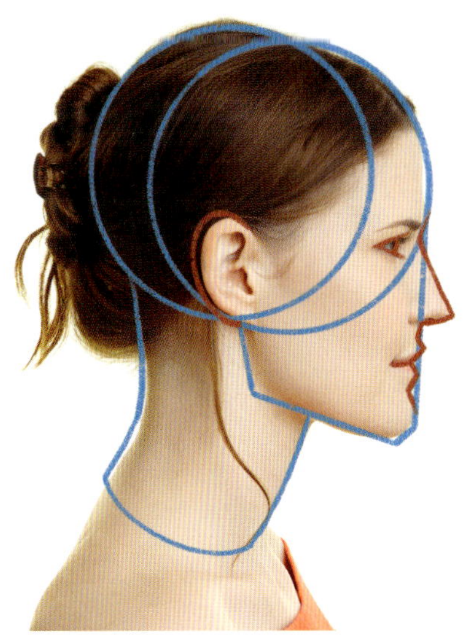

OTHER ANGLES

I recommend taking reference images and
tracing over them with these shapes to really
get a sense of how these shapes sit on the head
at different angles.

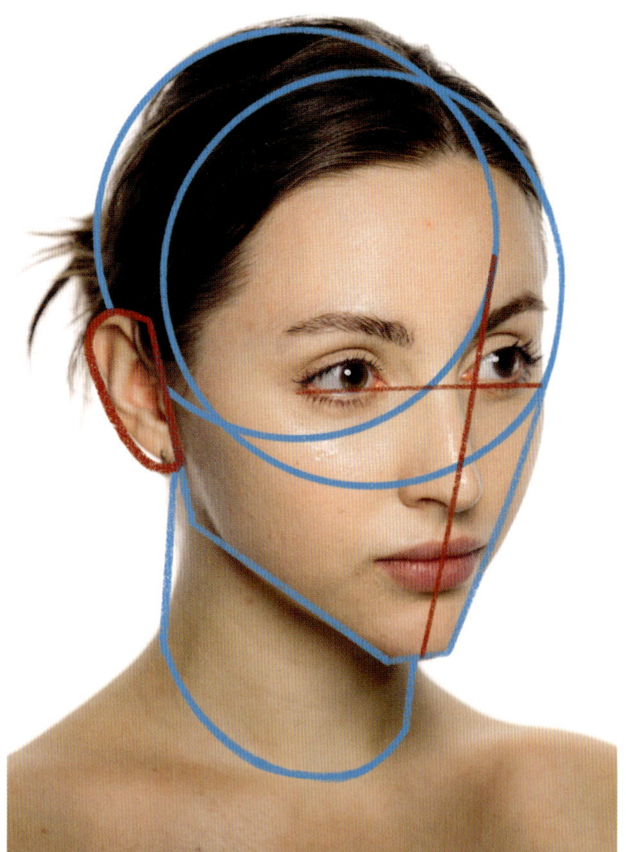

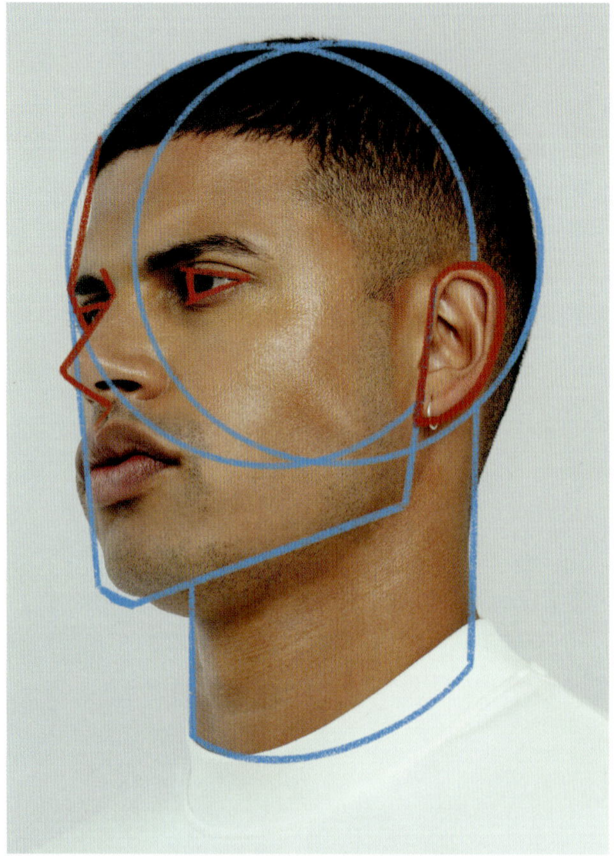

Remember, using basic shapes and getting
the "bones of the drawing" right is the best way
to ensure your faces are proportionally correct
and will make adding in your facial features a
lot easier.

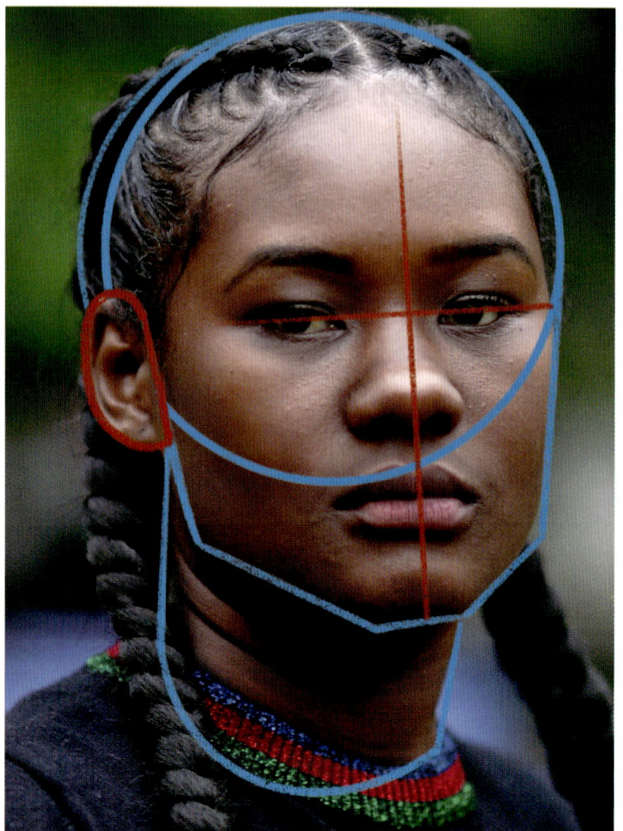

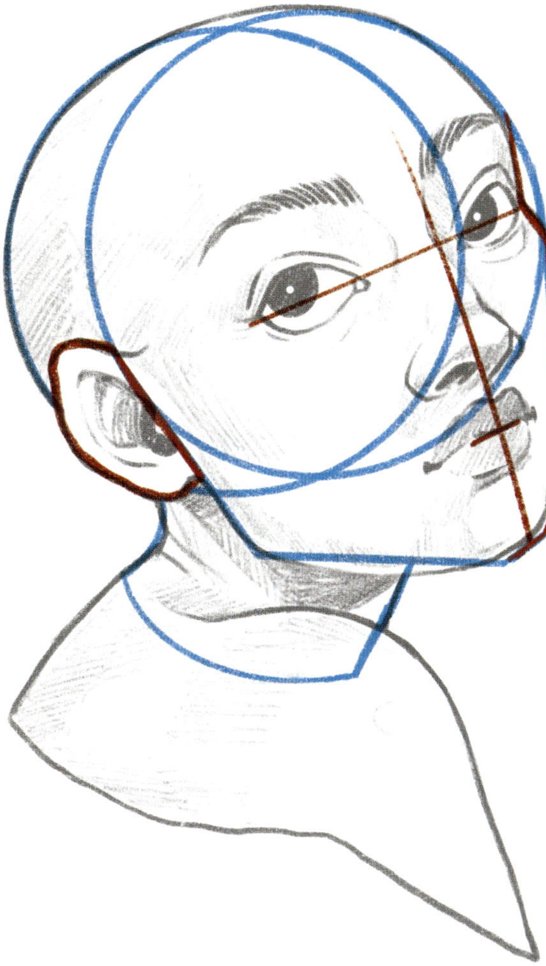

Here is an example of how you can use the same "rules," and even modify them a little to suit your own personal art style. This is how I structure a face using my own style of drawing.

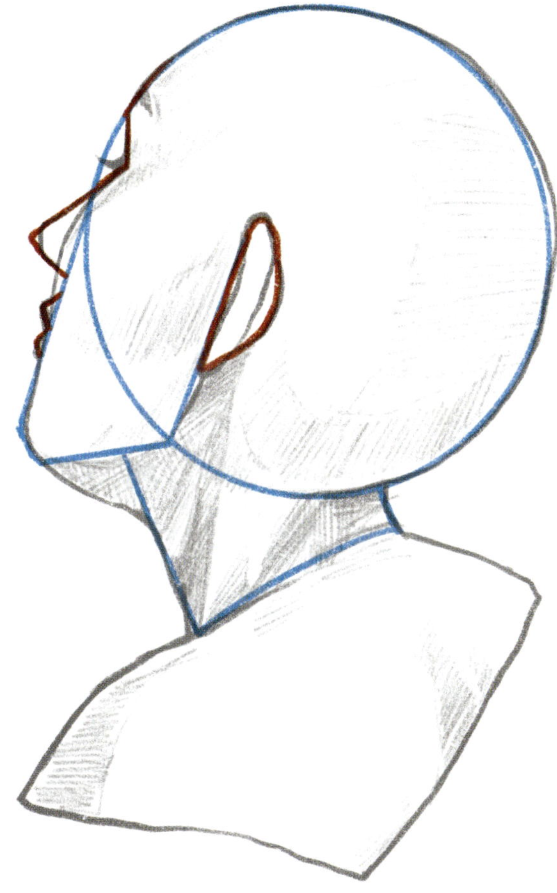

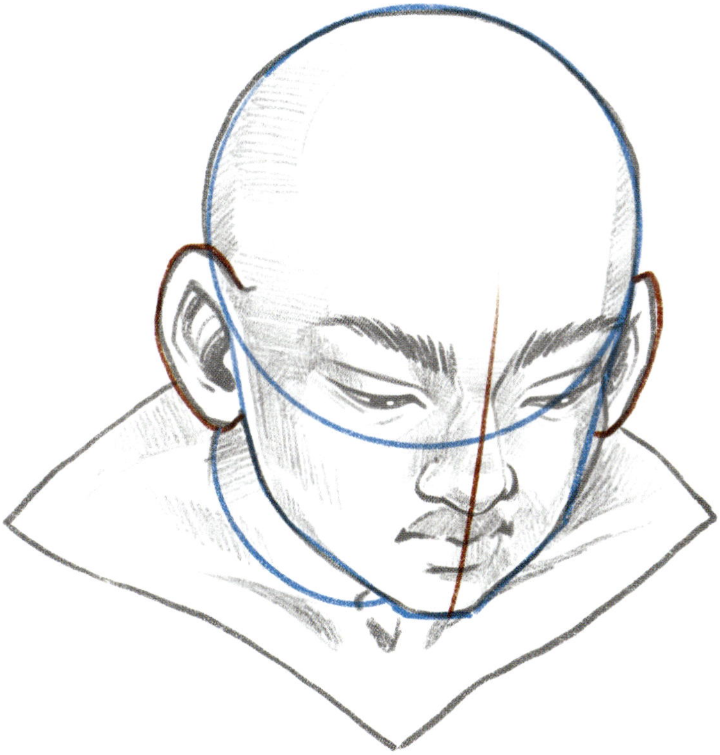

When it comes to drawing, once you learn the basics and the "rules," it's a lot easier to improve your skills. Then later you can "unlearn" some of these rules to complement your personal art style.

STUDYING THE SKULL

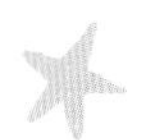

In order to understand the shapes and proportions of the human head, it's important to study and understand what lies beneath it.

Once you know the underlying structure, it's a lot easier to block out these shapes at any angle and then add the features, the fat, and the muscles on top. You start off with a little skull and its basic shape, and then you add cheeks, a nose, a chin, and eyes—making it as skinny or as chubby as you want.

Every single face on the planet is different, but everyone's skulls are somewhat the same. So understanding the skull's shapes and proportions will provide you with a great starting point.

I recommend looking at pictures of the skull and drawing as many of them as you can, making sure you focus on the shapes and angles rather than getting all the bones perfect.

You don't need to take a full anatomy class and know all the bones in the skull! Here are some of the main parts you may need to know:

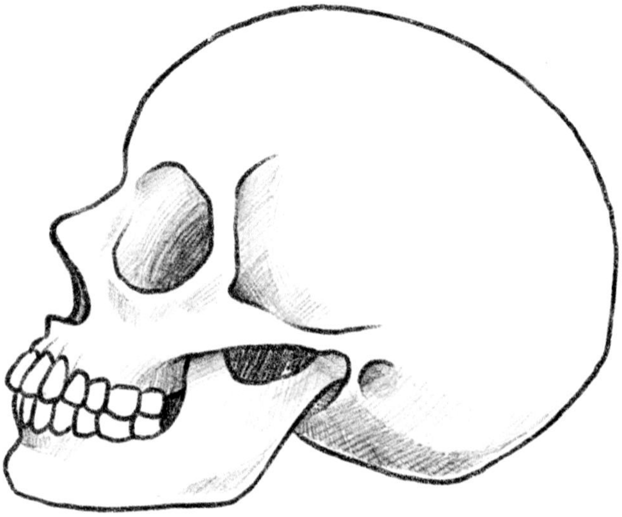

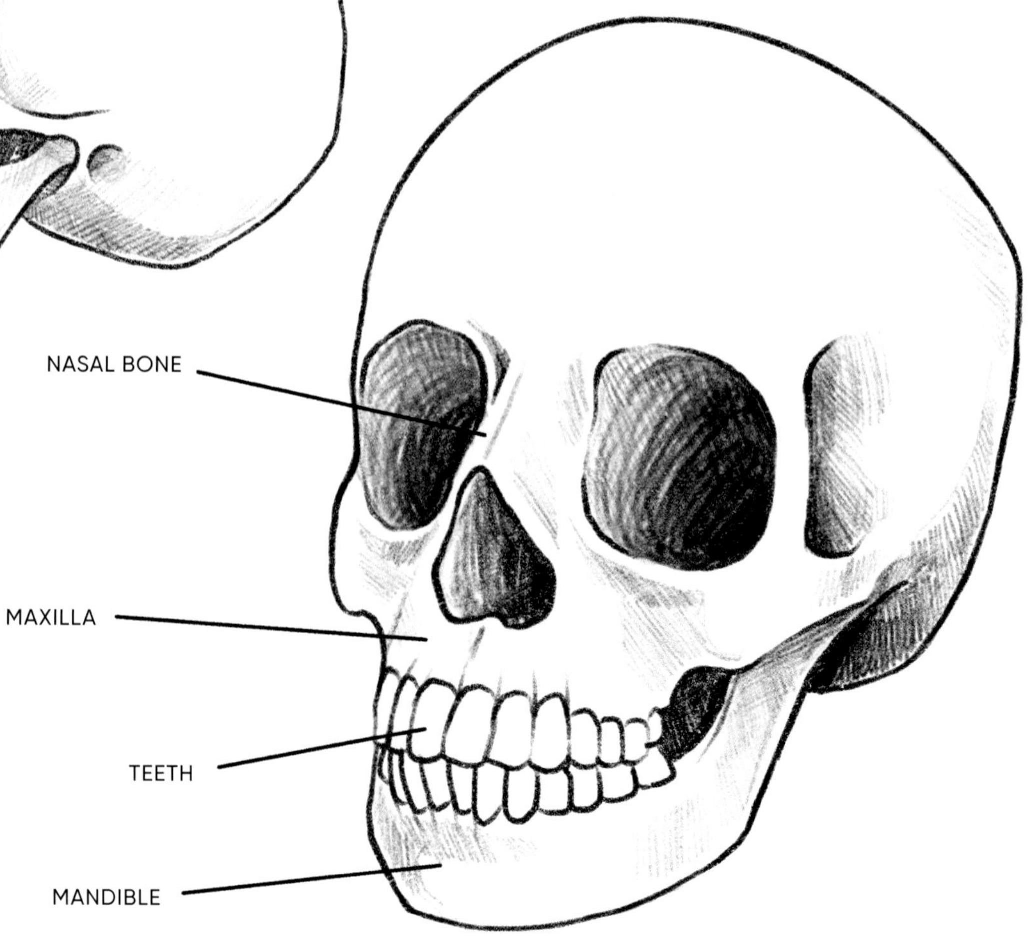

We have already discussed the basic shapes of the head, but it's important to understand the context of these shapes. We will explore this concept more very soon, but for now, take note of how the human skull looks differently at all these different angles.

In some of these we're looking down on the skull; in others we're looking up at it. These different angles completely change the shape and size of certain parts of the skull. In some of these examples you can't even see some of the features. That is what happens with the head and the face of the portraits you will draw, and that is why it's important to familiarize yourself with how the building blocks of the head look at these different angles.

Look up some images of skulls, try copying the ones on this page, or even get a model of the skull so you can draw it from real-life reference. This way you can easily rotate and place the skull at odd angles.

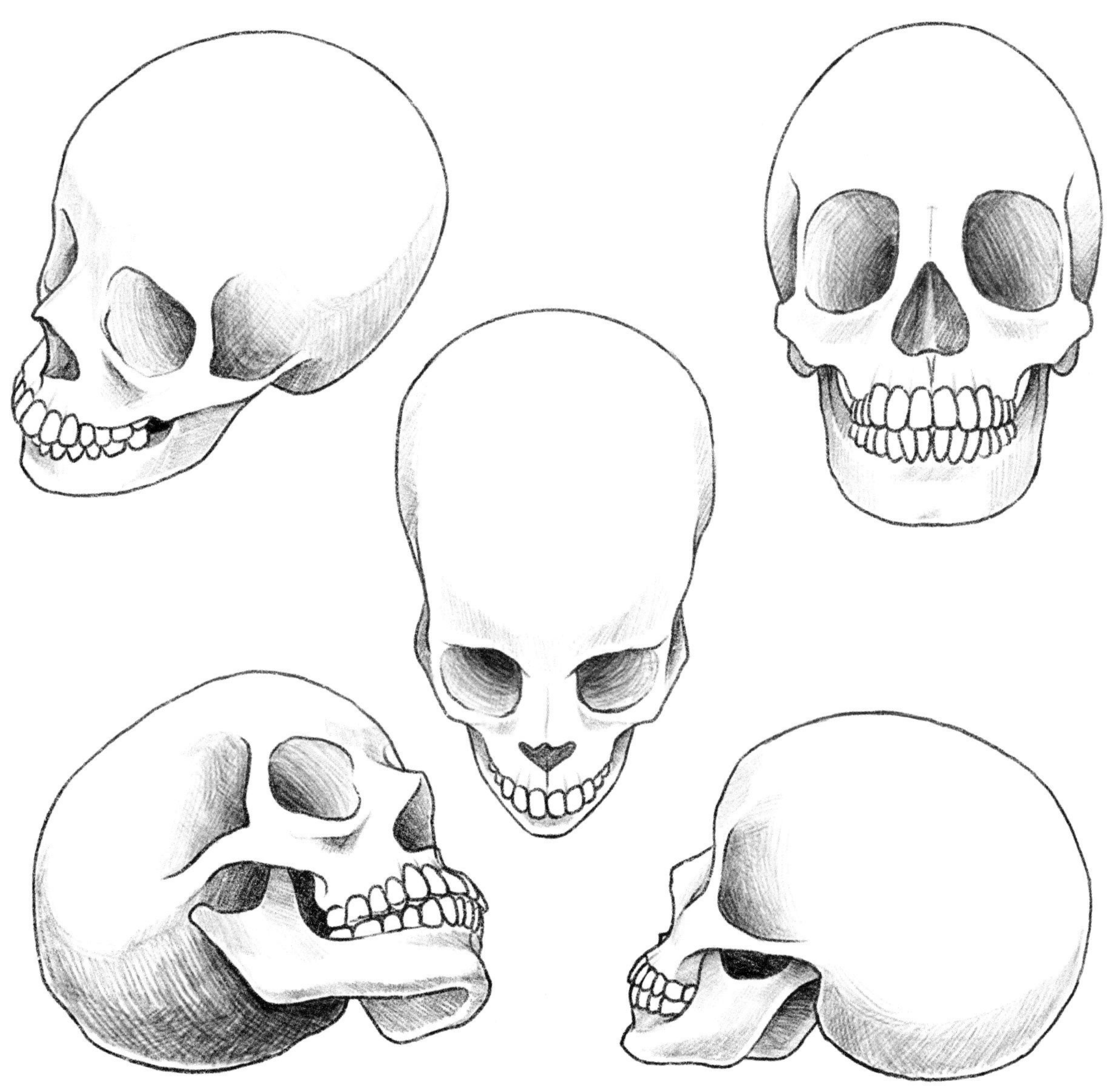

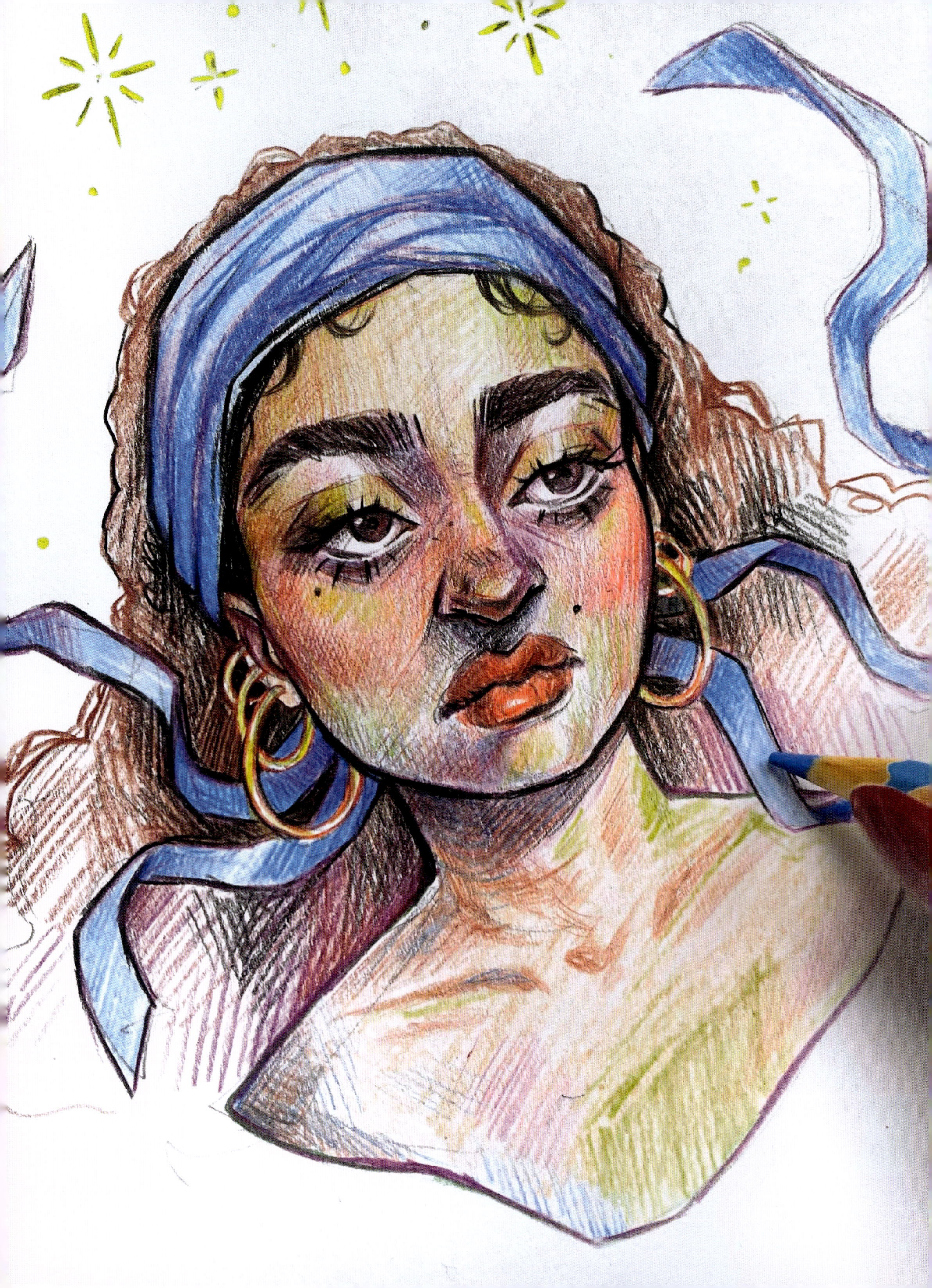

2

PROPORTIONS & PERSPECTIVE

Knowing where to place the eyes, nose, ears, and mouth can be very easy to learn—especially on a forward-facing portrait staring you straight in the face. The trickier part comes when you have to learn how the placement and size of these facial features can change depending on not only the angle the face is at but also the type of character you're drawing. You might have noticed that the places where the facial features change quite a lot from a baby's face to an adult's—this is what is called *proportions*. And these proportions can change due to *perspective*. They can be a little confusing at first to get a grasp of, but I've got a few different methods and tricks that will help.

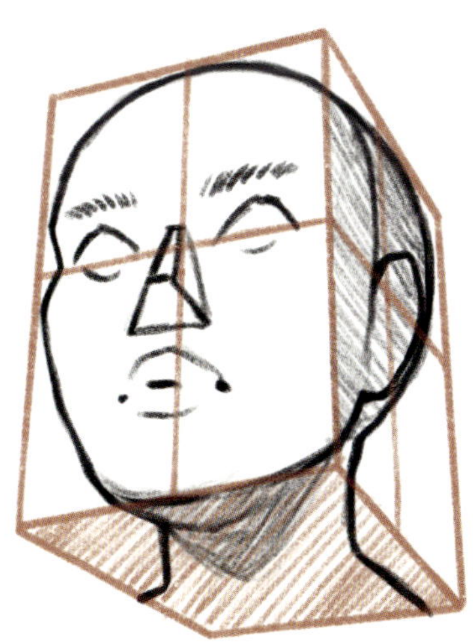

FACIAL PROPORTIONS

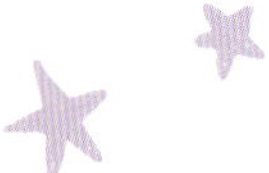

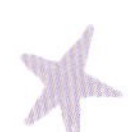

As you might guess, the placement of the facial features is incredibly important in how your portrait comes out. The size, shape, and placement of these features can change a face dramatically—it can change the age, gender, genetic background, and even disposition.

Now that we know the shapes of the head, we can add in the guidelines and general placement of the features.

You can use circles and basic shapes to sketch out the general area where the features will sit.

The sketches shown are only a generic example of placing these features. Using reference images and studying them will allow you to explore other examples of facial proportions on different kinds of faces.

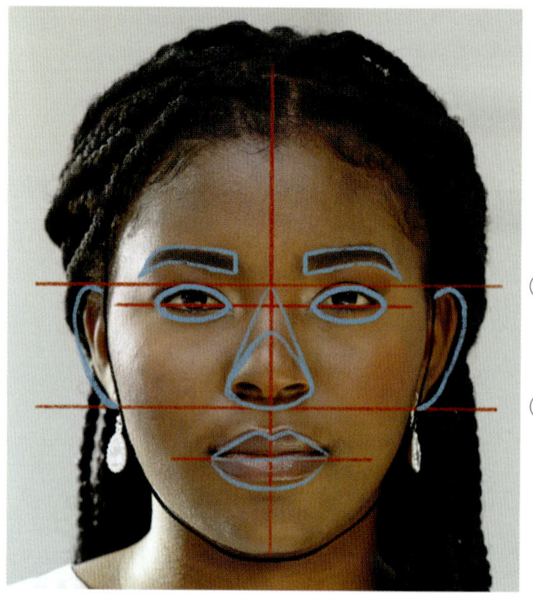

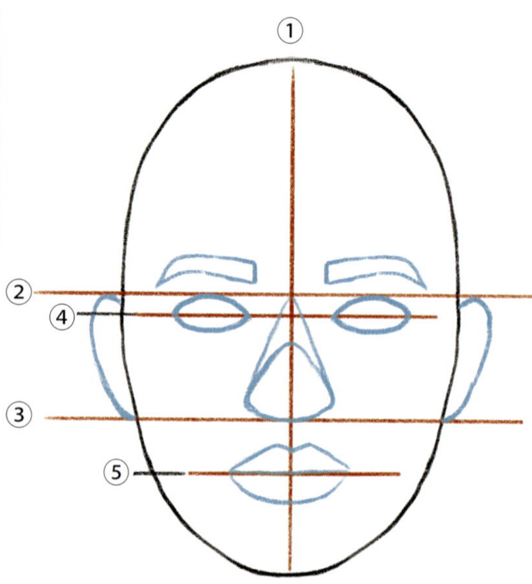

You can see above how to use a reference image to measure where all the features are placed on the head. You can even draw over the image to get acquainted with the placement of the guidelines you'll be using.

First, you should always start with your vertical middle guideline ①, as this will determine the direction in which your portrait is facing. You can see in the example that the top of the ears lines up with the top of the eyes ②, and the bottom of the ears lines up with the bottom of the nose ③. I then usually like to add in a second line just below the ② line, as that is where the center of the eyes lines up.

Similarly, another guideline can be drawn halfway between the bottom of the nose ③ and the chin, and this is usually where the mouth opening sits.

You can see how, by using these five guidelines, you can then start adding in some shapes to block in the features of the face.

But how about when drawing out a face yourself? Check out the next step-by-step page:

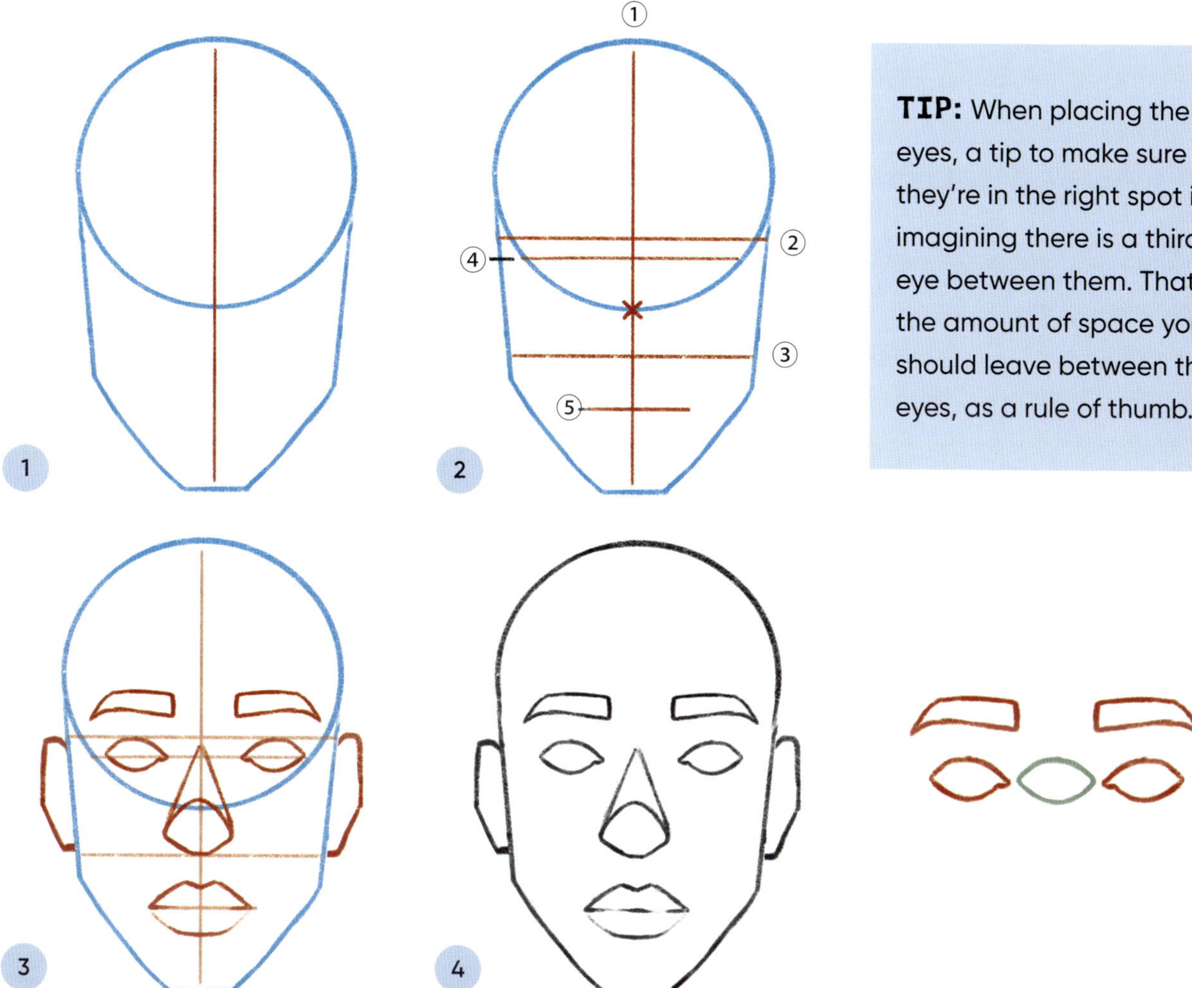

1. Using the steps we learned on page 16, sketch out the shape of the head and the vertical center guideline.

2. Use the spot where the vertical guideline meets the circle as your center point. Draw two equidistant guidelines above and below; one line near where the circle and the sides of the face meet ② and one just above where the jaw starts to turn inward ③. These are the guidelines for your ears but also for the top of the eyes and the bottom of the nose. From here on it's easy as you can then add the mouth guideline ⑤ halfway between the ③ guideline and the chin as well as the eyes' center guideline just below the ② guideline ④.

3. Now you can start placing features. The eyes (can just be oval shapes for now) sit so that guideline ④ crosses right through the middle of them and the top of them touches guideline ②.

The eyebrows go above guideline ②, but we will focus on eyebrows later in the book when learning how to draw the eyes.

The nose (a triangle for now) sits on guideline ③ and goes up to between the eyes. You can also draw in the ears between guidelines ② and ③ on each side of the face.

Finally, the mouth can be sketched out. Using guideline ⑤, sketch out the upper and bottom lip coming out of that line.

4. You can then erase all your guidelines and you should have something resembling a face!

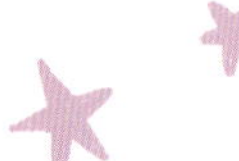
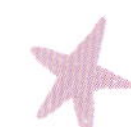

THE FACE IN PERSPECTIVE

Everyone's face is different, and some people's facial proportions may be different from others—that's what's so fun about portraiture! But the other main factors that can change the proportions of the face are age, perspective/angles, and sometimes even ethnicity.

As a base example shown here, you can see the facial proportion guidelines we just learned. These are usually the rules for a teenager and older. The face is fully formed and grown, and this is where the facial features sit for the rest of adulthood. But they don't really start like this.

In the examples shown you can see how the proportions of a human face change quite a lot as they grow up. The main thing to note is how the facial features go from being squished together as a baby to growing further and further apart.

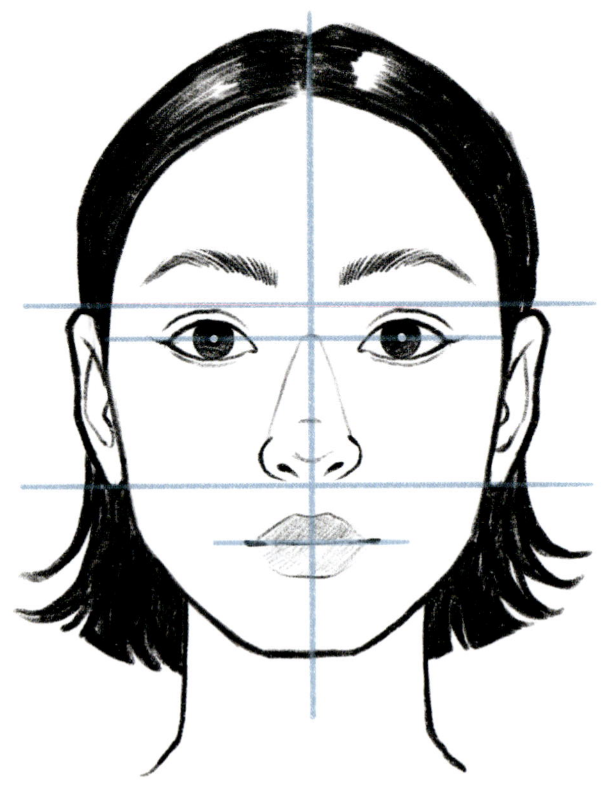

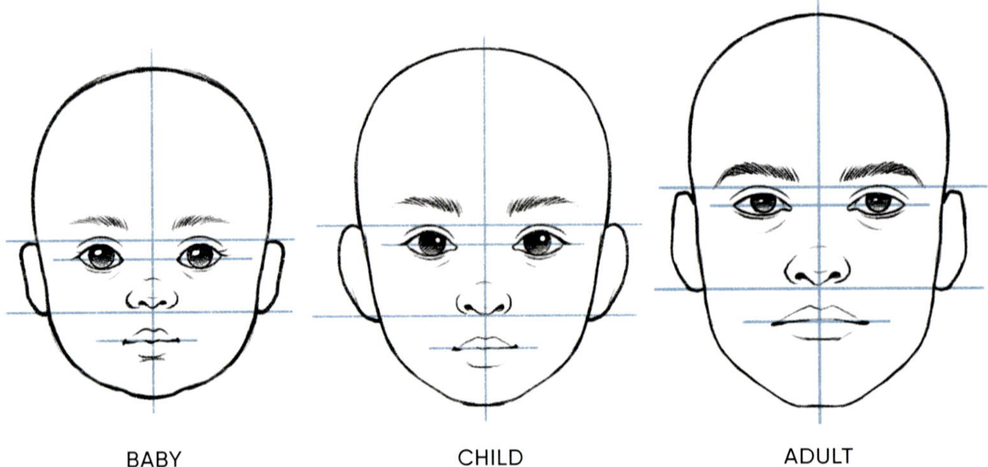

We always think of babies and children as having big youthful eyes, but the fact is that they're not that disproportionate when compared to an adult's eyes. What is different is the size and shape of the head. The eyes start off looking bigger and rounder, and they grow into their "almond" shape over time.

Overall, younger features are much closer together, and a child has a rounder head, which changes over time as the illustration shows.

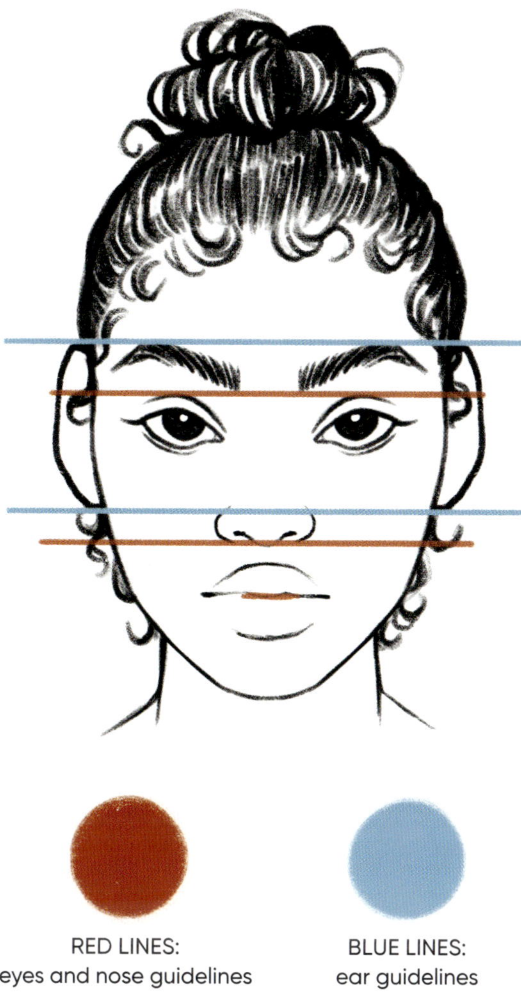

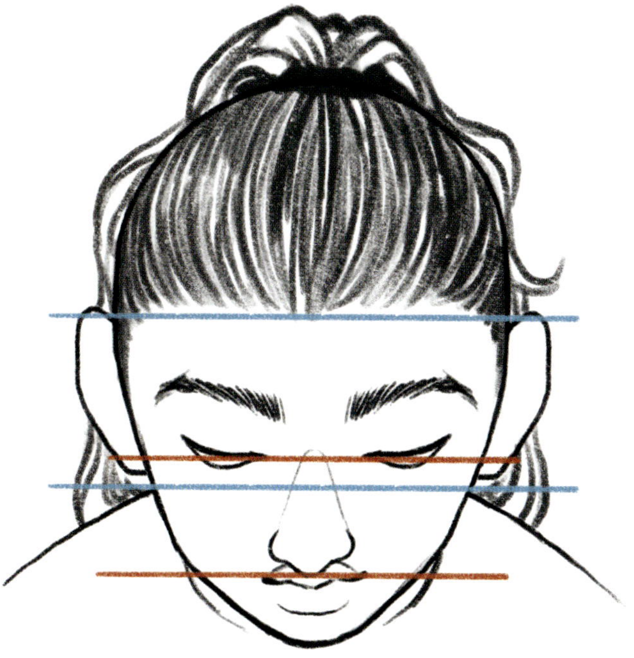

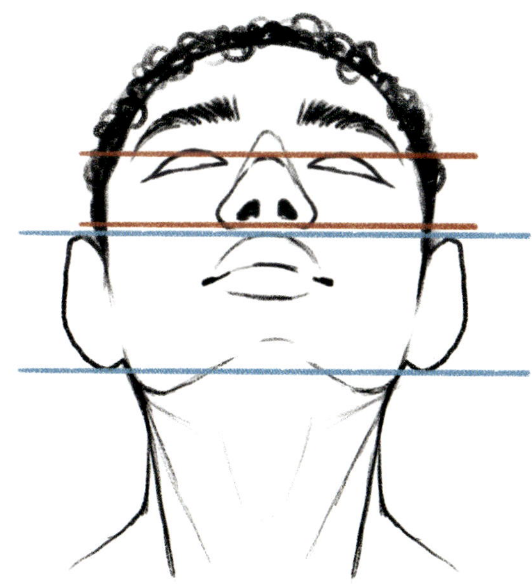

RED LINES:
eyes and nose guidelines

BLUE LINES:
ear guidelines

As we saw previously, on a face staring straight ahead, the top of the eyes lines up with the top of the ears, and the bottom of the nose lines up with the bottom of the ears. It's a rule that is generally anatomically correct on most faces. But this rule changes when the face is no longer looking straight ahead.

In the illustration above right, this head is tilted slightly down, looking up at us—the viewer. Using the guidelines you can already see how the eyes and nose immediately stop aligning themselves to the ears. This is how you create perspective with proportions.

For now, you can try using this exercise to see how drastically the guidelines changing position changes the angle and tilt of the head.

On a head tilted fully forward, you can see that the eyes almost line up with the bottom of the ears and the bottom of the nose even overlaps the mouth.

You can see in the more extreme example below, where the head is tilted backward and looking up, how the ears' guidelines sit completely underneath the nose and eyes and actually align with the mouth instead.

IT'S ALL ABOUT THE ANGLES

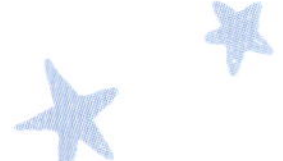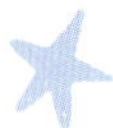

Things can start getting more complicated when the head is posed in different directions, and it might take some practice to figure out how you like to add in your guidelines.

If you think of a mask as being centered on the head (and keep in mind the three-dimensional structure of the head and skull), this might help you get a clearer picture of where the face should go. You can try imagining this mask capturing everything from the eyebrows to the bottom of the mouth.

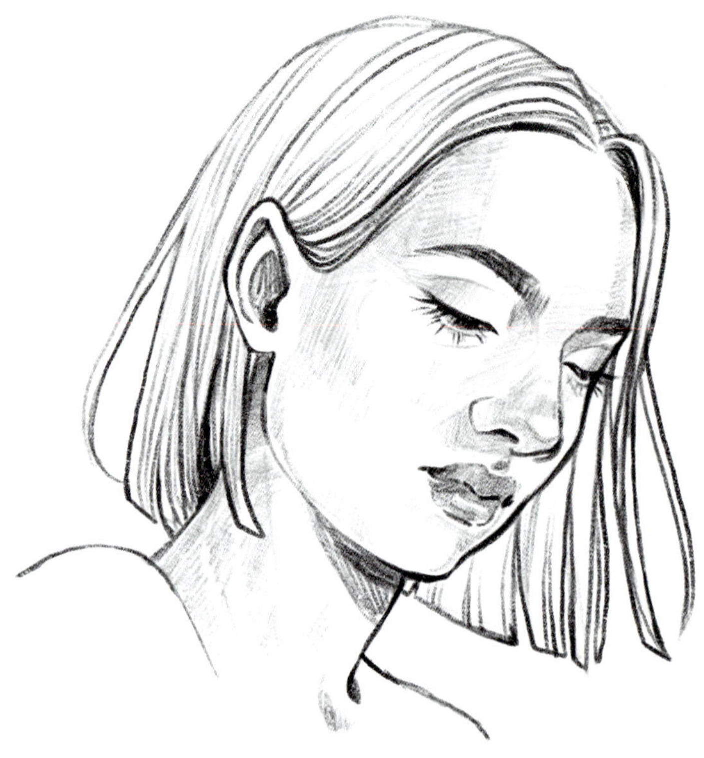

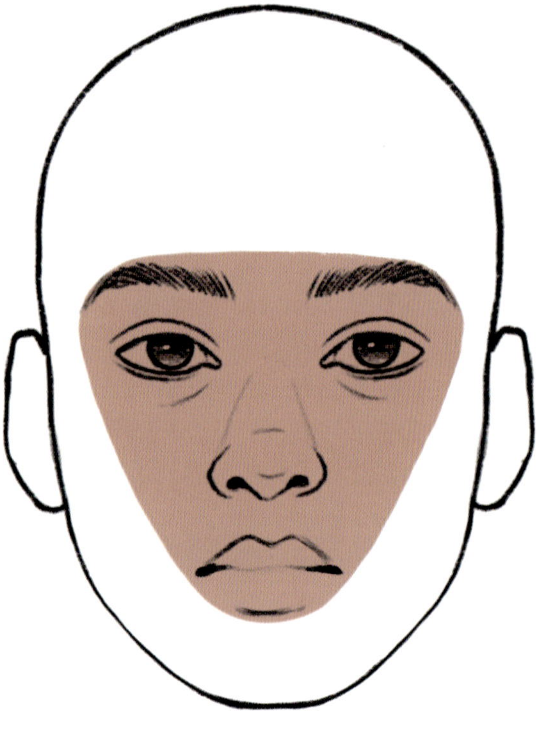

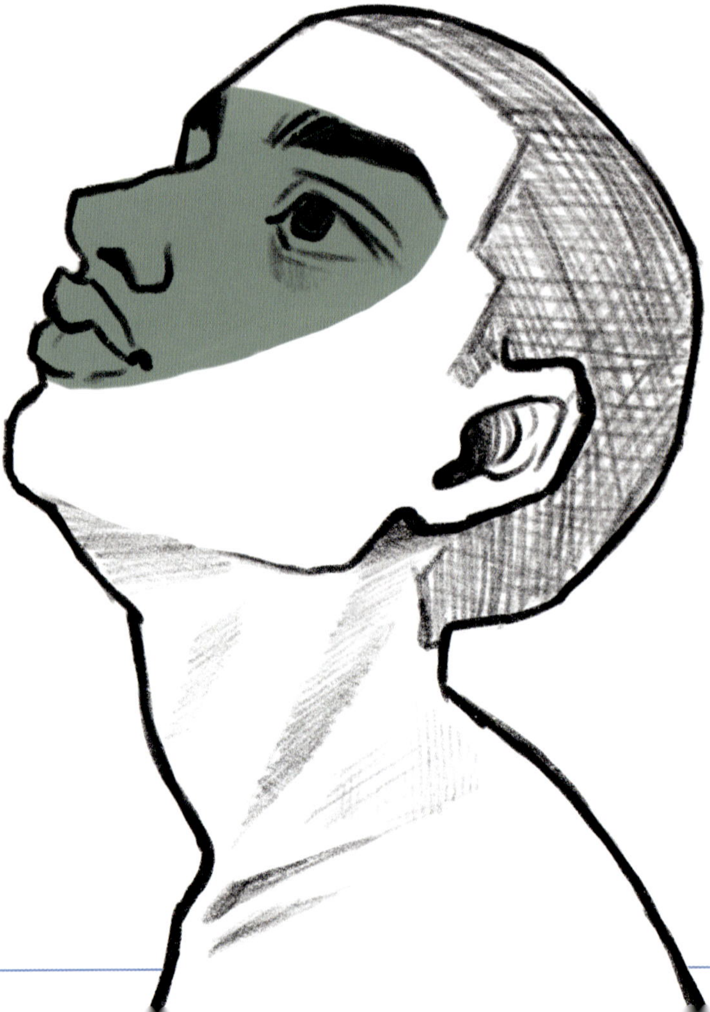

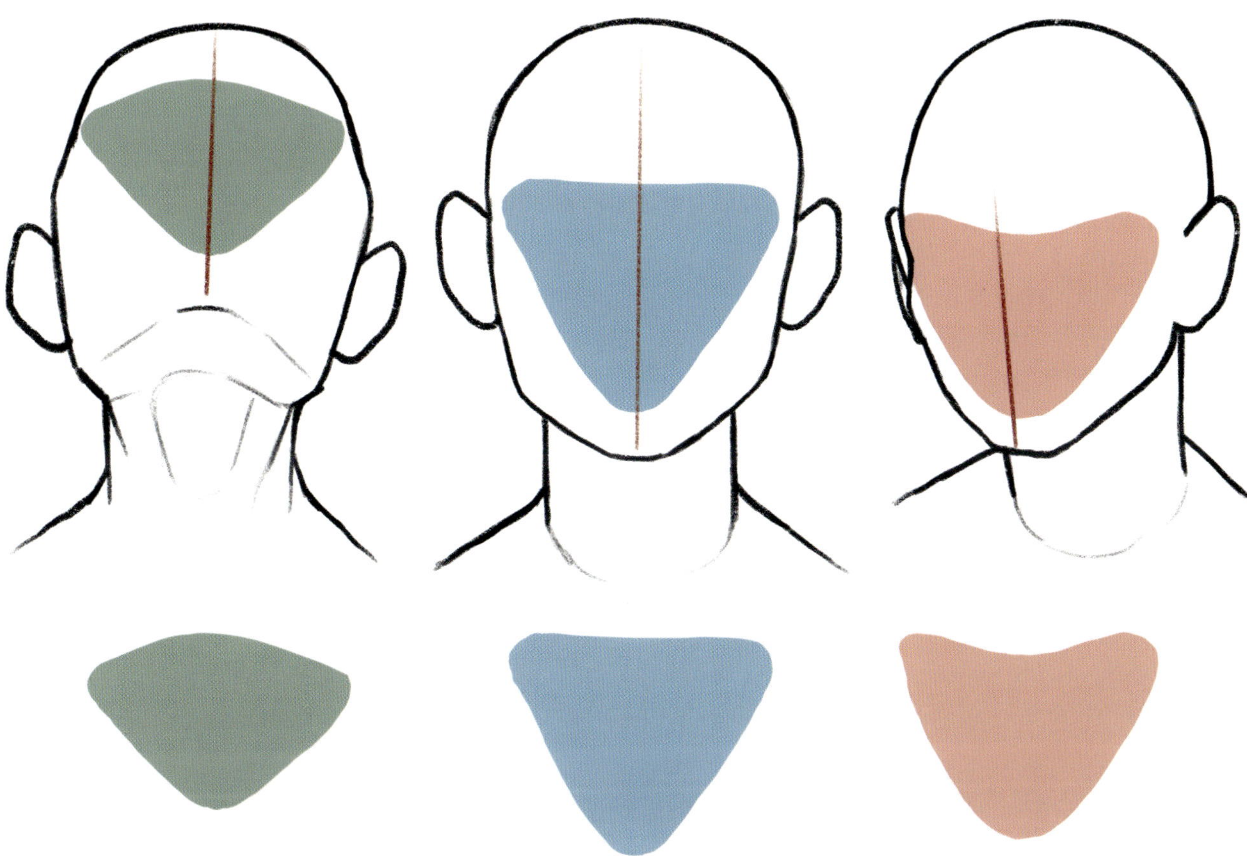

For example, shown here, the head is at a ¾ angle to the right. Considering the mask is to be centered on the head and imagining the strings of the mask tied back to the ears, this is where you should aim to block in your facial features.

You can see here how the shape of the "mask" changes when the head is at different angles. When the head is tilted upward, the "mask" looks squished together, as all the features look much closer together due to perspective. When at a ¾ angle, the "mask" shows how the curvatures of the head can skew the facial features and their placement at this angle.

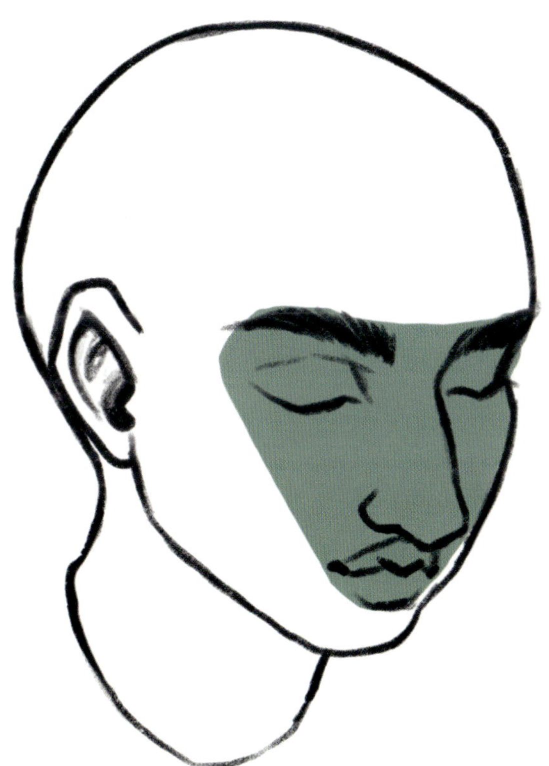

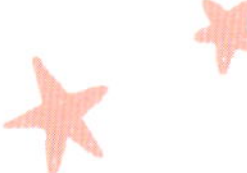

THE BOX METHOD

One method I like to use for posing the head is the Box Method. As the name suggests, it involves using a box to position the head in different angles, making sure the proportions and the shapes of the head are still accurate. The box is a little taller than it is wide (cuboid). You can also draw some guidelines on each face of the box to help with placing the head inside the box correctly.

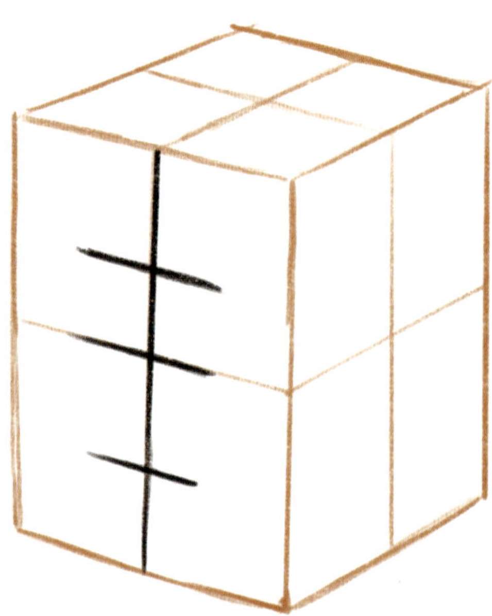

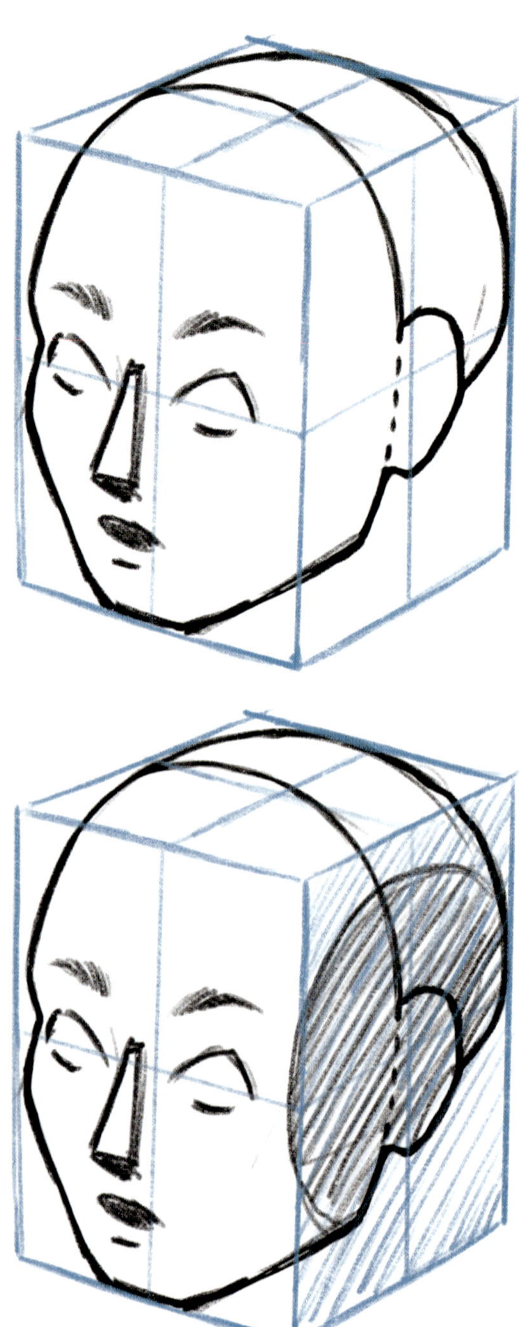

After the box is set up, you can place your head inside it following those guidelines. Once you have the shape of the head and the guidelines there, it's a lot easier to then place all the features of the face at the correct angle to match the perspective of the box.

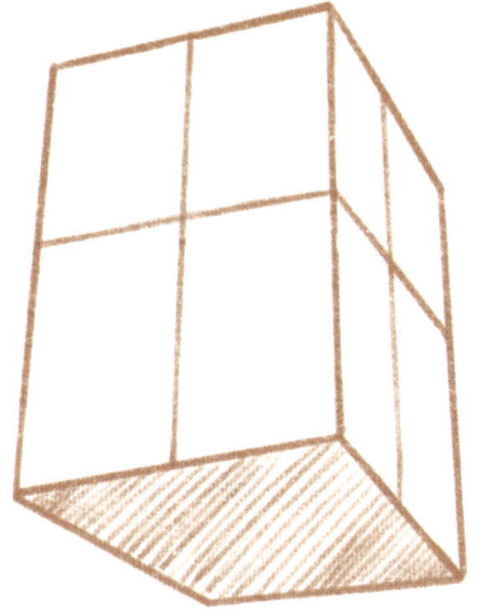

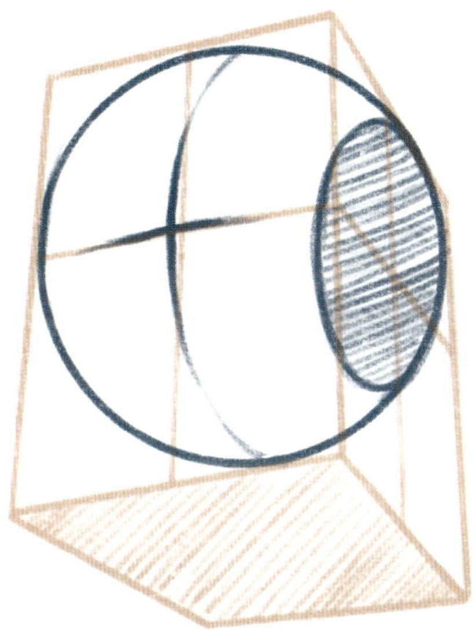

HOW TO USE THE BOX METHOD

Let's break it down a little bit:

1. First draw a box/cuboid at the angle you want your head to be. You can use an actual box as reference.

2. Add in the two guidelines on each of the sides of the box to make a cross right through the middle of the box sides.

3. Inside the box (closer to the top) draw out the main circle of the head. I like to flatten out this sphere on the sides a little to mimic the shape of the head. This can also help you place the ears and jaw.

4. Draw in some more curved guidelines while following the box's guidelines. The head is three-dimensional and curved, so it's helpful to make sure the guidelines reflect that.

5. From that sphere, add in the jaw and bottom section of the head. These two shapes together should now start resembling the shape of a skull. Once the jaw section is placed, start adding in the placeholder shapes for the facial features. Imagining that the box's cross guidelines are your facial proportions guidelines, you can place the features along them.

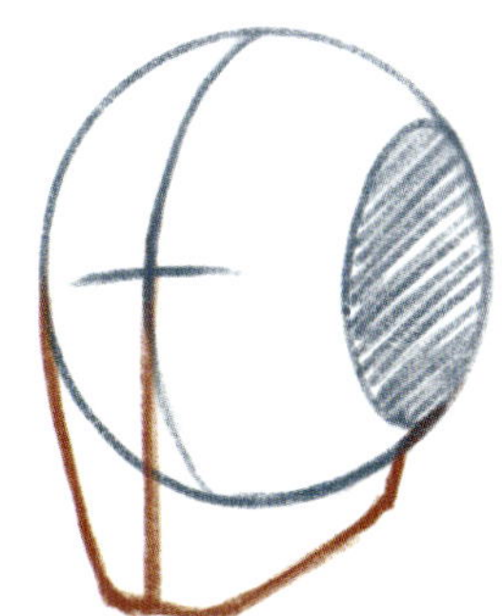

On the next two pages, you'll find a cheat sheet for you to reference whenever you need, showing the different angles of the face and how the facial features look at each of these angles.

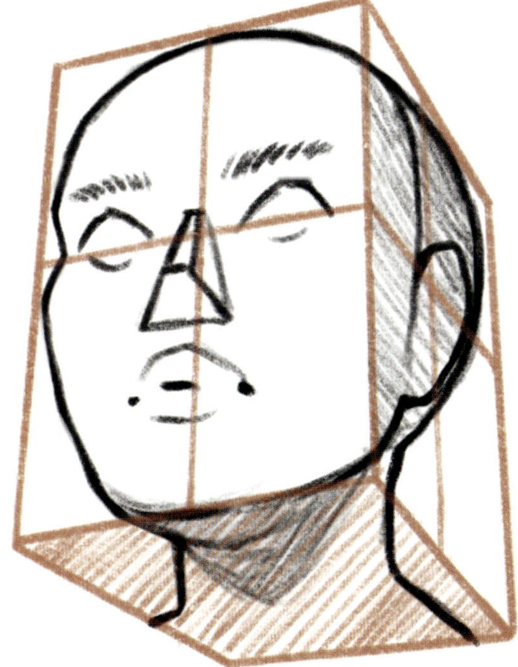

THE HEAD FROM DIFFERENT ANGLES

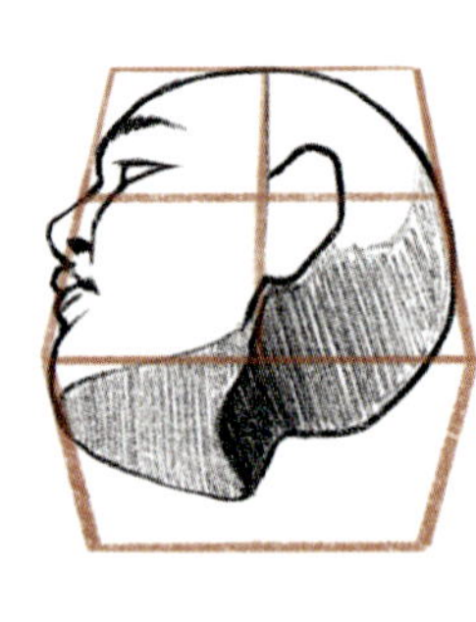
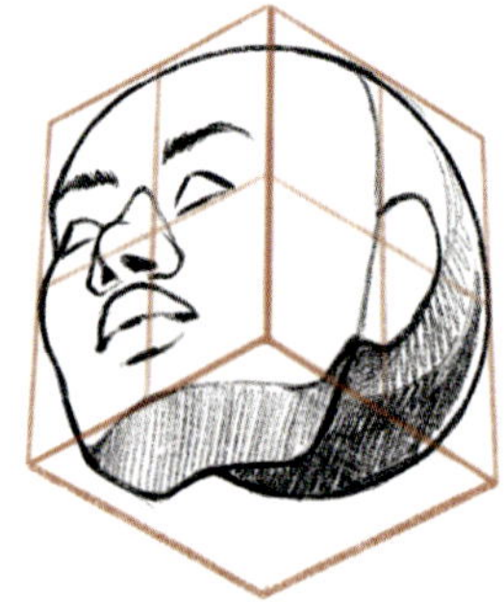
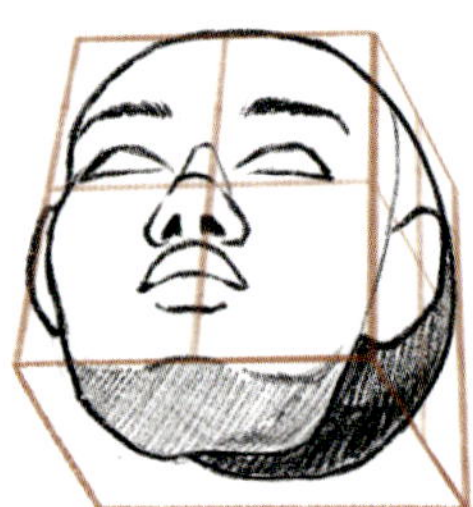
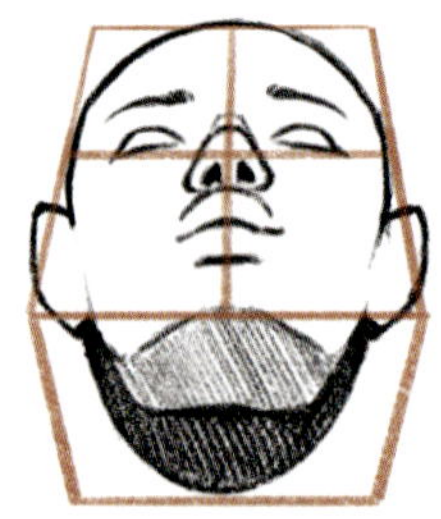
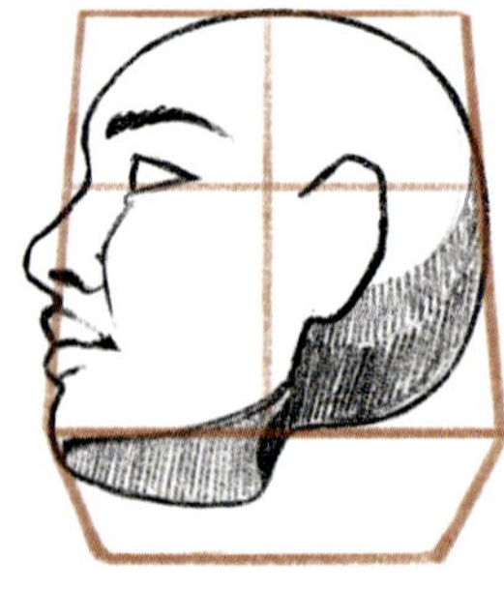
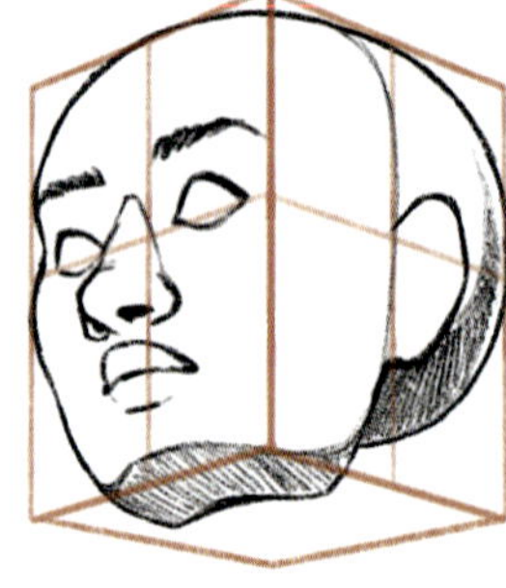
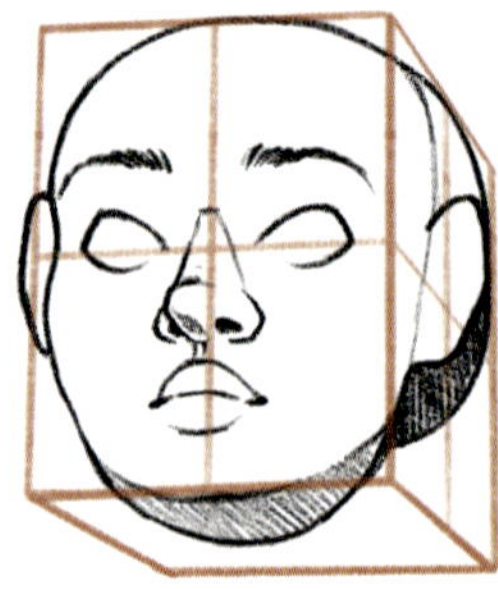
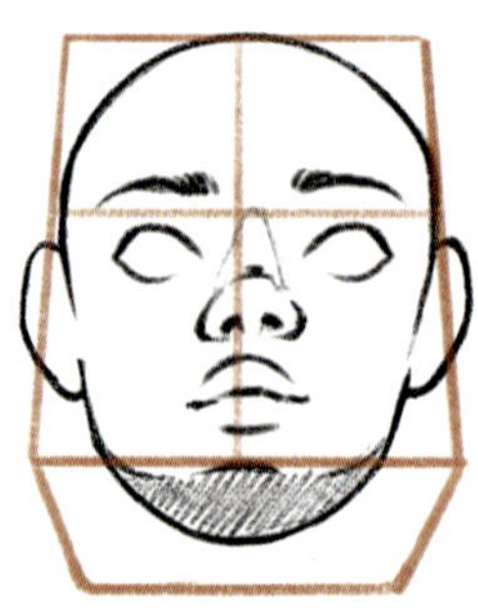
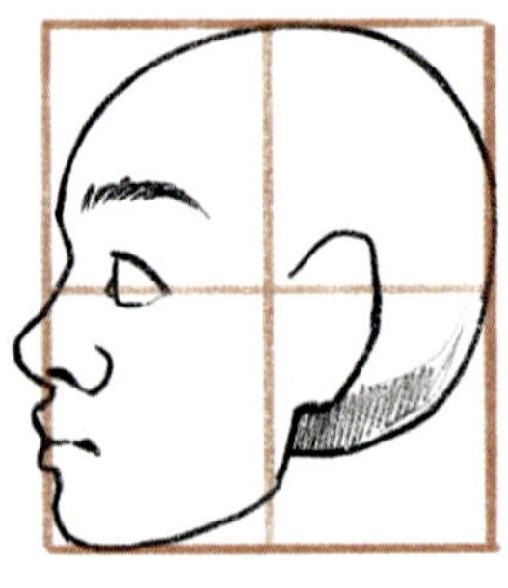
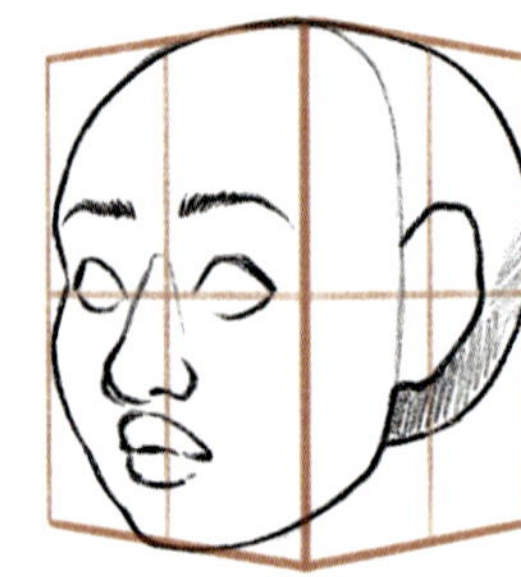
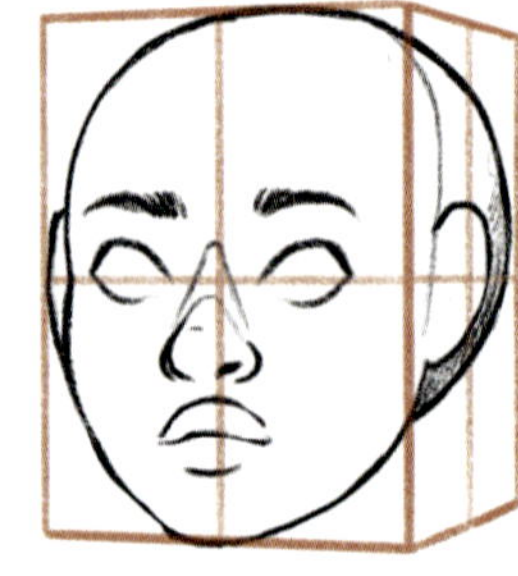
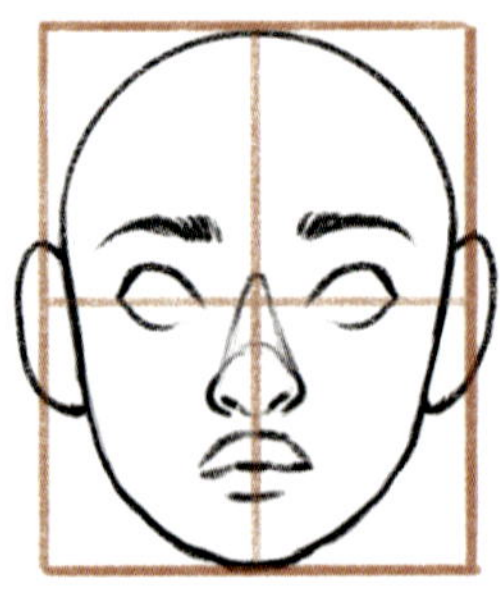
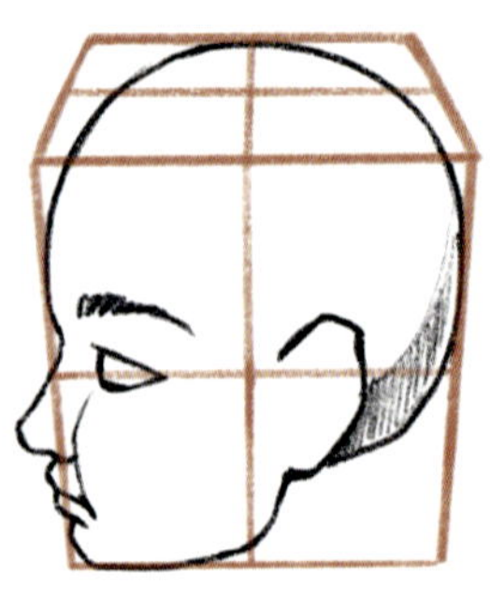
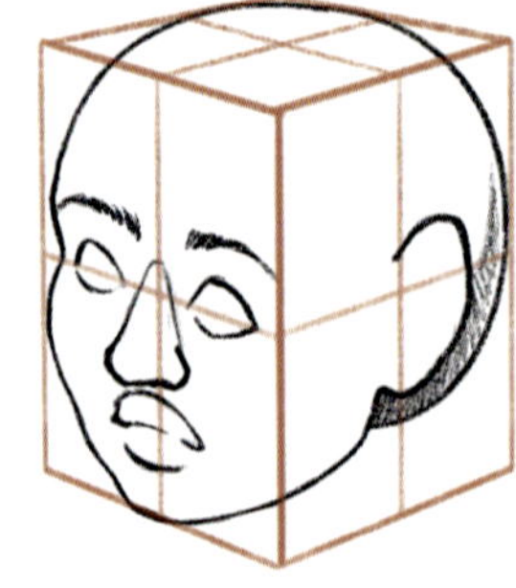
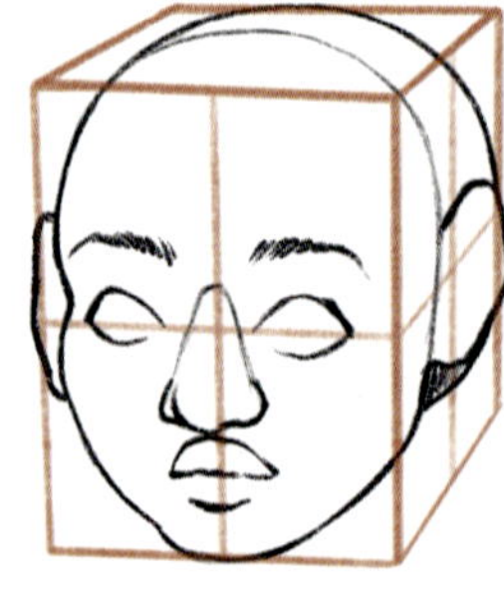
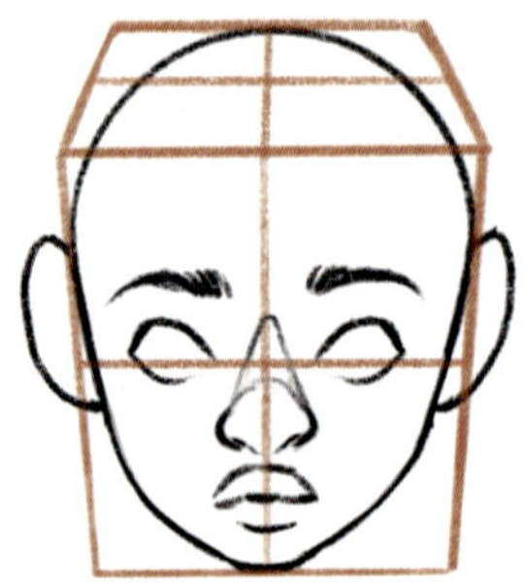
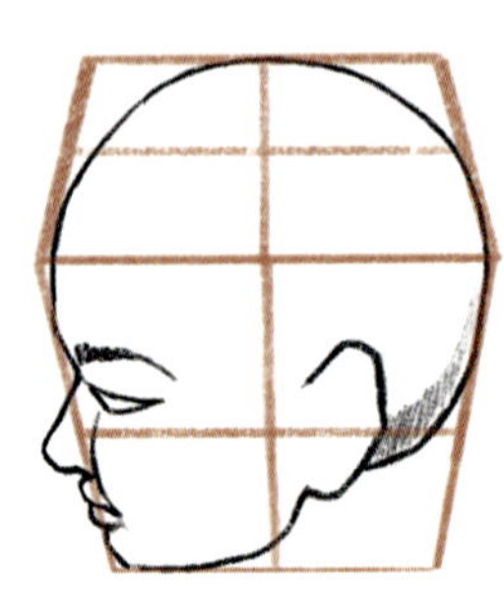
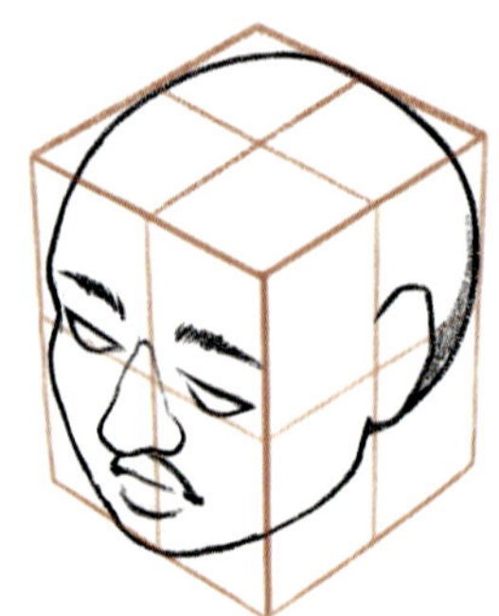
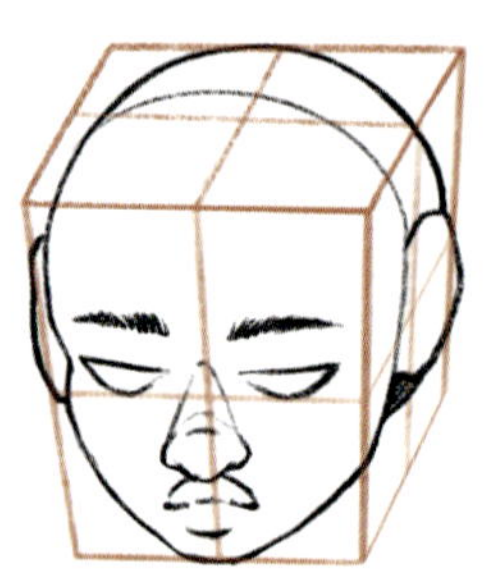
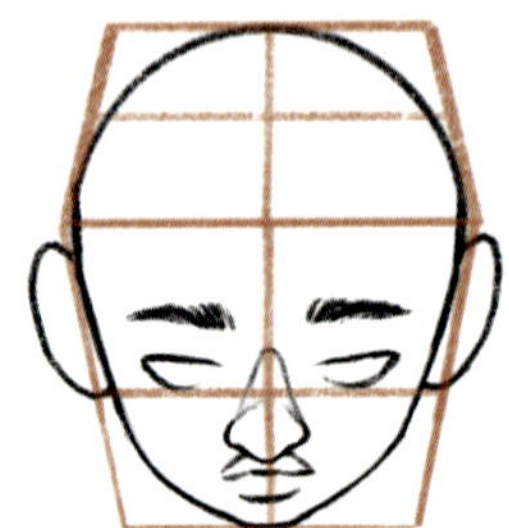

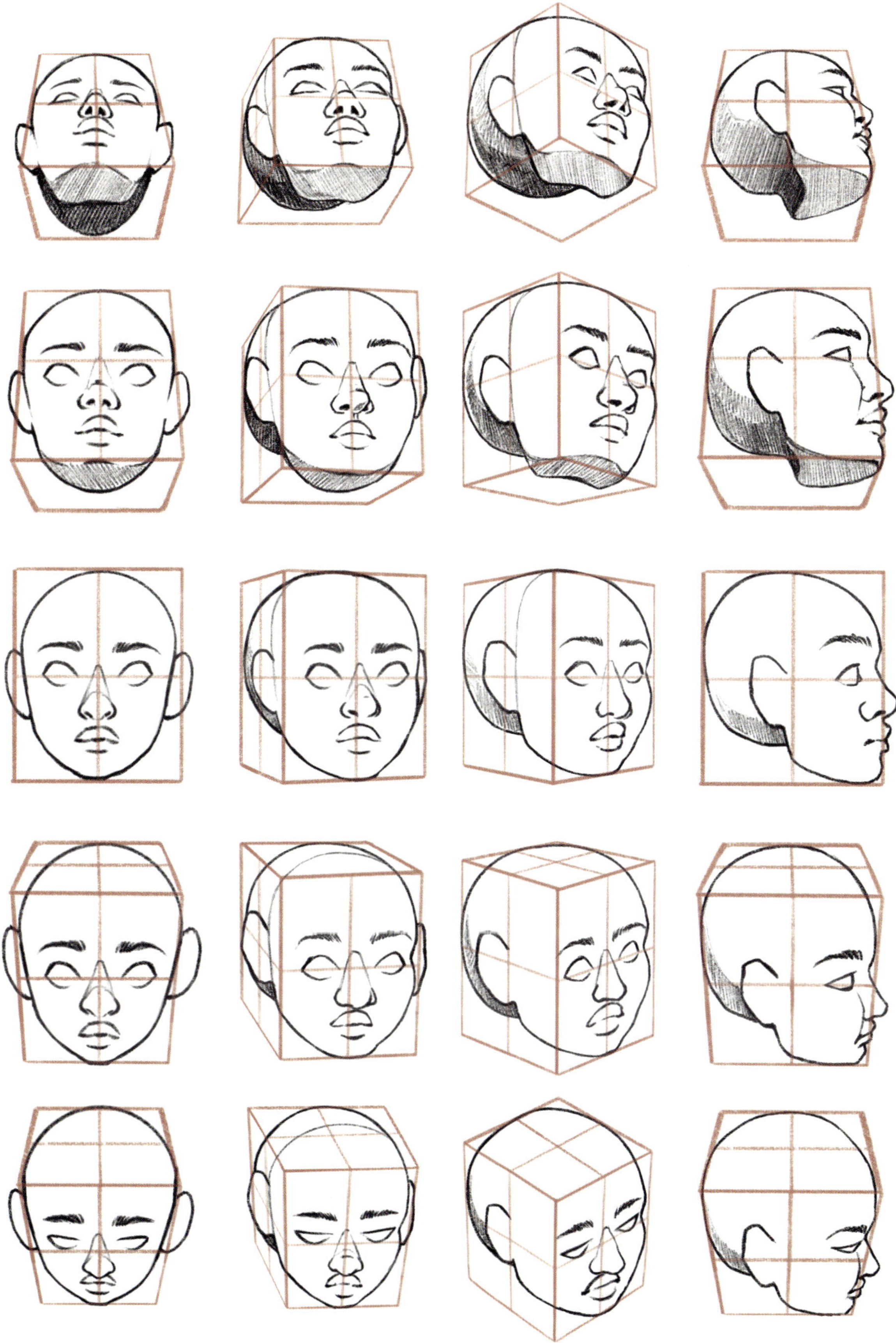

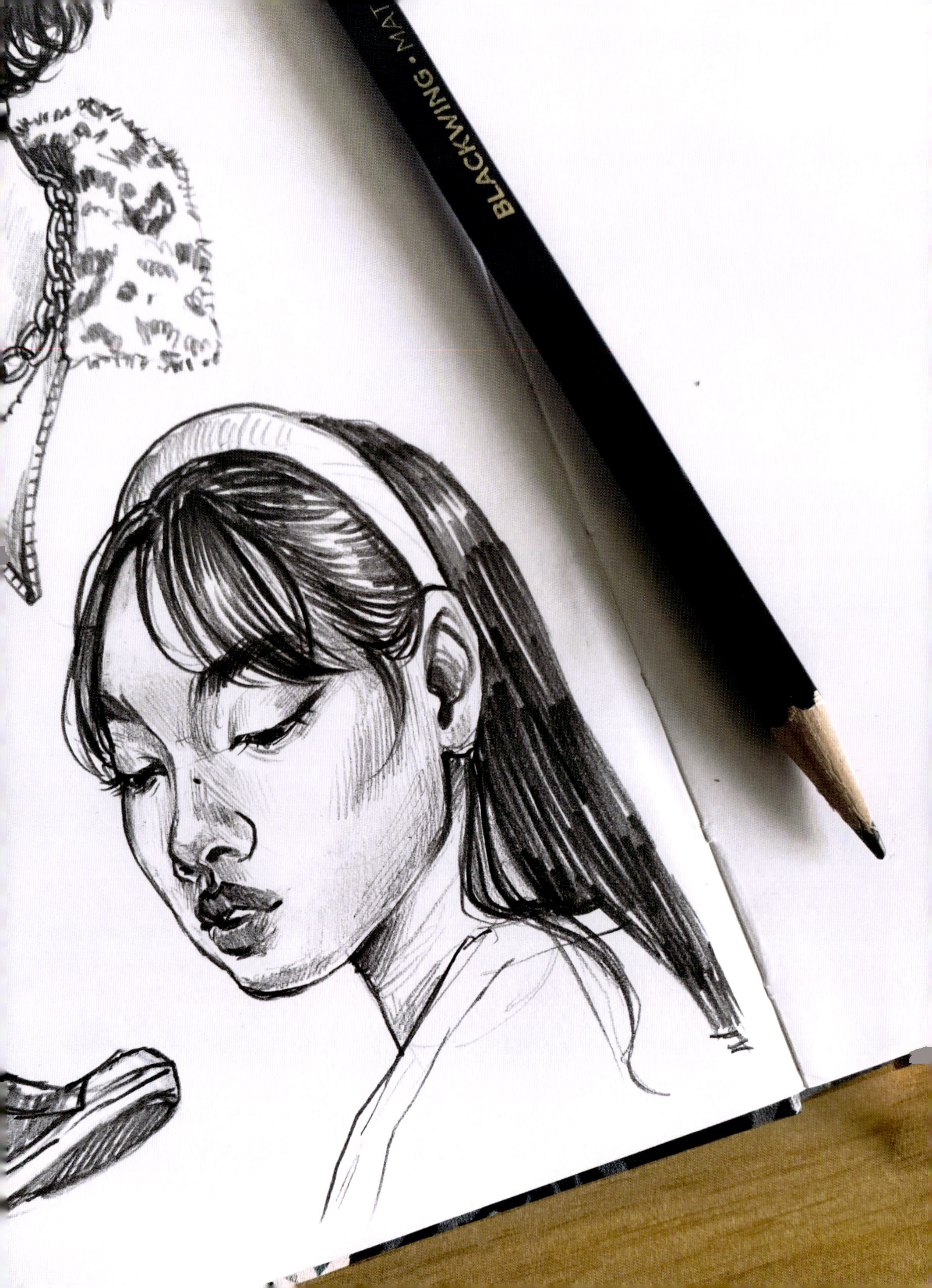

BLACKWING · MAT

3

SHADING, LIGHTING & RENDERING

Being able to draw a face is incredibly rewarding in itself, and that goes for most things. Knowing where to put the lines and how big to make them in order for a bunch of scribbles to resemble a human face—amazing! But drawing doesn't end there. In order to take your drawings and your portraits to the next step, you need to learn how to render your drawing. Don't worry, it's not as complicated as it might seem. We'll break it down and make it simple—and fun!

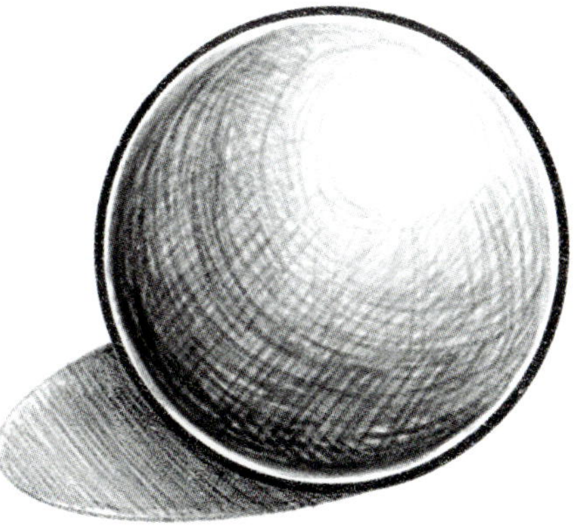

PENCIL SHADING TECHNIQUES

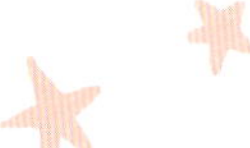

All you really need to create the illusion of a three-dimensional shape is the pencil you're already using.

Shadows are the absence of light, so we place shadows on an object to indicate where the light is and isn't. We'll get to lighting and how that works in a bit. For now, let's focus on shading.

For starters, there are many ways to shade in a drawing, and there isn't really a wrong way to do it. You can experiment with a number of different ways and eventually find a technique you prefer to use.

I will only be showing you the four most common ways to shade a drawing, but you might find some new ones you like better than these.

Here are four shading techniques you can try:

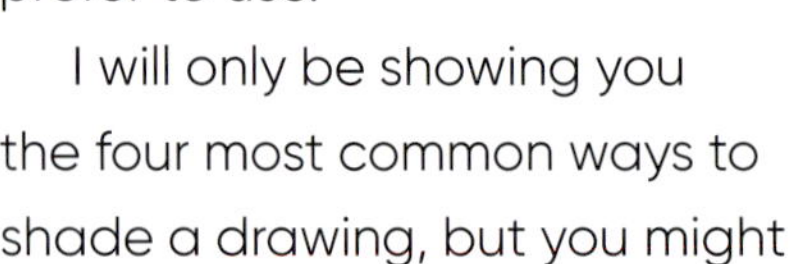
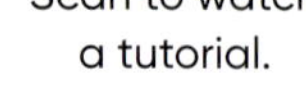
Scan to watch a tutorial.

HATCHING

Hatching consists of a series of "parallel" lines very close together. The closer together the lines are, the darker the shadow you'll create. When the lines are more sparse, an illusion of a lighter shadow is created. You can also mold the shading lines to the curves of your object.

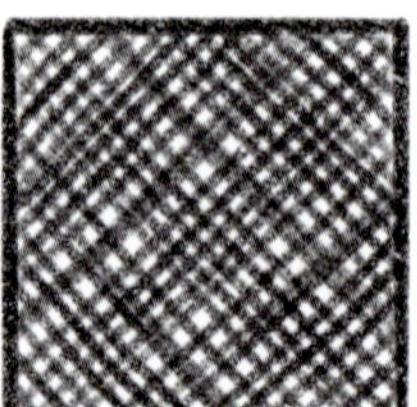

CROSSHATCHING

Crosshatching is another form of hatching where you layer a second set of hatching in a different direction on top of the original hatching. This automatically creates darker shadows but also creates a nice texture to them. I love this shading technique the most!

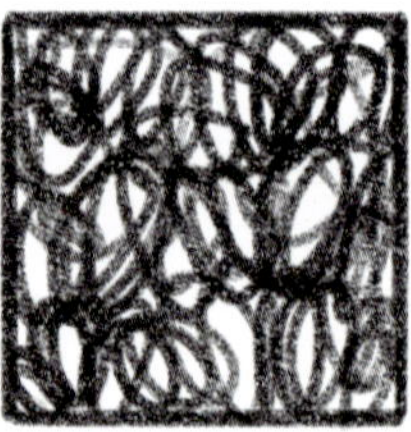

SCRIBBLING/CIRCLING

Scribbling is another very nice way to add texture and a fun look to your shadows. It's exactly what it says: scribbling. You can darken the shadows by scribbling over areas that have already been scribbled and layering the shadows.

FINGER BLENDING

This shading technique is the easiest one for beginners. Just sketch in some shadows and then use your finger (or a *blending stump*) to smudge the pencil around on the paper. This one works well only with graphite and some other pencils.

As you might have noticed, shadows aren't always a solid blob of color in one area with a harsh line around it. Most often than not, shadows taper off in a gradient-like fashion as they become closer and closer to the light source.

Either way, there are a few ways to create a gradient shadow with these four techniques.

The easiest and most obvious one is layering. Go slowly and as light-handed as possible when blocking in your shadows—you can always darken your shadows later!

The other two ways to manipulate your shadows' darkness are **sparseness** and **pencil pressure**.

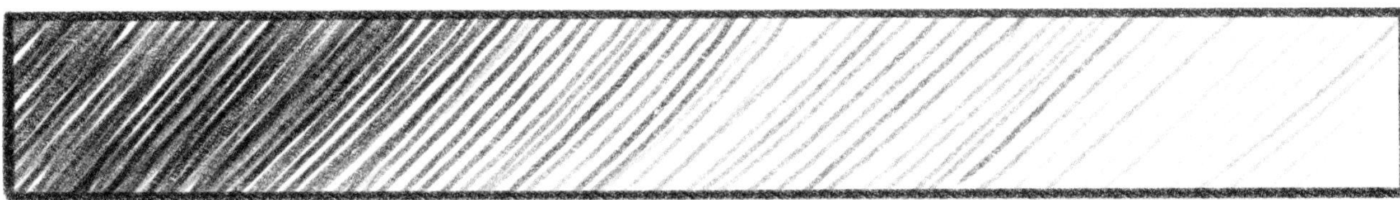

HATCHING

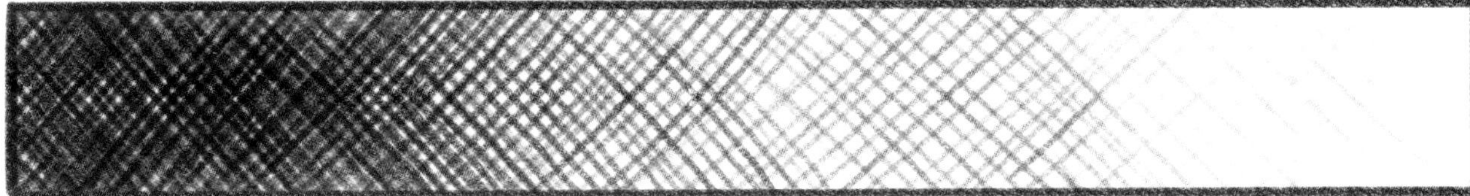

CROSSHATCHING

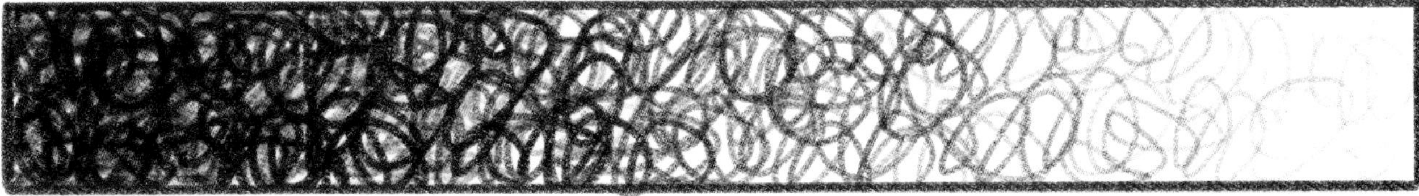

SCRIBBLING/CIRCLING

FINGER BLENDING

As you can see in the example, the more pencil strokes that are layered on top of each other, the darker that area becomes. And on the lighter side of each rectangle, the strokes are faint, light, and more spread out. Using less pressure on your pencil will create an illusion of a lighter shade, even though you're using the same pencil color! It can take some time to get the hang of quickly changing the pressure, but with practice that action will become second nature and you won't even need to think about it.

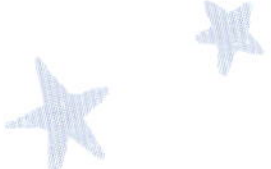
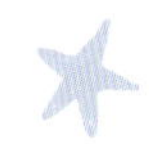

LIGHT SOURCES

Light is the main factor in making your drawings look 3-D. Light creates shadows and makes shapes pop off the page. You can't have shadows without a light source, and you can't have a light source without shadows being cast!

Take this sphere for example: If the sun doodle is our light source, the area closer to the top right of the circle would be getting directly hit by the light. So this area would be the lightest and brightest spot on our drawing (i.e., no shadows at all).

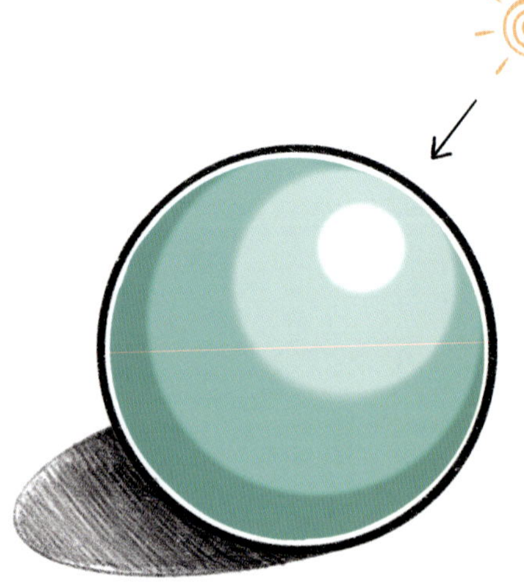

But as we travel down the shape toward the bottom left, the light is no longer able to hit this area (as light bounces off whatever surface it hits immediately). Therefore, the closer we get to the surface where our sphere sits, the darker the shadows are.

In green, I have blocked in the areas where there would be shadows and how strong they would be. The white area is a strong highlight, so no shadow at all. The light green is our midtone shadows and the dark green is our dark-tone shadows.

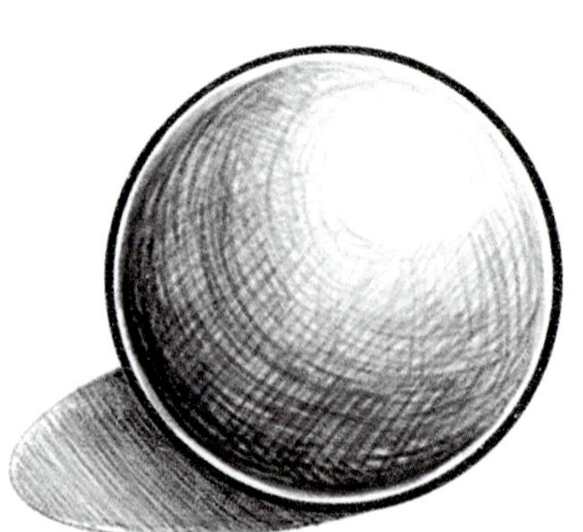

Here is the same sphere with the same light source but rendered with a pencil. Darkening the bottom of the sphere the most creates *contrast*.

Contrast is the visible difference in tones in an image. The more contrast you can create with your shadows, the more depth you will create in your drawing. And creating contrast is very simple. You just have to remember to create a balance between your **highlighted areas**, your **midtones**, and your **dark tones**. Having these three in your drawing will create depth and give the illusion of a three-dimensional space!

- Different tones = Contrast
- More contrast = Depth
- Depth = 3-D shapes

Shown here is what shading and lighting looks like on a cone, for example.

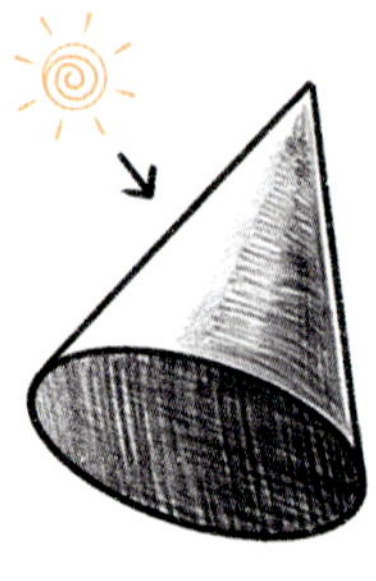
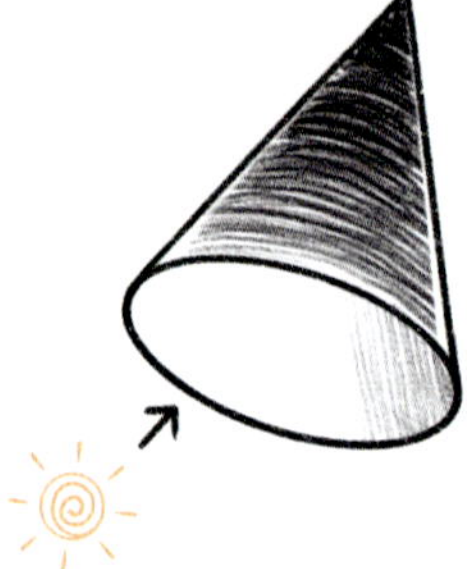
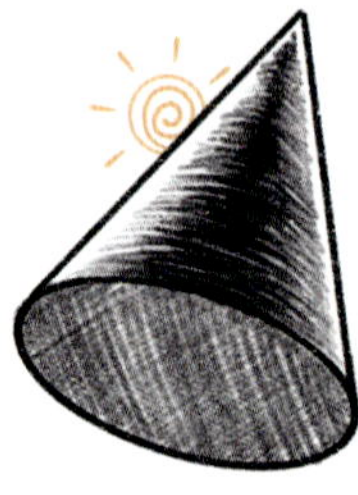

The placement of the light is obviously very important. As you can see in the cones examples, where you have your light source in your drawing changes the placement and darkness of the shadows considerably.

It's important to understand the basics of light and how it works so you know where to place your shadows—or where not to place them—when that time comes. But don't worry too much, as the more drawings you do from reference and from life, the more you will understand how lights and shadows work.

Take a few objects and place them on a table with a light you can move about to test out different light sources. If you do this, you will also notice that sometimes there is a little bit of highlight on the back side of your objects, completely obscured by the light source. How can that be? This is what is called backlight, and it's a very common detail you might like to implement in your drawings.

Backlight can be added in the form of rim lighting. I love adding a hint of rim lighting to my drawings, as it breaks up this darkness and allows the viewer to see the boundaries of our shape more clearly.

Light bounces off objects, and it can bounce off anything: the surface your object is on, a wall behind your object, other objects around it, etc. When the light bounces off something that is behind our main object, it comes back to hit it from behind (albeit less strong, of course—it's already lost some light along the way). This causes a little soft shadow where you would expect to be only shadow.

You can use either an eraser or a gummy eraser to take away a little bit of the shadows here along the edge of your shape.

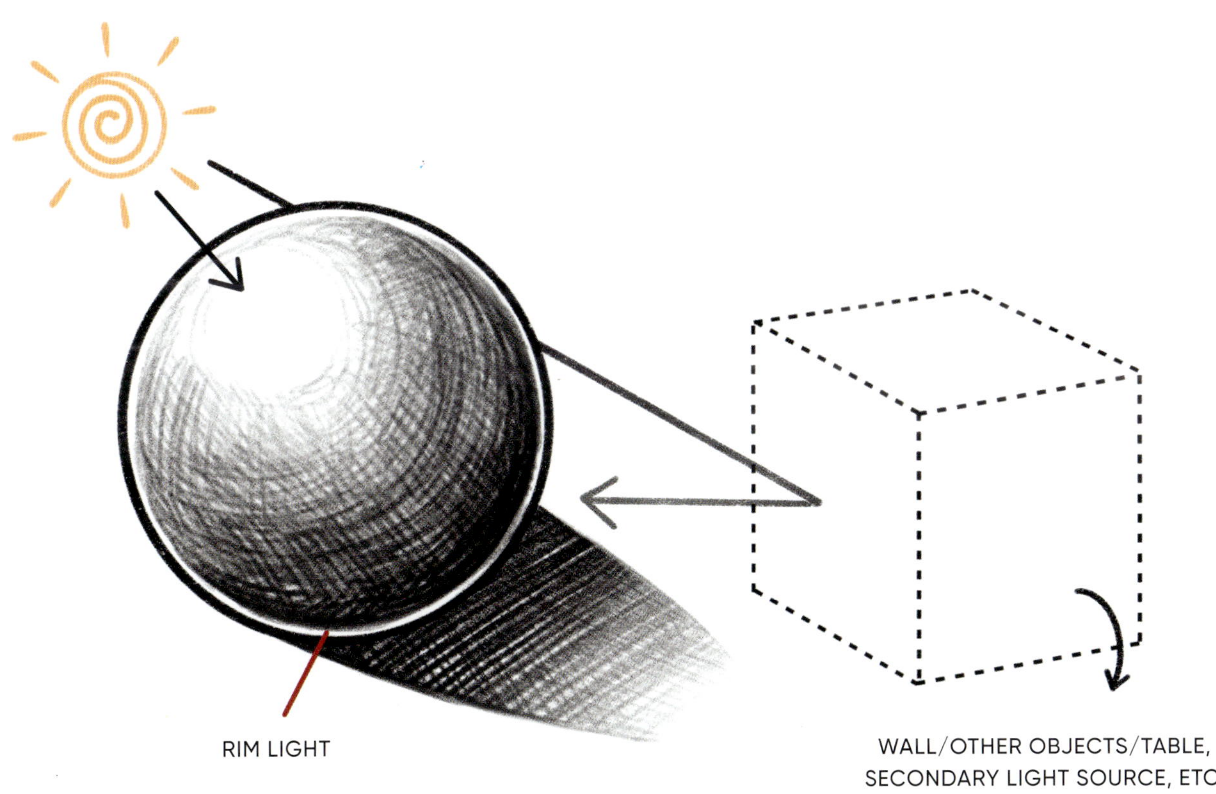

RIM LIGHT

WALL/OTHER OBJECTS/TABLE,
SECONDARY LIGHT SOURCE, ETC.

SHADOWS & HIGHLIGHTS

As we have learned, areas of a shape closer to the light source will be highlighted and lighter in color, whereas areas farther away or even obscured from the light source will be darker or have shadows cast upon them. The same rules apply to the shadows and highlights on the face.

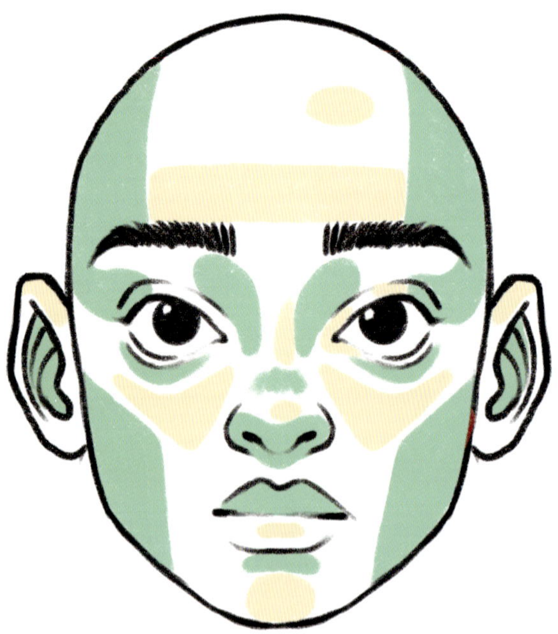

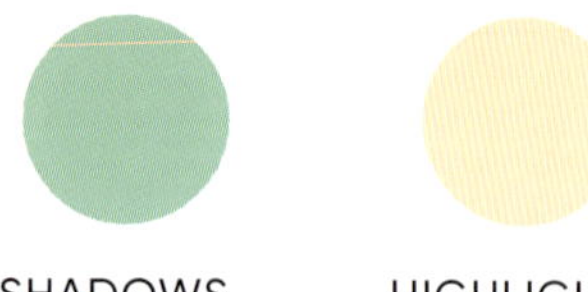

Here is an example of a face where the light source is right in front of it, being lit straight on. You can see, using the different colors, I have shaded in which areas would have shadows and be darker and which areas would be highlighted and very light. All other areas that have not been shaded in would be your midtone.

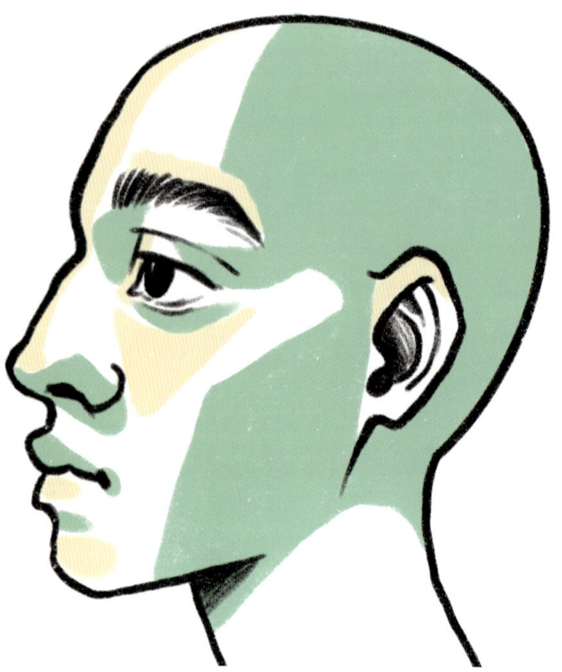

Here is the same lighting example, but from the side. The tip of the nose, forehead, chin, and front of the cheekbones are still being touched by the light the most, and the farther into the back of the head you go, the darker it gets, since the light cannot curve around the head and reach those areas.

This is just one example of light hitting the face, however, so let's look at some other scenarios.

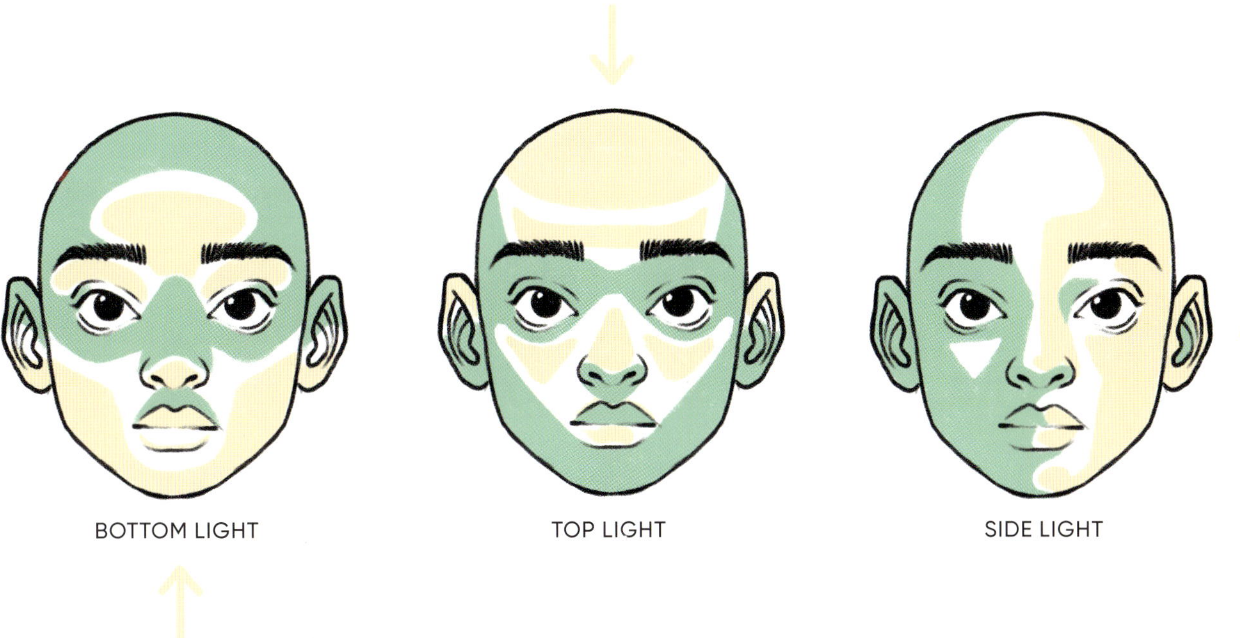

The direction in which the light comes from and hits the face changes the placement of the shadows and highlights drastically.

When light hits from below the face (like when you shine a torch under your chin to make yourself look spooky), the whole chin and jaw area are completely highlighted, as well as the bottom of the nose and lips, the upper eyelids, etc. The nose also casts a big shadow all the way up the nose bridge, whereas when light hits from above, the nose casts a shadow downward onto the cupid's bow and mouth. Most of the face appears to be darker with overhead lighting, as the forehead, brow bone, and nose will cast shadows onto most of the face—this is why overhead lighting is not very flattering in photos!

From the side, as you can guess, half the face will be highlighted and half the face will be in shadows cast by the nose, mouth, and rest of the face.

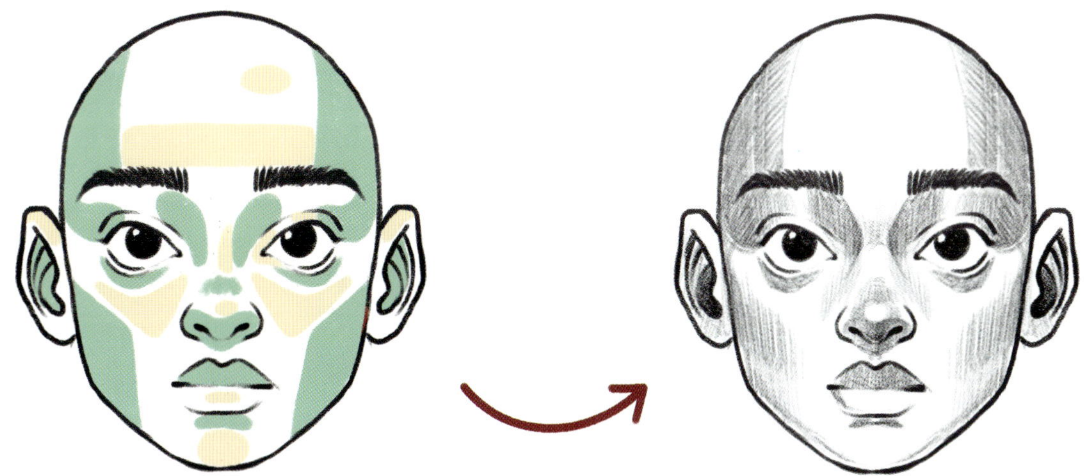

In this example, the green areas can be shaded using the techniques on page 36, making sure to taper off along the edges. The yellow areas are the highlights and should be left untouched when shading with pencils.

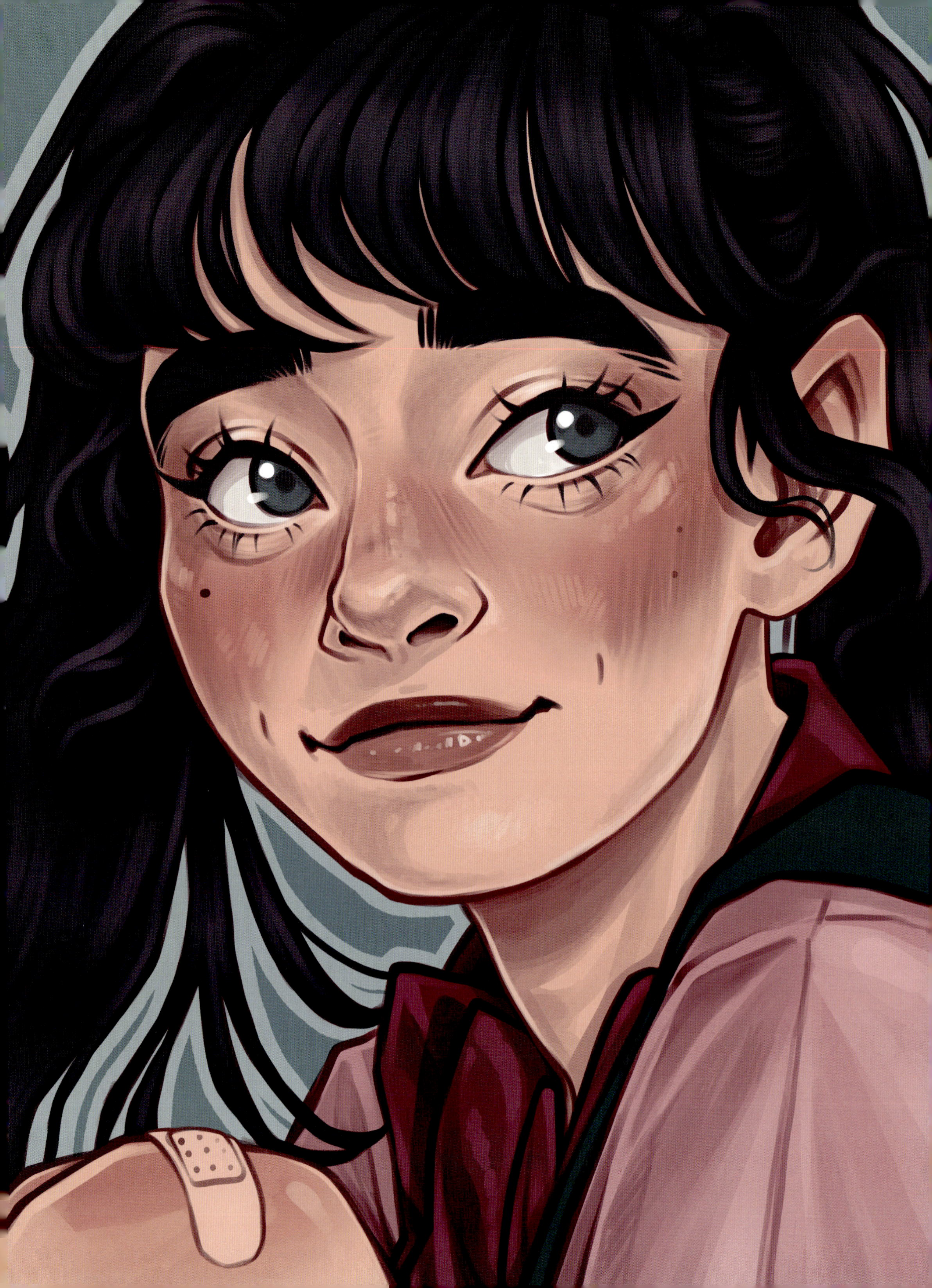

4

DRAWING THE EYES

Eyes are an incredibly important part of the face—they take up a big chunk of the head, they're centered on the skull, and they're incredibly emotive. When you look at a face, you are usually drawn to the eyes to get a sense of how that person is feeling, which is why eye contact is so important in communication! All this to explain why I always recommend drawing your face eyes-out. Once you get the eyes placed and drawn out well, the rest of the face just naturally comes together.

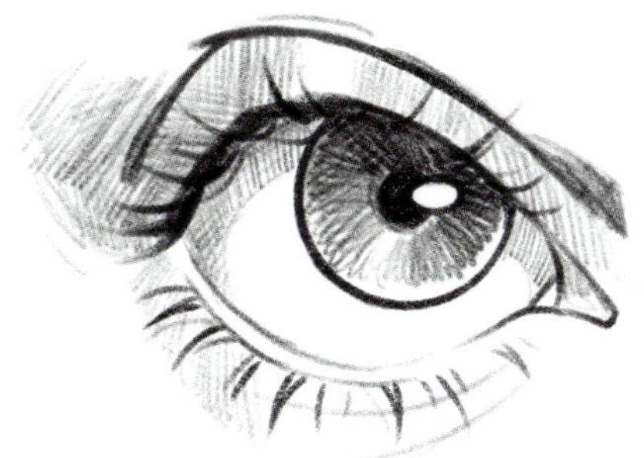 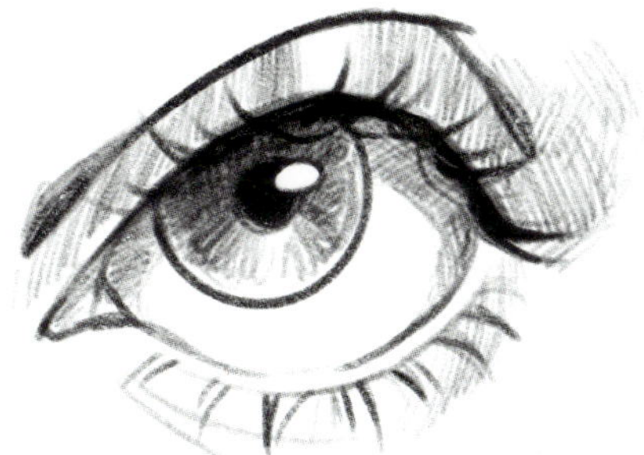

STARTING WITH THE EYES

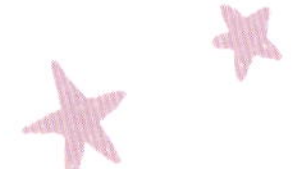

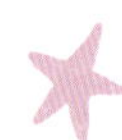

Because the eyes are such a crucial and emotive part of a face, it can be quite intimidating to draw them. I'm going to show you ways you can study the eyes and how to easily draw them yourself.

There are three basic elements to the eye: the eyeball, the eyelids, and the hair (eyebrow and lashes). Once you break it down into those three elements, it feels a lot less daunting to tackle the eye, wouldn't you agree?

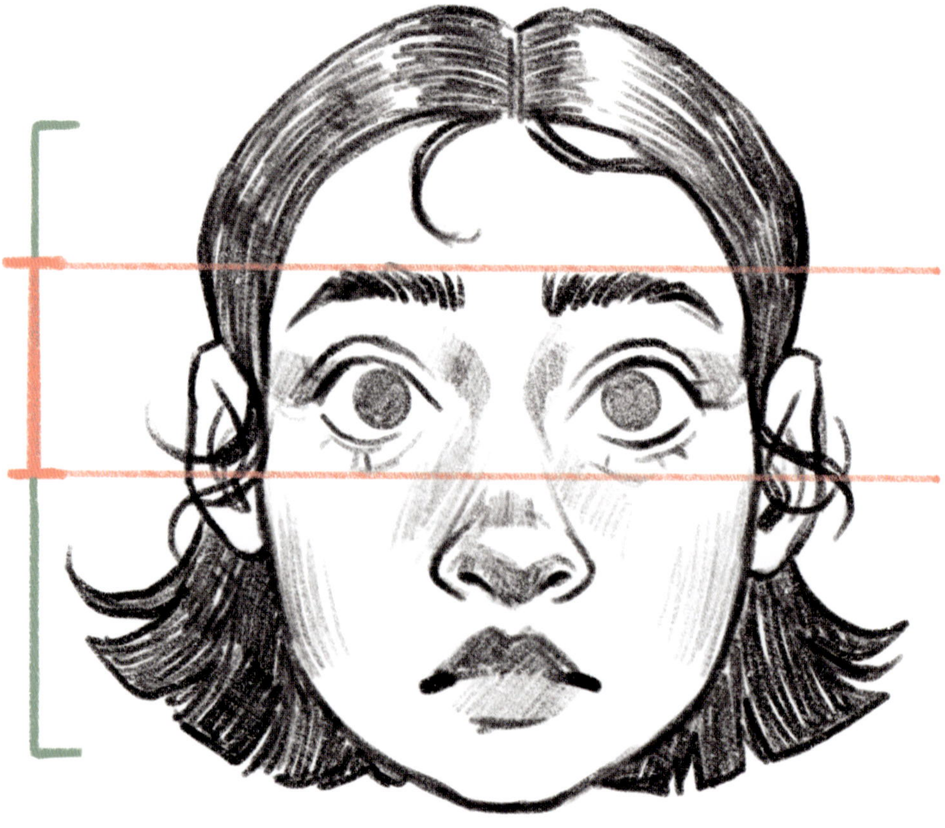

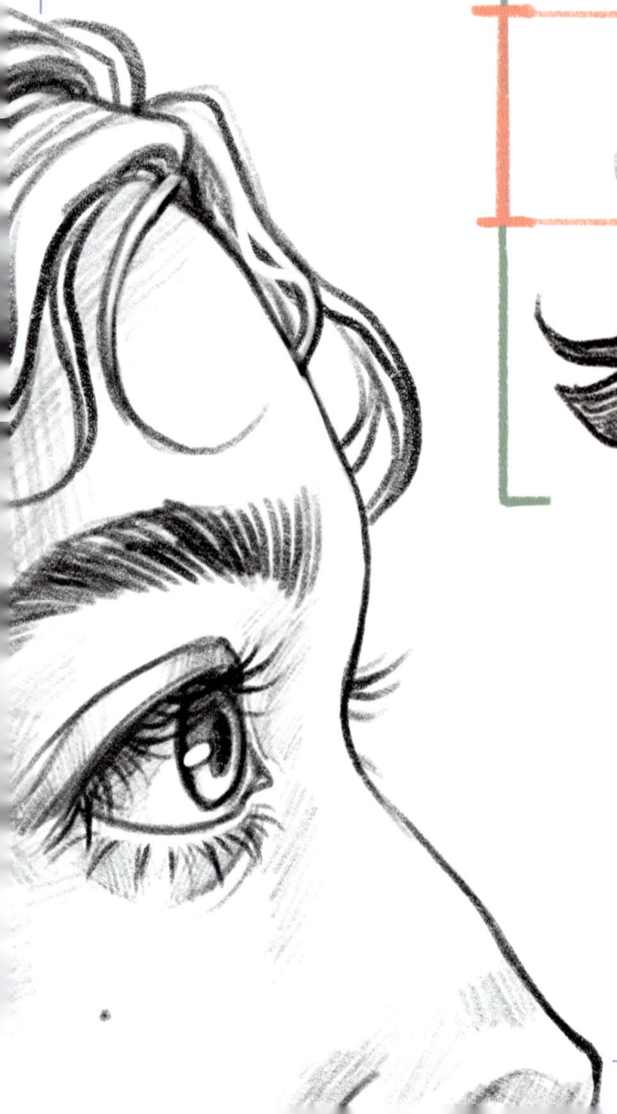

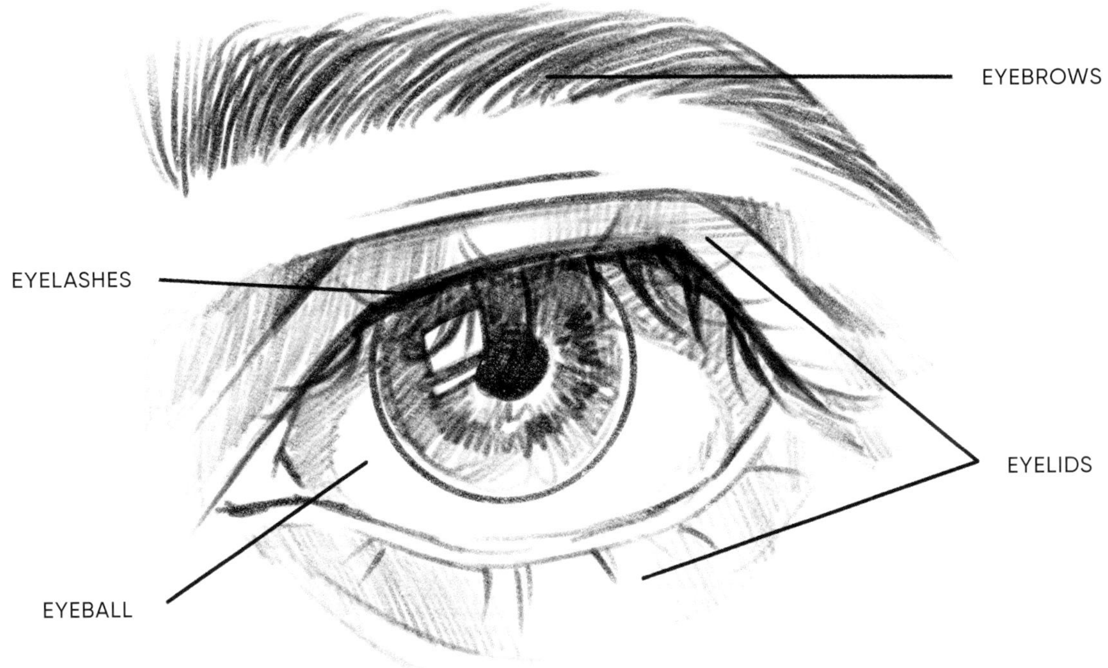

THE EYEBALL

The eyeball contains the iris and pupil, which dictates the direction in which your character is looking. The eyeball itself does not change much on its own.

THE EYELIDS

The eyelids control how open or closed the eye is and can showcase a lot of emotion depending on their shape.

THE EYEBROWS

The position and shape of the eyebrows assist the eyelids in showing feelings and are what cause the eyelids to move and change shape.

And of course, these elements all look differently at different angles, ages, and ethnicities. Therefore, it's important to first study these shapes and grasp the basics so that over time you can create a shorthand for drawing eyes at any angle (and emotion!).

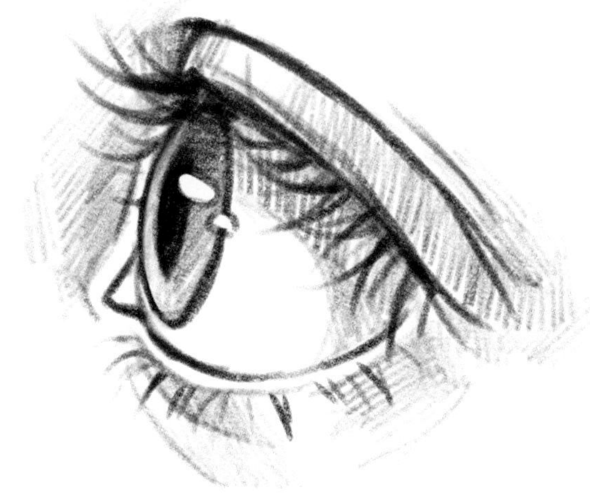

ANATOMY OF THE EYE

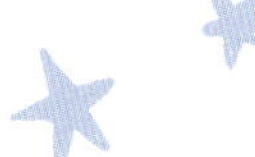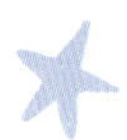

It's important to know what is going on not only on the surface but also behind the eye to get a better understanding of the shapes you'll be drawing and why. Knowing the anatomy of an object gives you a three-dimensional understanding of how that object might look at different angles.

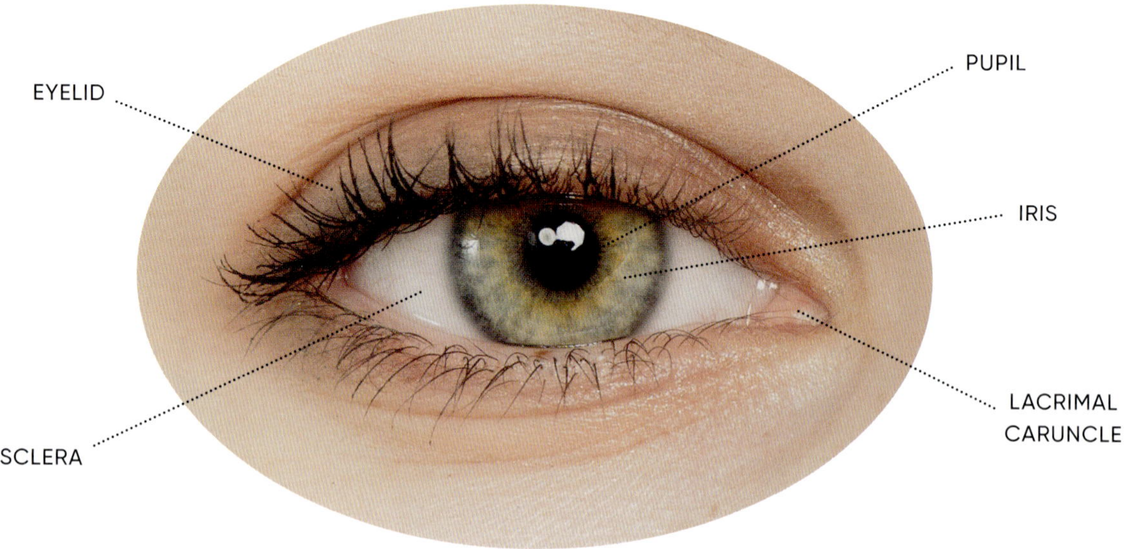

The eye from the outside is composed of two eyelids that open up. The upper eyelid is the more pronounced one, usually creating a crease.

In the inner corner of this almond shape, we have the *lacrimal caruncle*, a very fancy term for what most people call the tear duct.

Then inside the eye we have a small amount of the eyeball that we can actually see. We can see the *sclera* (the white part of the eye), the *iris* (the colorful part of the eye), and the *pupil* (the black center of the eye).

We also have the extra bits, like the eyelashes and the waterline of the eye, but we can get into those when learning how to draw the eye in more detail.

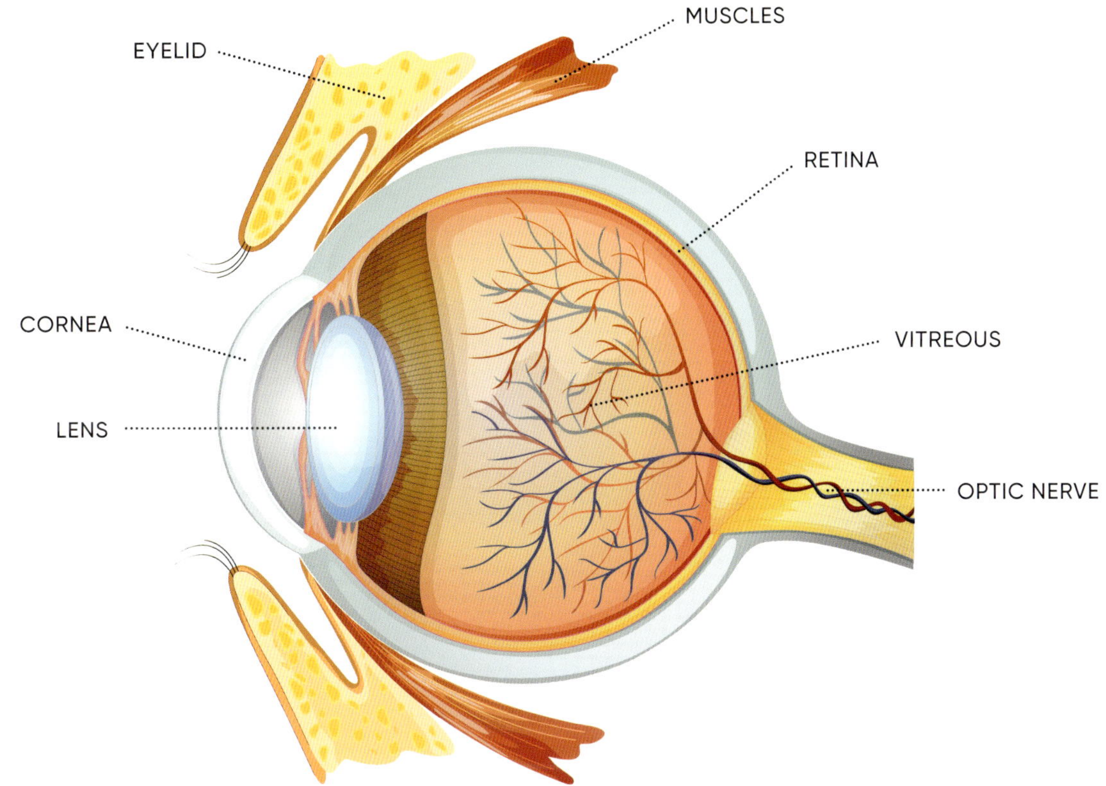

As I said, the eye from the outside actually only shows a small fraction of the whole story. There's a whole eyeball behind the skin that we don't see but whose anatomy creates a protruding spherical shape on the eye. It's why the eyes aren't flat—they curve outward, and this is most evident when you see the eyes from the side.

The *cornea* is the bit with the iris and pupil I mentioned earlier. This area protrudes even farther out from the spherical shape of the eyeball, but it can usually be seen only from the side.

From here on out, imagining the eye as a sphere covered by two eyelids can be helpful for drawing the eye not only at different openings but also at different perspectives.

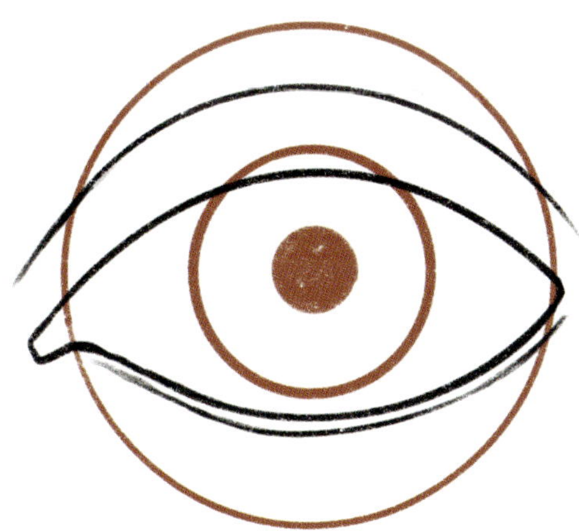

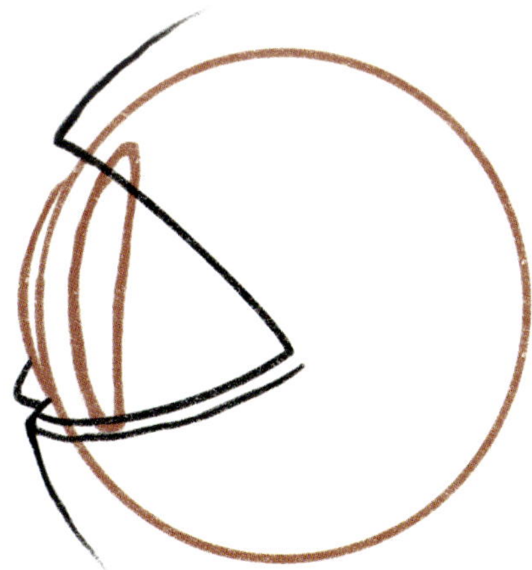

BASIC SHAPES OF THE EYE

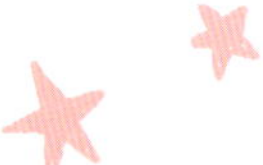

Now that we know about the anatomy and the structure of the human eye, we can learn how to understand it in a way where we can draw it. The best way to understand how to draw the eyes is to understand the shapes that make them up.

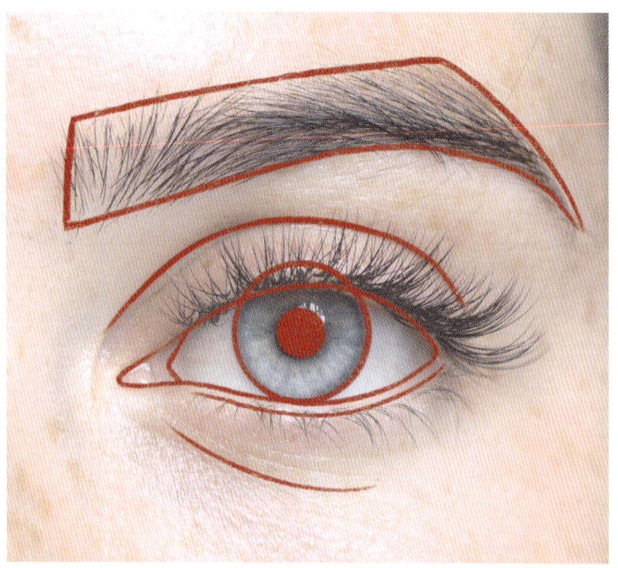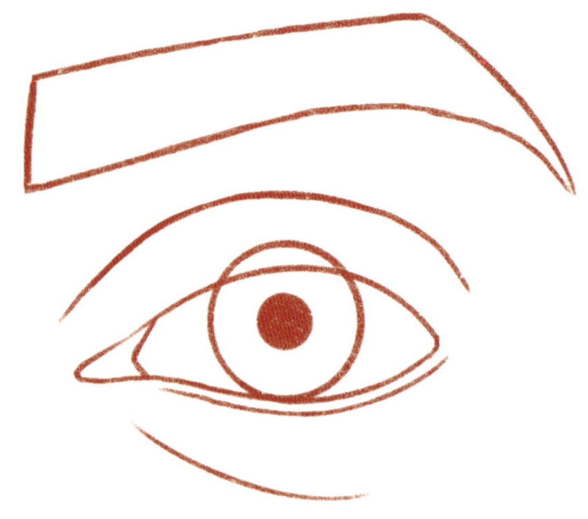

In the example shown, you can see there are a few shapes to think about when constructing an eye. The first ① is the eye opening, which is usually a variation of an elongated almond shape. For the iris, you'll want to draw a circle in the middle of the eye, where usually a part of it's obstructed by the upper eyelid ②. You should also draw in the pupil right in the middle of the iris.

Above and below the original almond eye shape ①, there is usually a crease line ③. These two lines are usually parallel to the eye shape lines (following the same curvature).

The eyebrow is usually a curved rectangular shape, tapered off at the end into a point ④. Finally, the little sideways V shape in the inner corner of the eye forms the *lacrimal caruncle* ⑤.

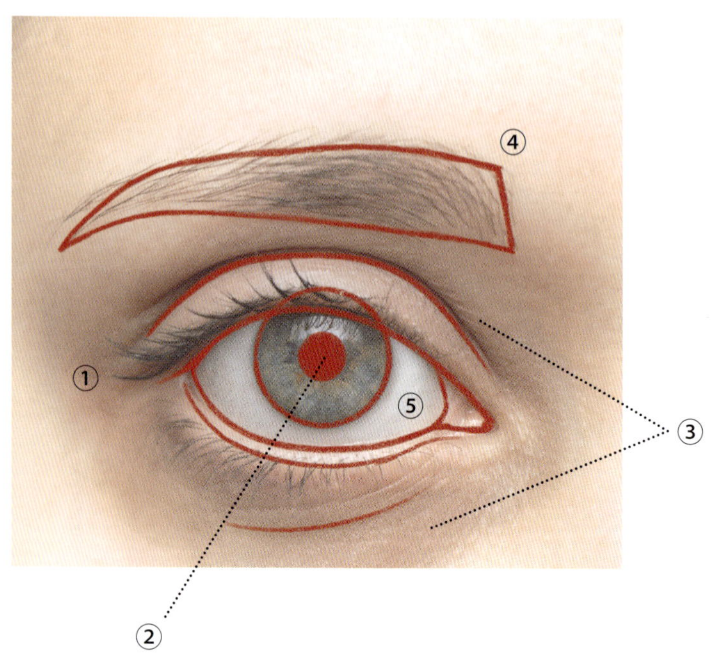

But of course, the eye also looks very different when viewed from the side (in profile). In profile, the eye doesn't look so much like an almond but more like a capital letter A lying on its side.

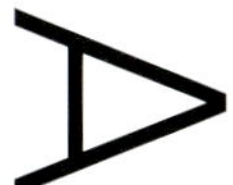

When drawing the eye in profile, it's as if all the shapes and lines we learned about on the previous page get more and more squished from the sides until some of them are not even visible anymore.

The eyebrow is shorter than before and rounder at the inner corner ④. Again, the eye itself goes from an almond shape to a triangular shape ①.

You may also notice that the pupil is no longer centered inside the iris in profile ②. This goes back to the anatomy of the eye earlier in the chapter, and if you'll remember, in front of the pupil sits the cornea, which shoves the pupil back.

As you can see in the illustrations, the main differences in the eye in profile have to do with perspective: the inner corner of the eye with the tear duct are not as visible, if at all ⑤.

Once you get the hang of the eye straight on and in profile, it becomes a lot easier to "fill in the blanks" and draw the eye at any angle in between these two.

The waterline and eyelid creases follow the same principles as before, following the same curvature of the eye shape and staying somewhat parallel to it. The upper eyelid's inner corner area is no longer visible, however (much like the inner corner of the eye), and that crease line now connects to the top of the eye ①.

Another thing to note about the eye in profile is that the eye opening is not flat. Thinking back to the sideways "A," imagine the bottom line of the A is curved downward. This is because of the bulging nature of the eye—as we know, the eyeball is a sphere. So when it is in profile, we must draw the exposed part of the eyeball as such.

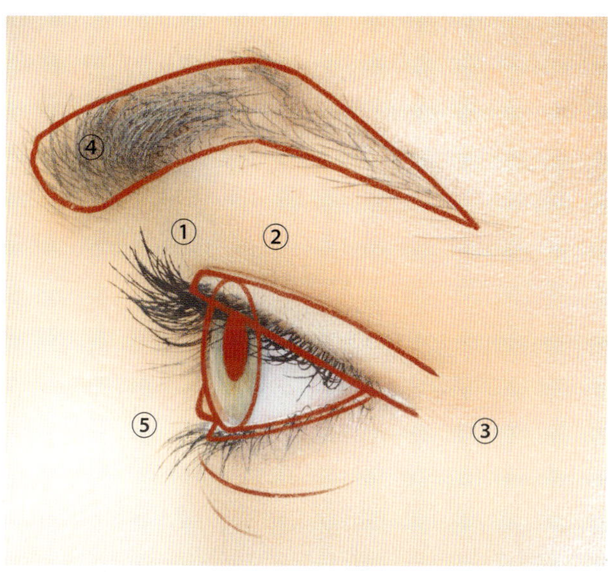

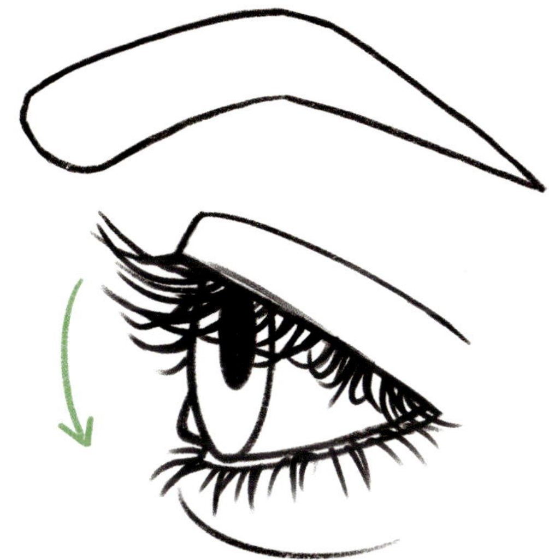

THE EYE HAS CURVES

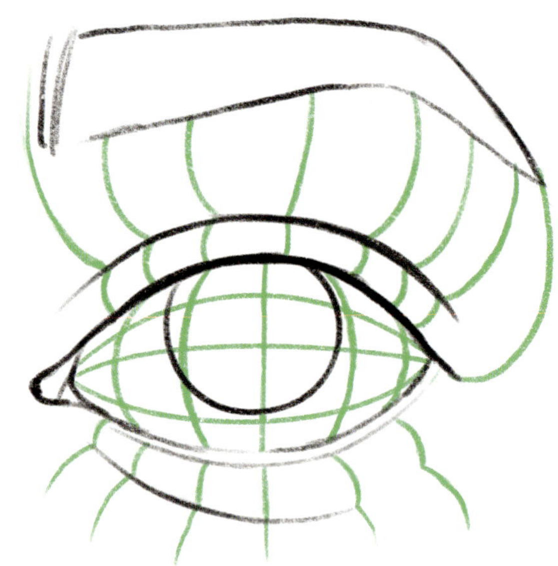

As we previously discussed, the eyeball is a spherical shape and it causes the eyes on the face to have a bulging, rounded shape to them.

When thinking about the eye in the 3-D space, you can use directional lines to map out the "faces" of the shapes.

The human eye is formed of many shapes all interacting and colliding with each other, and the skin itself stretches and moves, so we cannot think of the eye as a flat plane.

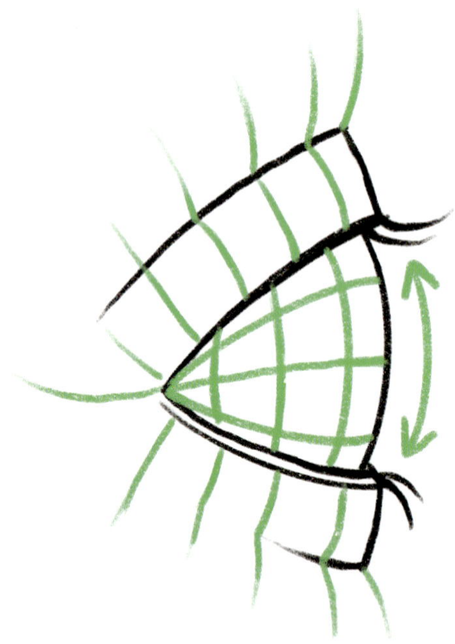

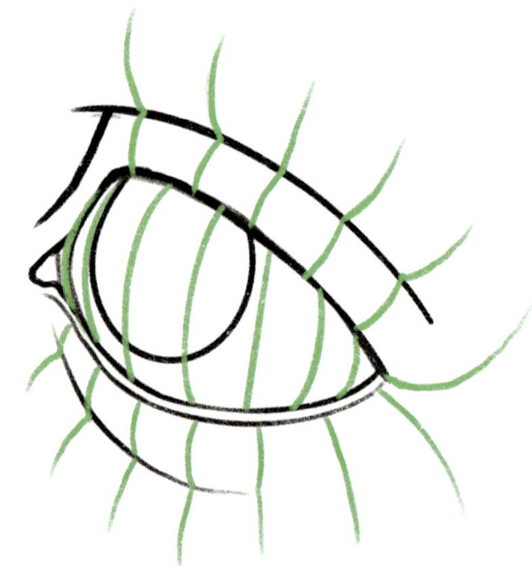

On the almond-shaped eye on the left, you can see how the green guidelines show the way the eye and the skin around it have curves, as well as how the skin puffs out, creases, and curves back out again to meet the rest of the face.

In profile, we can see how the eye protrudes from the face, and even the eyelids, and how the eyelids follow that curvature up into where they fold into a crease. The eyelid is just skin that folds over the eyeball, so its shape matches the curvature of the eyeball underneath it and then follows the rest of the bone structure of the skull.

You can even use some guidelines like the ones shown to help you understand where to add in shadows in the rendering stage of the drawing.

We've been looking at the eye when it's open and staring straight ahead so far. But the eye looks different depending on where your character's eyes are looking, the perspective of the face, and how open or closed the eyes are.

The best way to always make sure your eye is anatomically correct is to think of it like an anatomy drawing: imagine the eyeball as a circle behind the eye, with the pupil and iris placed in the direction you'd like the eye to be looking, then draw the eyelids and the "eye opening" over the top.

This way you know that the eye will always be aligned with the eyelids no matter where it's looking.

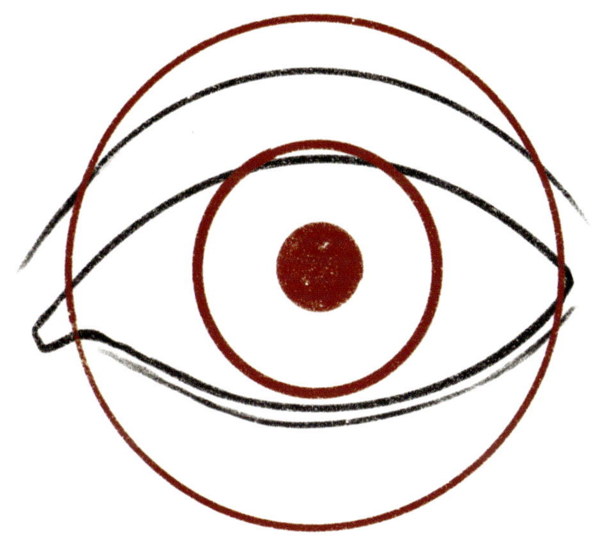

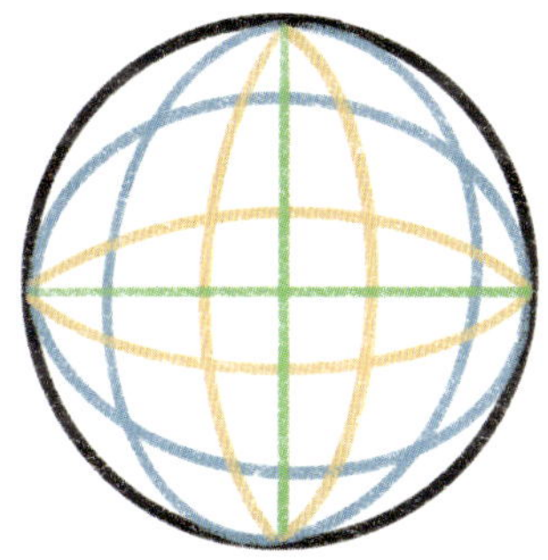 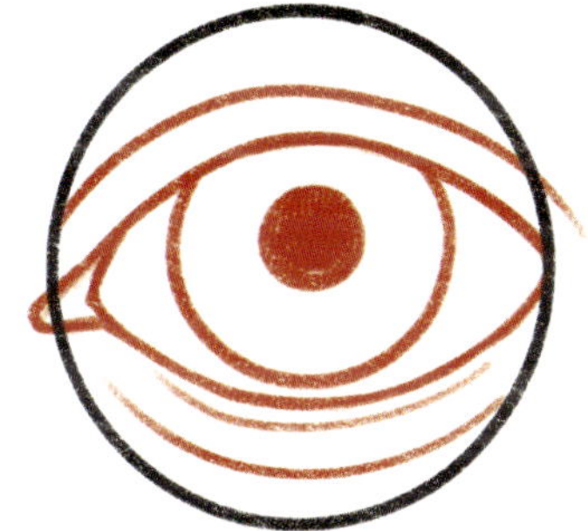 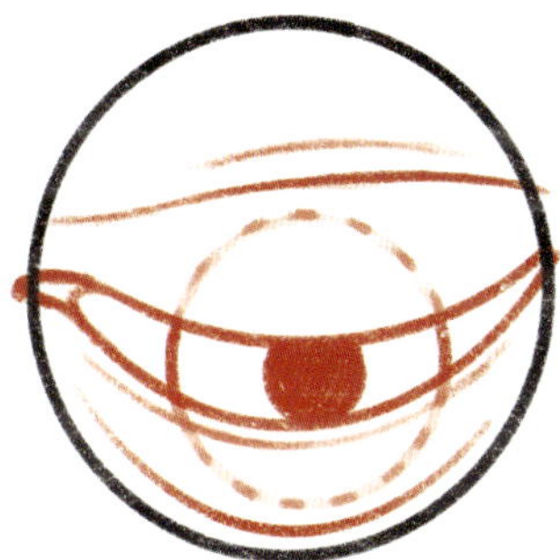

Make sure to keep the spherical shape of the eyeball in mind whenever you draw the eyes. For example, you can follow the yellow guidelines shown in the illustration when drawing out an eye that is more closed, or even squinting, or use the blue guidelines for an eye that is extra wide open.

Overall, using guidelines like these will not only keep the 3-D space in the back of your head but also offer you some help when drawing the curvature of the eyelids, the eyelid creases, etc.

This works for perspective too. In the example here, you can see how you can use this method to draw an eye being looked at from above while still using the spherical guidelines. You can also see how the iris and pupil are placed in a different place and where they sit behind the eyelids.

A way that I like to think of the eye is comparing it to a rugby ball. If you think of the eye-opening shapes and curves similar to those of a rugby ball, you will be starting off on the right foot!

These shapes and curvatures will become a lot more important later on when adding in shadows and highlights to your drawing, which will make your portraits look more realistic and alive!

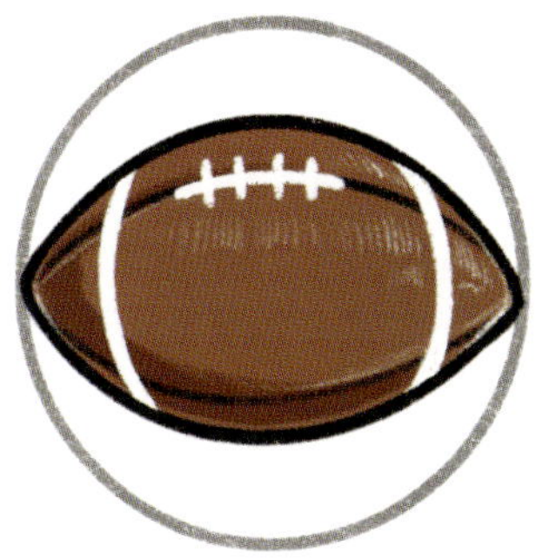

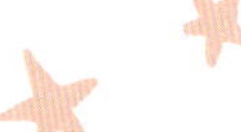

DRAWING AN EYE STEP BY STEP

Now that you are aware of the basic building blocks that make up the eye, you can translate that into drawing one yourself. It might seem like a lot of complicated parts, but take it one step at a time:

Scan to watch a tutorial.

FRONT VIEW

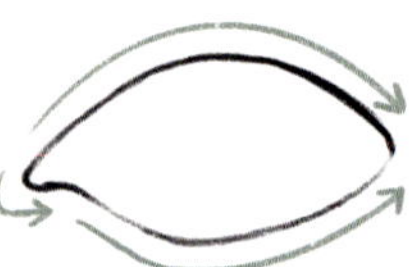

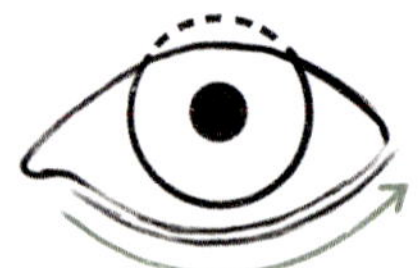

1. Start off drawing the eye opening, which, for this example, resembles an almond with a little droopy point on one of the corners.

2. Add a parallel line to the bottom part of the almond slightly below it for the waterline. You can also add in the iris as well as the pupil right in the center.

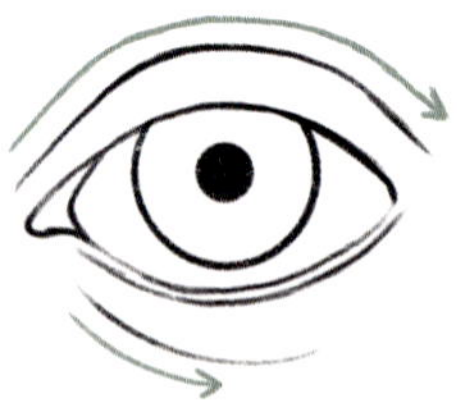

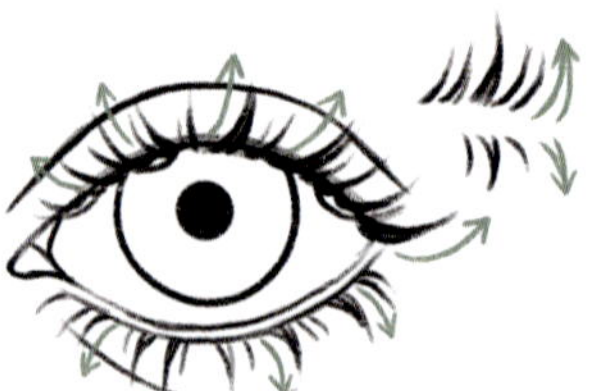

3. Add in two lines: one above the eye, parallel to the top of the eye, and one smaller line below the eye, following the curvature of the bottom of the eye. These are the eyelid creases. You can also add in the little line in the corner of the eye to create the lacrimal caruncle.

4. Now add in the eyelashes. These will look more natural the more randomly you place them. The curvature and direction of the lashes should coincide with where they are on the lash line.

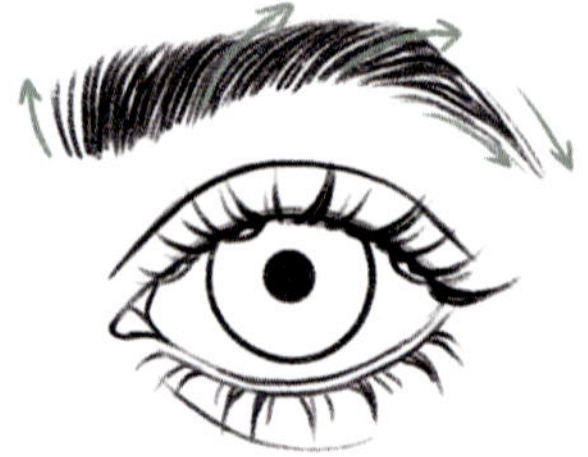

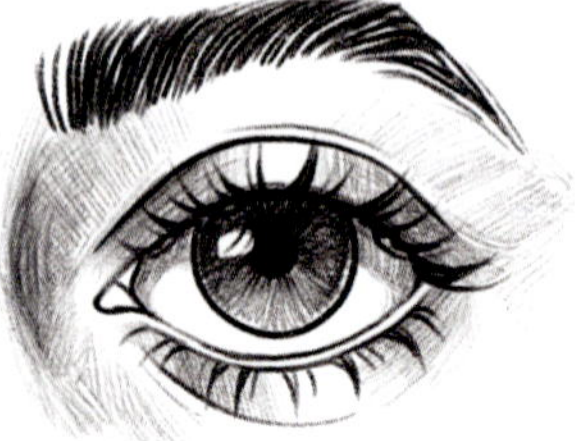

5. Add the eyebrow above the eye. For this neutral expression, the eyebrow sits comfortably on top of the eye, stretching slightly longer than the width of the eye. The hairs of the eyebrow should move in the direction shown.

6. Finally, add lights and shadows to the eye. All the areas on the highest point of the eye are hit by light and therefore have little to no shadows on them. The deepest areas will have the darkest shadows.

PROFILE

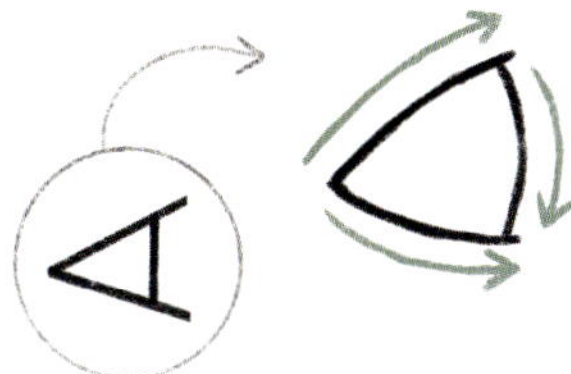

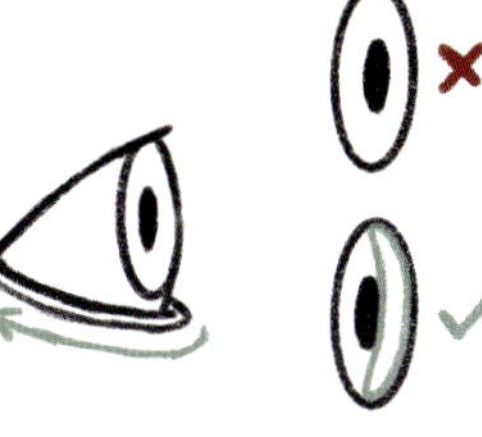

1. In profile, we know that the eye resembles a sideways capital A and not an almond. So start off by drawing a rounded sideways A with curvier lines, as shown.

2. Add in the waterline like before. You can also add in the iris and pupil. In profile, the pupil is not centered like before. It's actually positioned slightly closer to the inside of the eye (allowing space for the cornea in front of it).

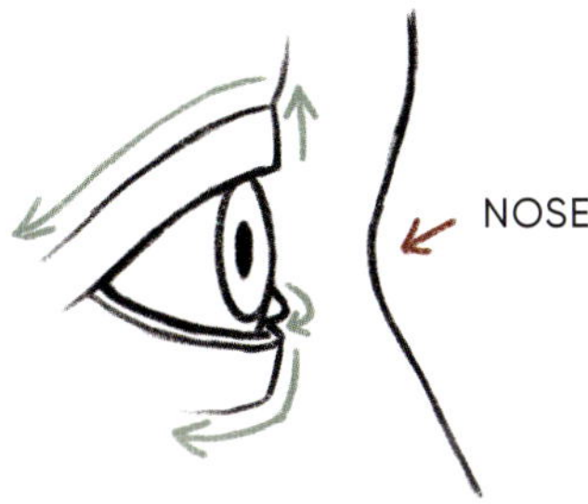

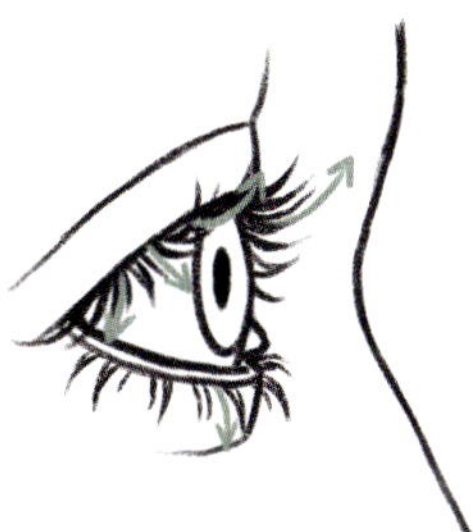

3. At this point, you can draw in a line to depict the nose outline and add the eyelids. These lines will go out from the bottom tips of the A and then inward, following the curvature of the eye. The little tip of the lacrimal caruncle can also be seen sometimes in profile.

4. Now for the lashes: the general rules apply, except that in profile, the lashes closer to the outer corner of the eye appear as if they're pointing downward and into the eye. Try drawing guide arrows before adding these in.

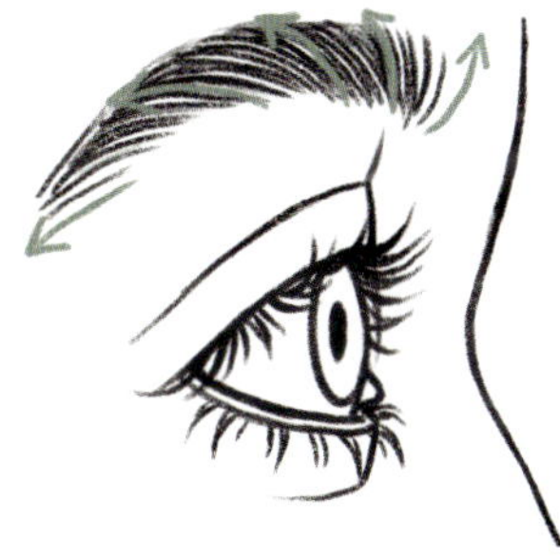

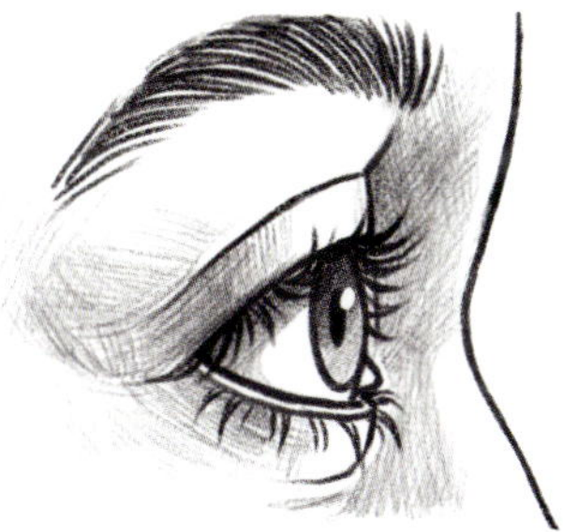

5. Then we can add in the eyebrow. The eyebrow, like the eye, looks a lot shorter from the side, due to perspective.

6. And finally, we can add in shadows. Areas like the inner corner of the eye and areas around skin creases will have shadows. Flatter areas "bulging" out of the face will be highlighted.

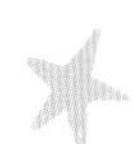

HAVING FUN WITH EYE SHAPES

There are many different eye shapes you can play around with when drawing your characters. These different eyes stem from a combination of genetics, ethnic backgrounds, age—and that's before we even get into facial expressions!

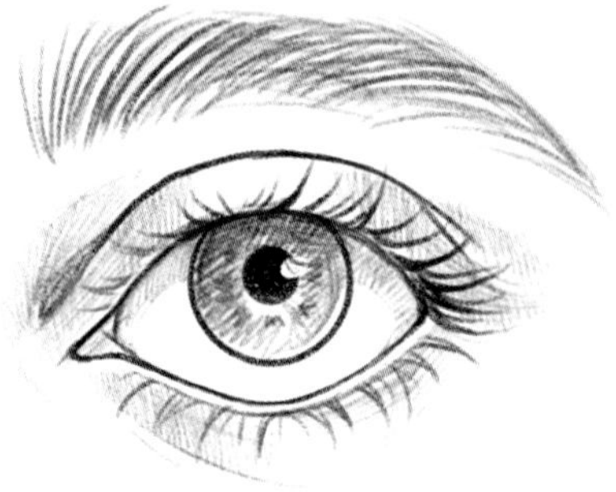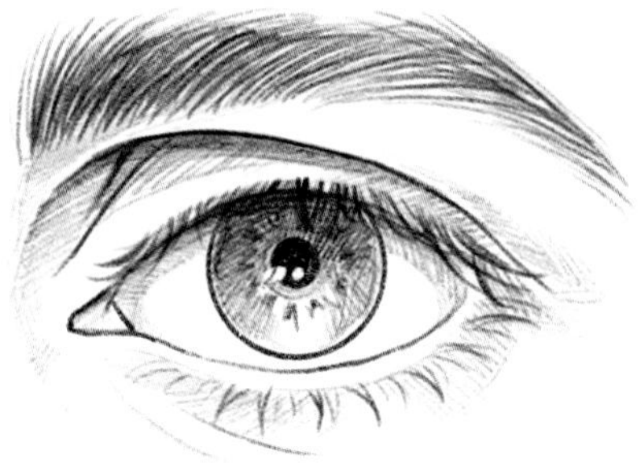

ALMOND EYES

I have mostly been using almond eyes as examples, as they are big and wide open, which makes it useful to showcase all the elements of the eye clearly. They resemble the shape of, well, an almond.

HOODED EYES

As the name implies, hooded eyes usually have a very low and creased upper eyelid that sits so close to the eye that it creates a "hood" over it.

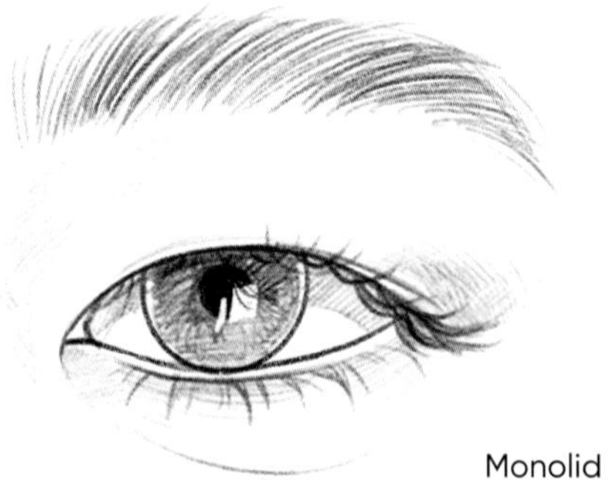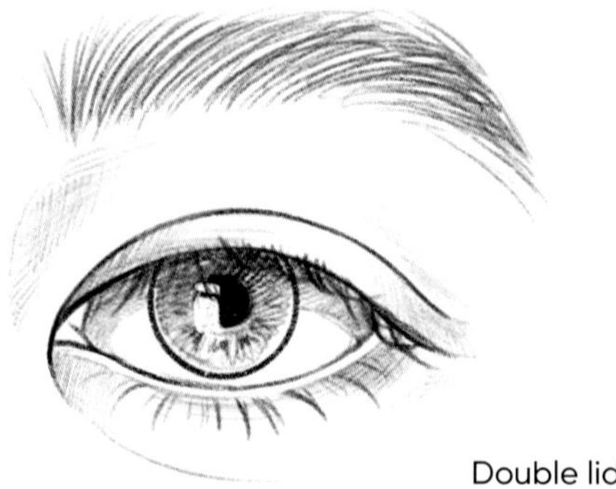

Monolid

Double lid

EPICANTHAL FOLD EYES

Epicanthal fold eyes are predominantly found in people of Eastern and Asian background. *Monolid eyes*, as the name suggests, seem to have only one lid above the eye since the eyelid crease sits so close to the eye, rendering it invisible. In both of these examples, the eyes are a lot pointier at the corners, and the eye may appear more closed. The inner corner of the eye will also have the *epicanthal fold*, which is where the skin fold of the upper eyelid touches and, in some cases, covers the inner corner of the eye.

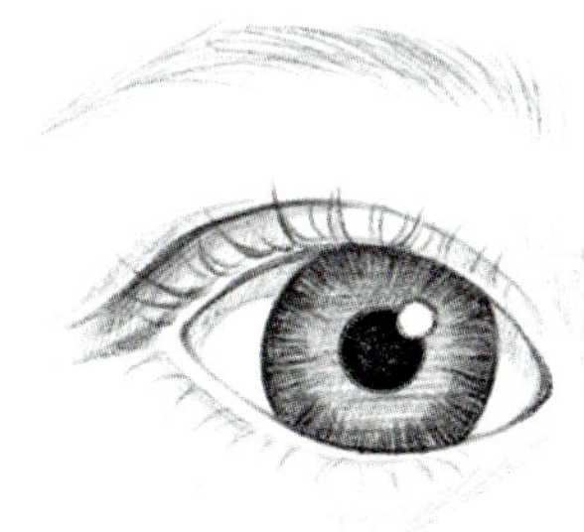

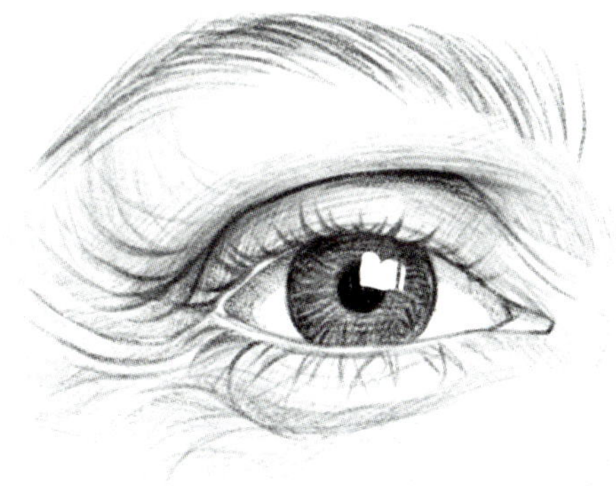

BABY EYES

Infant eyes have a much smaller eye-to-iris ratio, meaning that the iris and pupil appear much larger inside the eye itself. The eye shape itself is a lot shorter and rounder before it eventually grows into a more stretched-out, almondlike shape. Also, as you might have guessed, babies have much fainter creases around their eyes, and their eyebrows are also much fainter.

ELDERLY EYES

As the face and skin ages, there are more and more wrinkles in areas where the skin creases. This happens the most around the eyes and mouth, as these parts of the face are the ones that move the most in our lifetime. On top of the usual increase in wrinkles, we begin to see the wrinkles known as *crow's-feet*, as well as the upper eyelid becoming more and more hooded.

But these are not the only factors that can change the shape of your character's eyes. The way that the face itself moves and emotes can drastically change the appearance of the eyes. This is where facial expressions come into play. We'll look at them more later in this book.

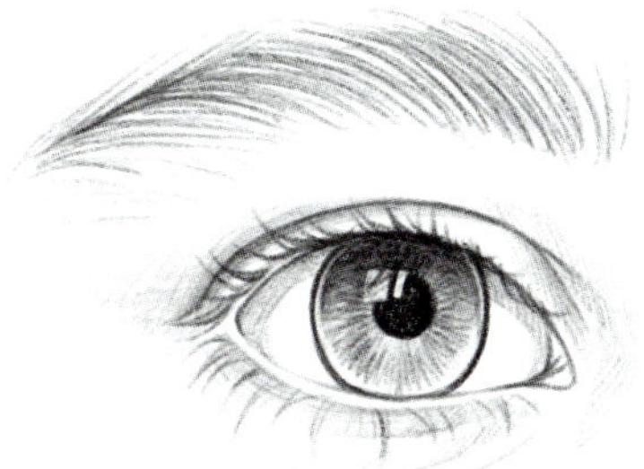

CHILD EYES

Children's eyes are a perfect balance between a baby eye and an adult eye. They are still not as stretched out and are still a little rounder. A child's iris looks a little more to scale inside the eye. As the eye ages into an adult, it looks almost as if the iris gets smaller and smaller, but in fact, the eye around it just gets bigger and bigger as it grows.

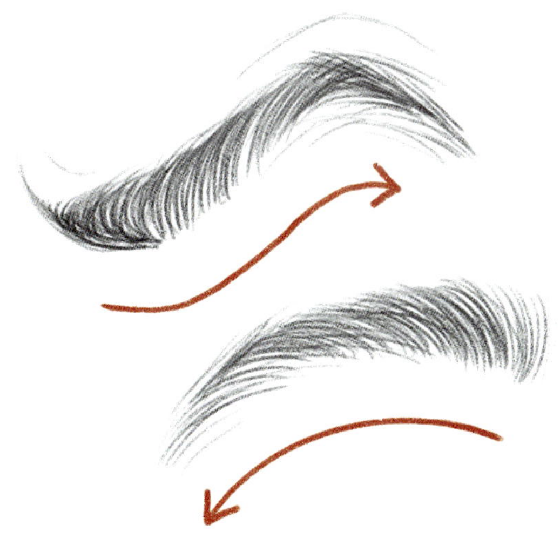

 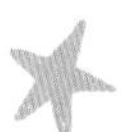

THE EYES AT DIFFERENT ANGLES

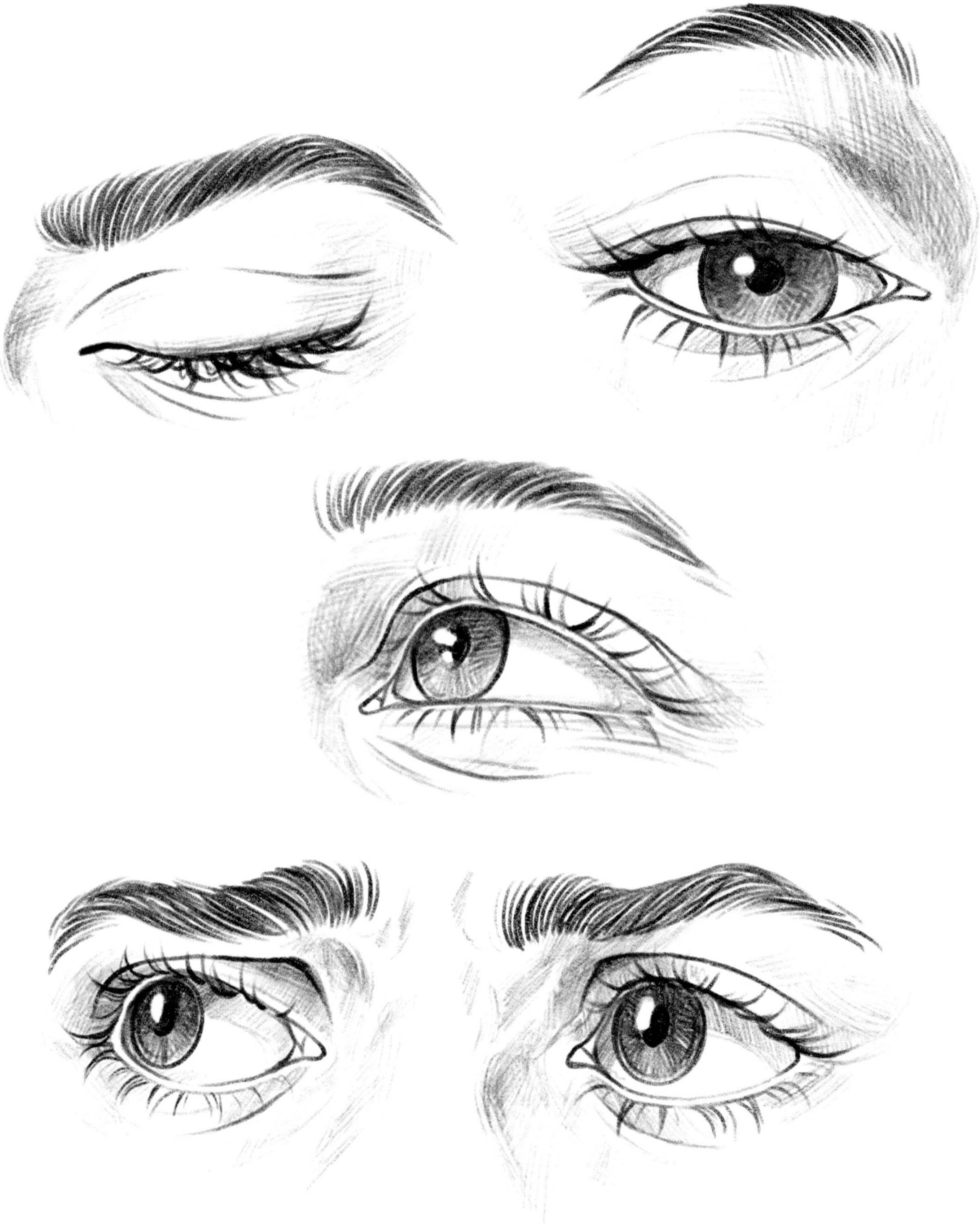

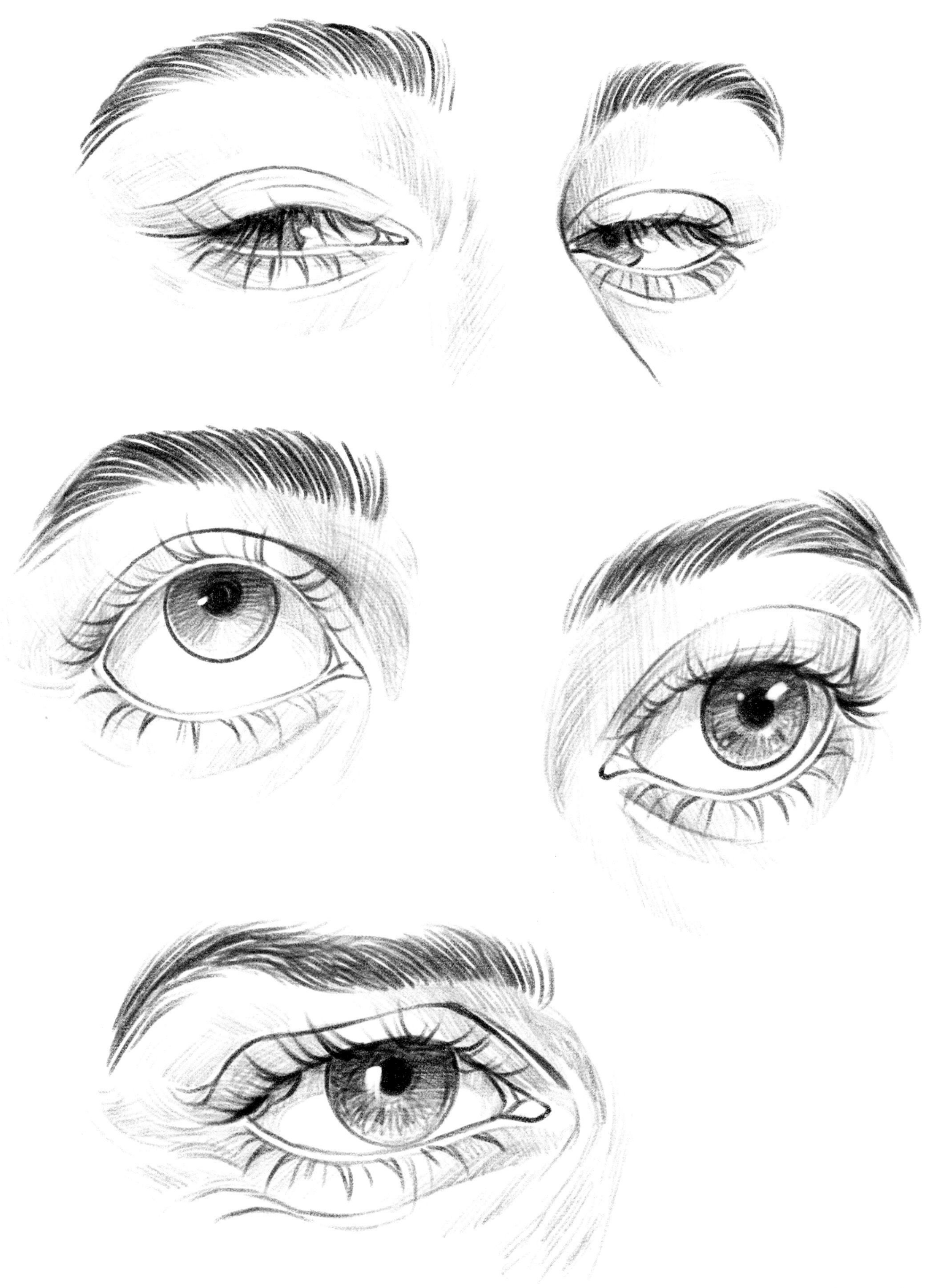

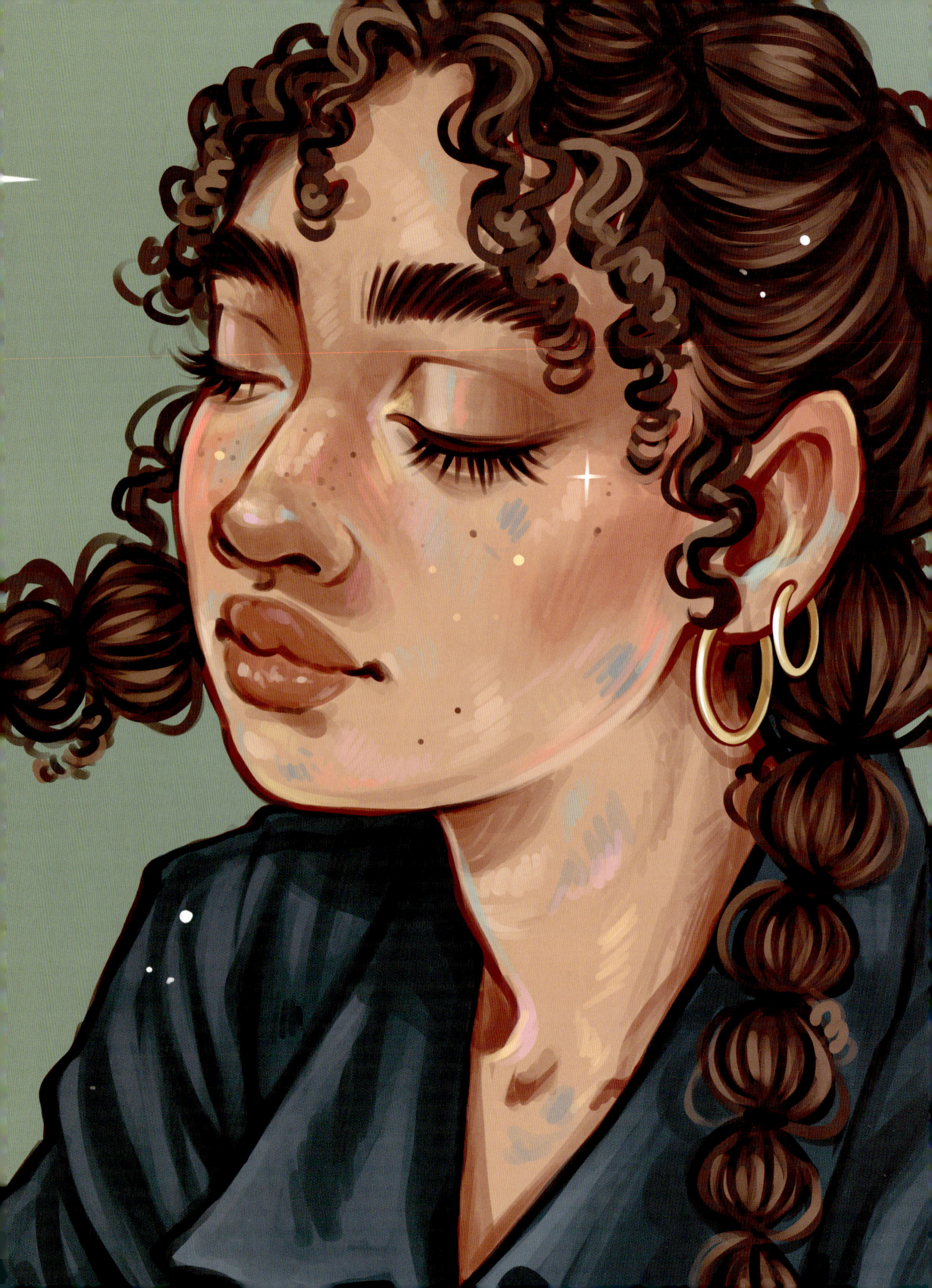

5

DRAWING THE NOSE

The nose is smack bang in the middle of the human face. You might not think about it often, but it's quite an important feature, not only for helping with placing the other features of the face but also for carrying a lot of emotion. The nose moves alongside the eyes and the mouth since it's connected to both and can really help with stretching out a facial expression. So the nose not only allows your portrait to breathe, but it's your main middle point of reference when drawing the face.

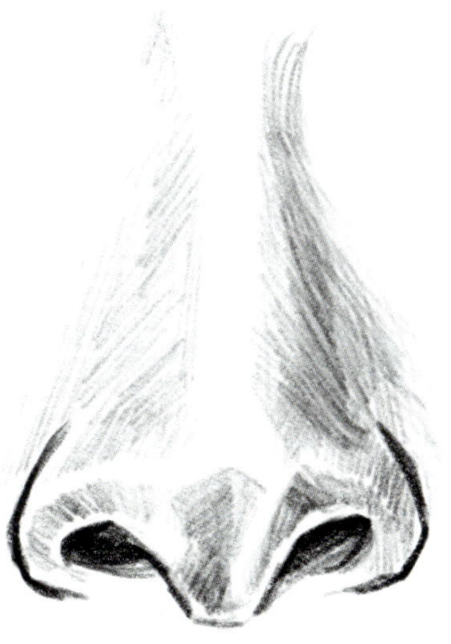

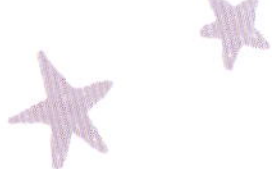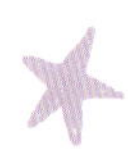

BREAKING IT DOWN INTO EASY SHAPES

Let's look at the nose and start off by identifying the basic shapes behind it. This will be a great help when we get into drawing the nose.

FRONT VIEW

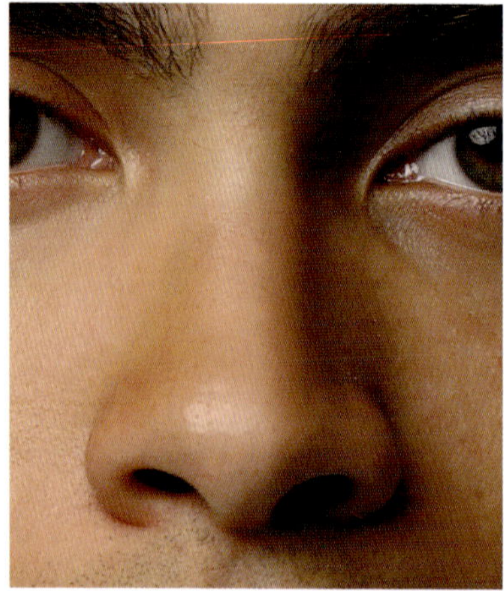

Let's take this nose, for example.

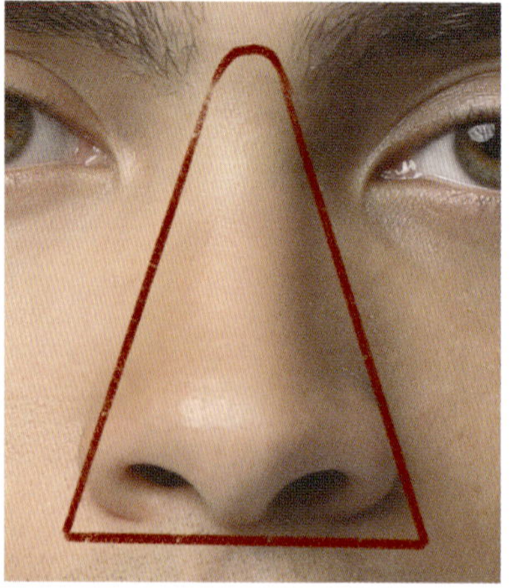

As you might guess, the main shape encapsulating the entire nose is a large, tall triangle, going from the top of the nose bridge down to underneath the nostrils.

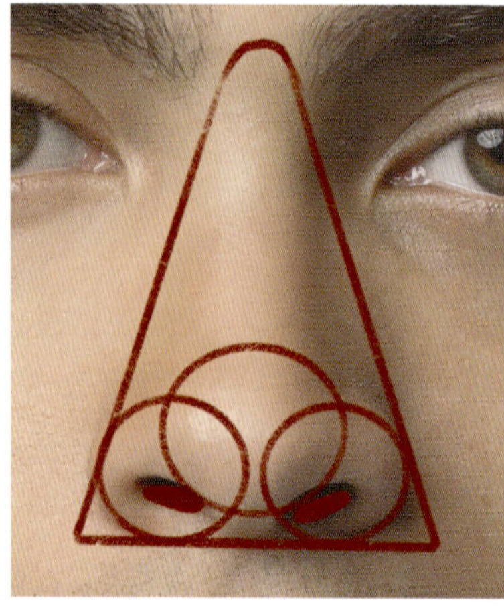

We then have the protruding masses of the nose. These can be identified with three circles, almost like a Venn diagram, where the middle circle (the tip of the nose) is usually bigger.

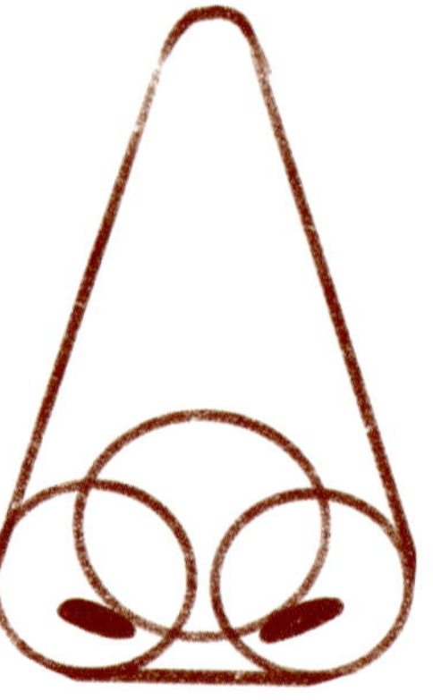

The nostril holes usually sit underneath the middle circle, almost centered in each nostril circle. And that is the nose broken down into shapes!

PROFILE

In profile, however, the nose looks slightly different—as most of the features of the face do at a different angle.

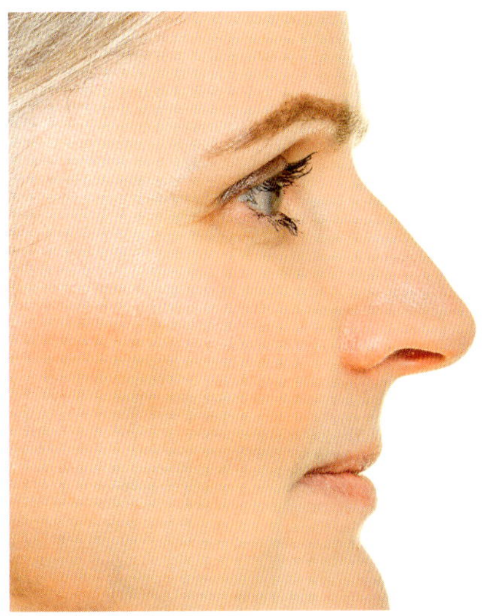

Let's use this profile as an example to study.

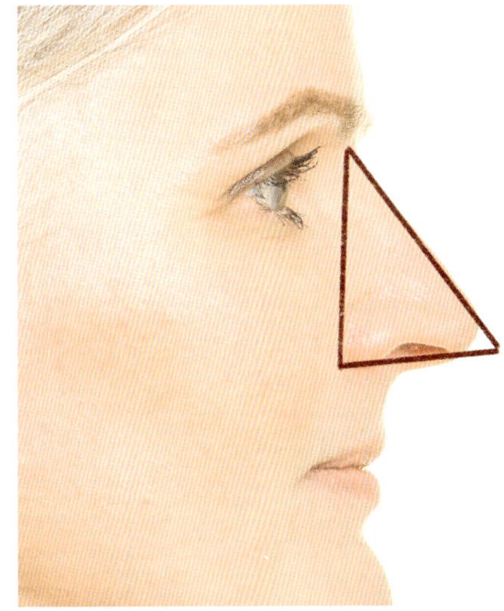

The main shape of the nose is still a triangle. But in profile, this will be a more right-angle triangle, almost sitting in line with the face.

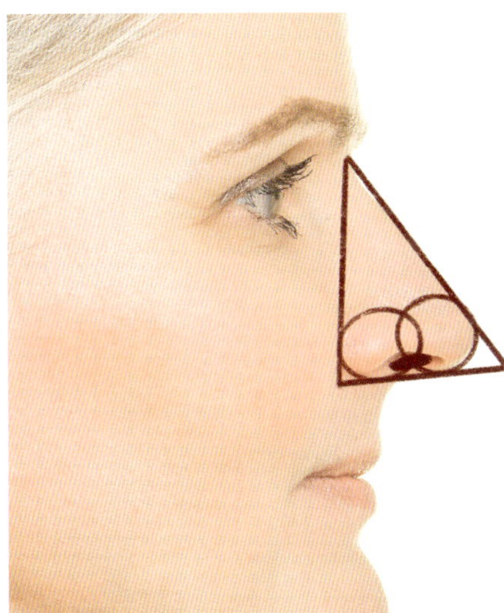

Then within that triangle we can add in the middle circle for the tip of the nose and then only one of the nostril circles, since in profile, we can usually see only one of the nostrils.

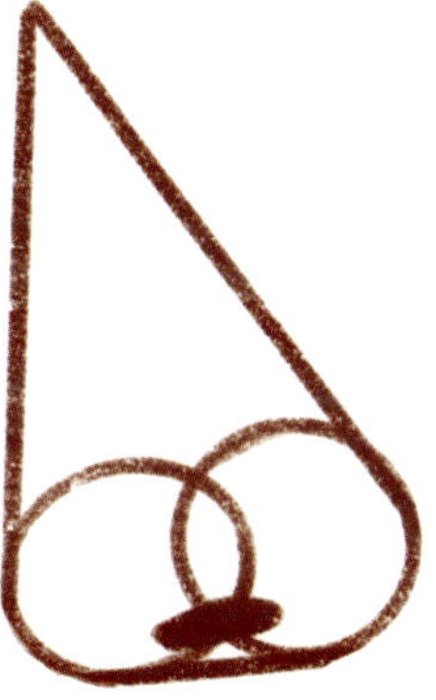

The nostril hole sits in the middle point where the two circles meet. So now you understand the basic structure of the nose at two different angles.

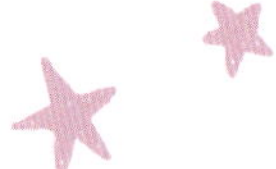

DRAWING A NOSE
STEP BY STEP

Follow along as I draw the nose first from the front and then from the side.

FRONT VIEW

Drawing the nose is actually not very complicated when you get the hang of the shapes we have just looked at. Next you just need to know where to place those shapes in order to draw any nose you want.

Scan to watch
a tutorial.

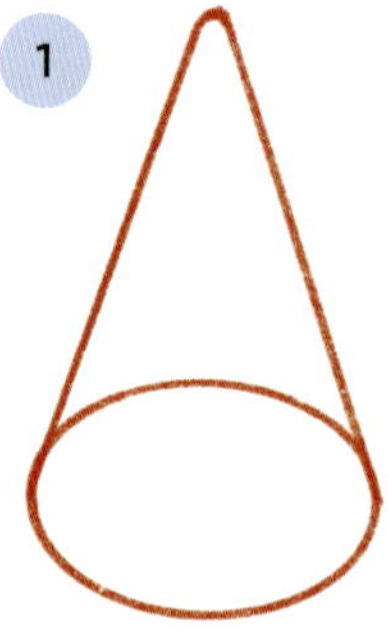

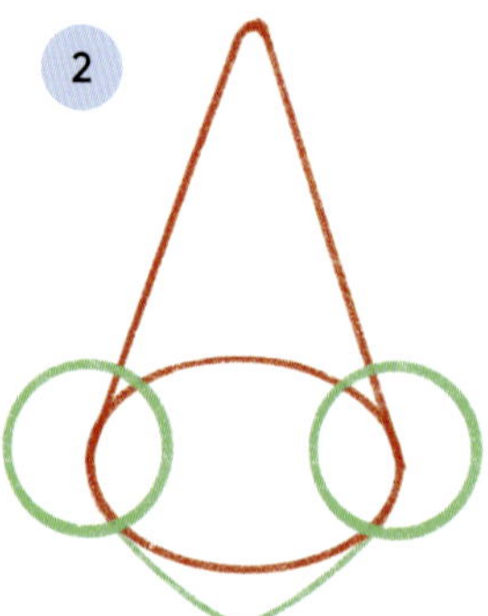

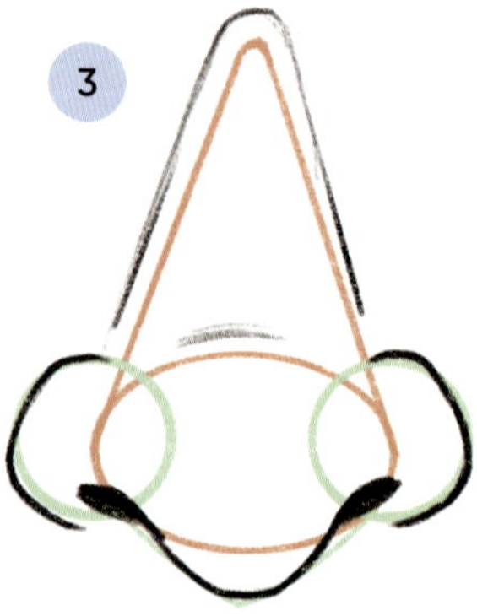

1. To start off, draw a circle or an oval shape for the "tip" of the nose. Then draw two lines connecting to the sides of that oval shape and meeting at the top. This will be the bridge area.

2. Next, draw two little circles around the spot where your nose bridge lines connect with your oval shape. Also go ahead and draw a flat upside-down triangle under the oval nose tip.

3. Now that you have the guidelines for the nose, you can start drawing in the shape of the nostrils and the nose tip, following those shapes.

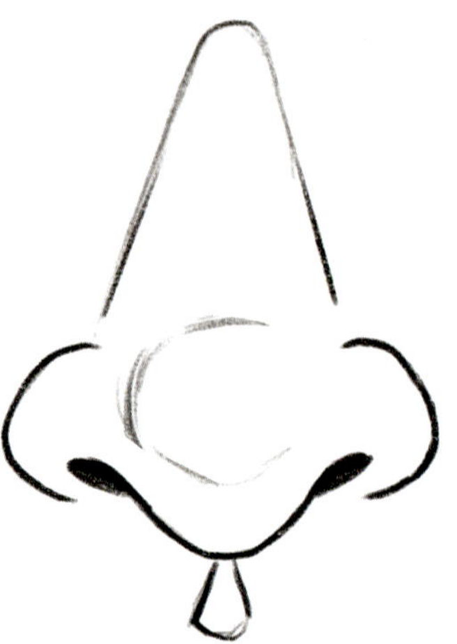

Finally, you can erase all your guidelines and add in other details, such as the divot under the nose known as the *philtrum* and some sketchy lines to indicate the apex of the tip of the nose.

All these sketchy lines will come in handy at the shading and lighting phase, but it's good practice to pencil them in when drawing the outlines of the nose so that you know what the overall shape of your nose is.

There are many different types of noses with different shapes and sizes, but the guidelines shown in steps 1 and 2 should help you be able to draw any nose you want.

PROFILE

In profile, the nose looks a little different.

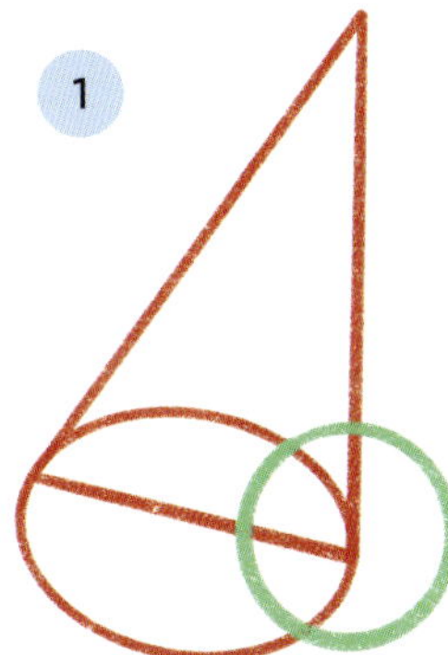

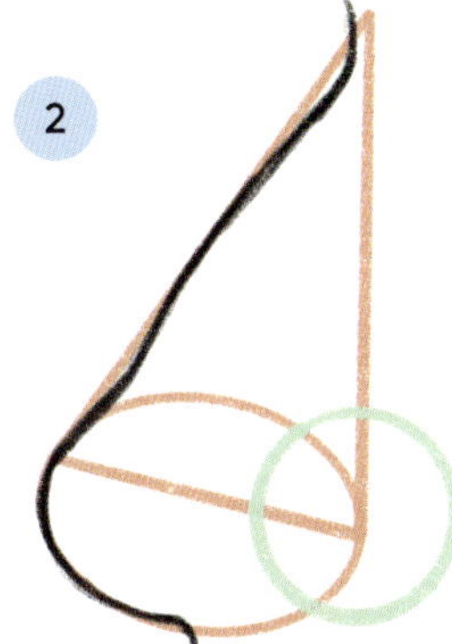

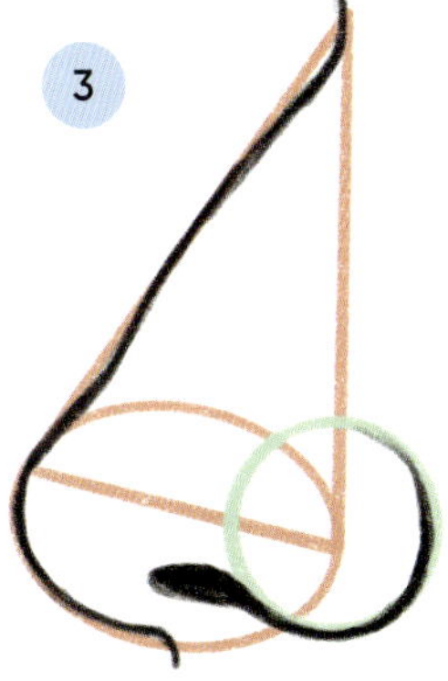

1. First, draw a tall triangle tilted so that the right side is vertical. Then draw the oval shape connected to the bottom of the triangle like before. The nostril circle should also go in the same spot (where the other two shapes connect).

2. Using these guidelines, start drawing the curvature of the nose bridge: First dip in at the top, then curve slightly out and then in again to go back out into the apex of the nose. Then the line can flick back out once you've reached the center of the oval shape.

3. Then you can draw the nostril following the little circle on the side. This line will then connect into a dark flat oval shape that is the nostril itself. Generally the nostril hole is located around the middle of the oval guide shape.

Once again erase your guidelines and see the nose you've drawn. As always, the nose will look very different at different angles (looking from underneath, from the top, at a three-quarter angle, etc.). However, using these steps and shape guides, you should be able to draw the nose at any angle or perspective.

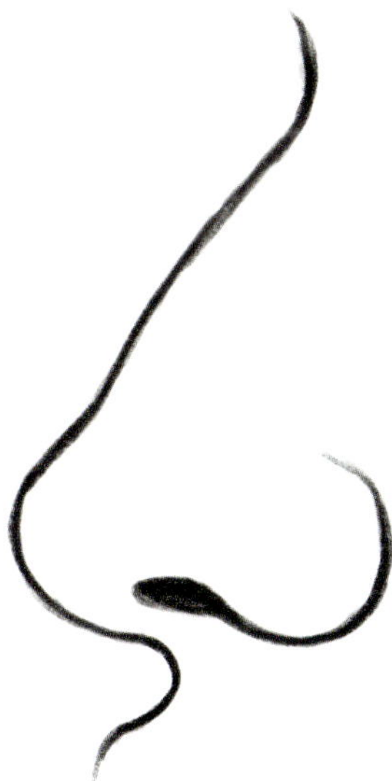

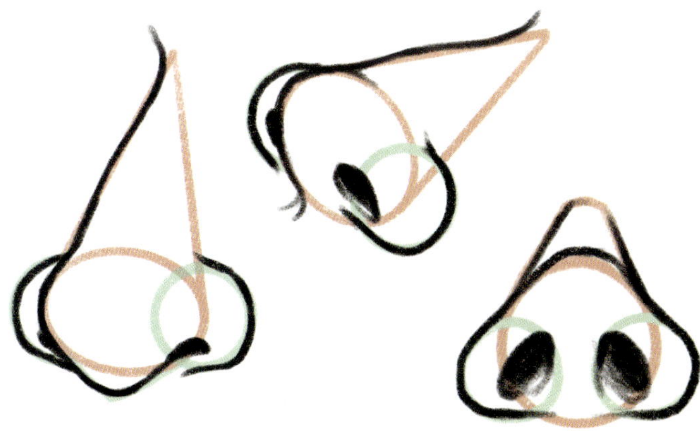

SHADING THE NOSE

Now to add three-dimensionality to the nose. As we saw before, we need to first establish our light source so we can accurately place our shadows.

There are also three plane levels of the nose to consider when shading it in: the tip of the nose, the nostrils and the bridge of the nose, and the area surrounding the nose. These three areas sit at different heights, so some of them might cast shadows on each other.

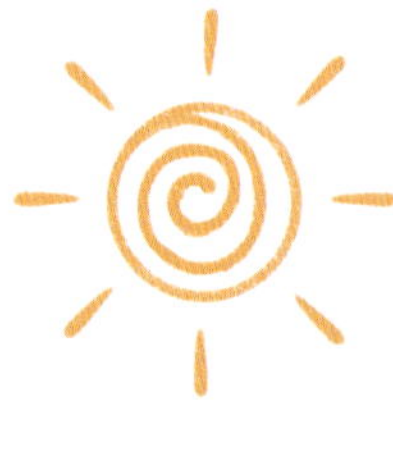

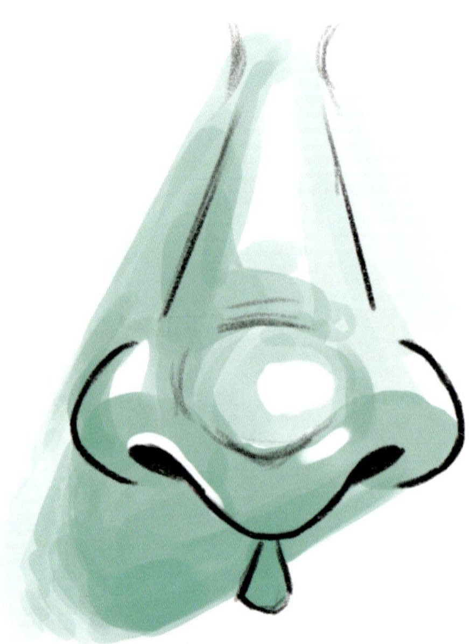

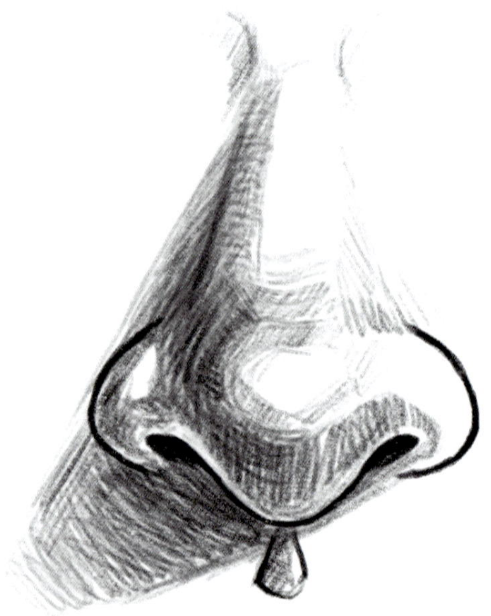

Here is an example of how I would plan out the shadows on the nose using the above light-source direction.

The tip of the nose and the right-hand side of the nostrils are hit by the light, as well as the top right-hand side of the nose bridge. The nose bridge and tip of the nose then cast a shadow to the bottom left of the face in a triangular fashion.

Because the light is coming from the top right, everything in the bottom left areas of the nose is in shadow (darker shadows near areas that are covered or near creases), and the shadows get lighter the farther away they get. When shading, always soften the transition areas between shadow and highlight.

I used the hatching and crosshatching methods of shading, as I find them the most useful to create different amounts of shadow and darkness.

Here are some more examples of how the shadows of the nose could be placed with different light sources coming from different directions.

As you can see, the shadow cast from the nose onto the face is usually triangular in shape, due to the nose being triangular. When light hits an object from one side, the shape of that object obstructs the light from going past it, which is how harsh shadows are created. So the general rule is that whatever shape is casting the shadow, that is the shape you should make the shadow.

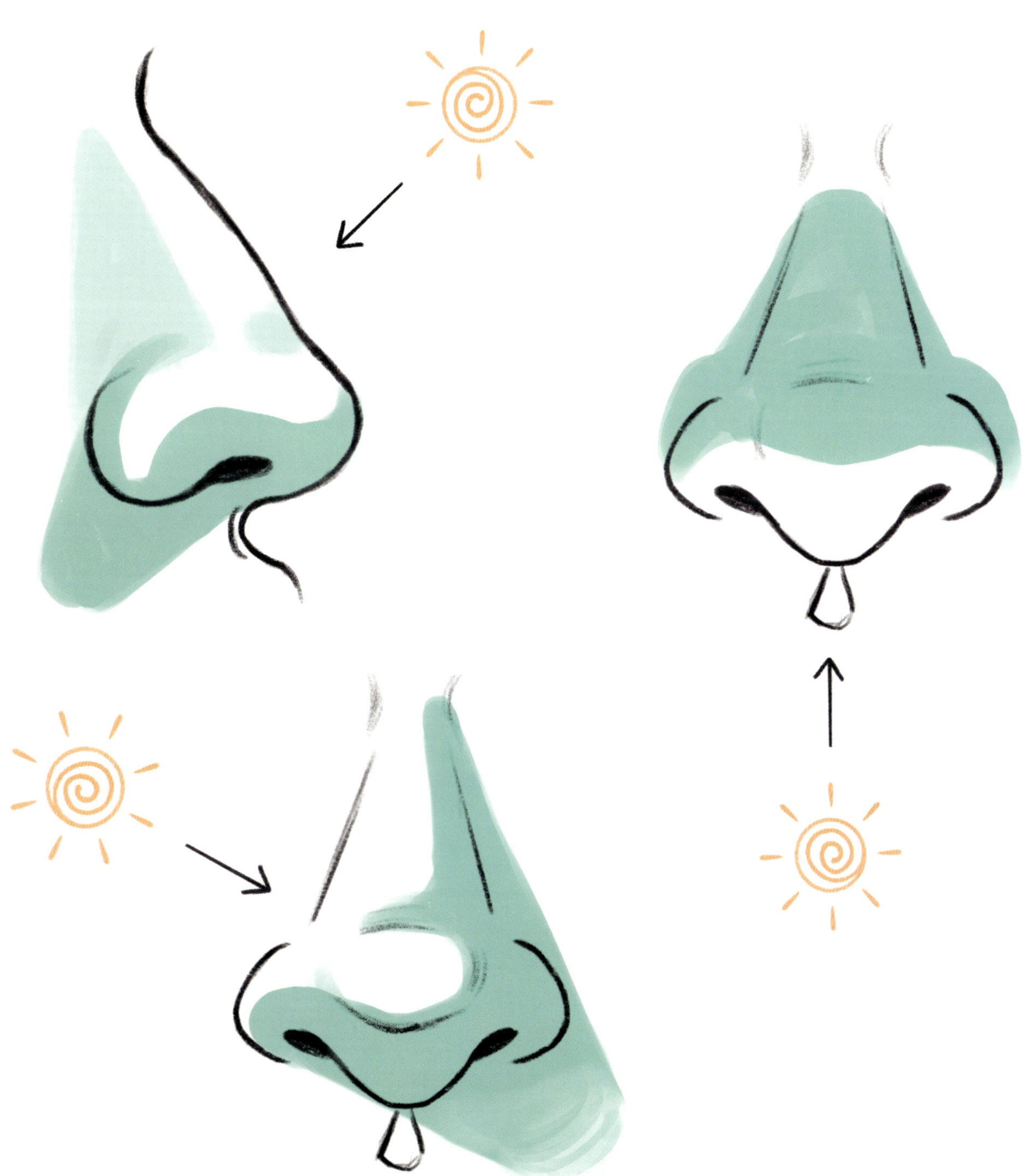

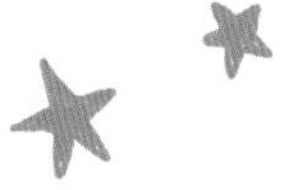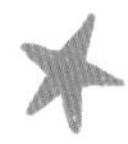

SO MANY NOSES
TO CHOOSE FROM!

There are so many different noses you can play around with. You can change the shape of the nose bridge, the length, the width, the shape of the tip, etc.

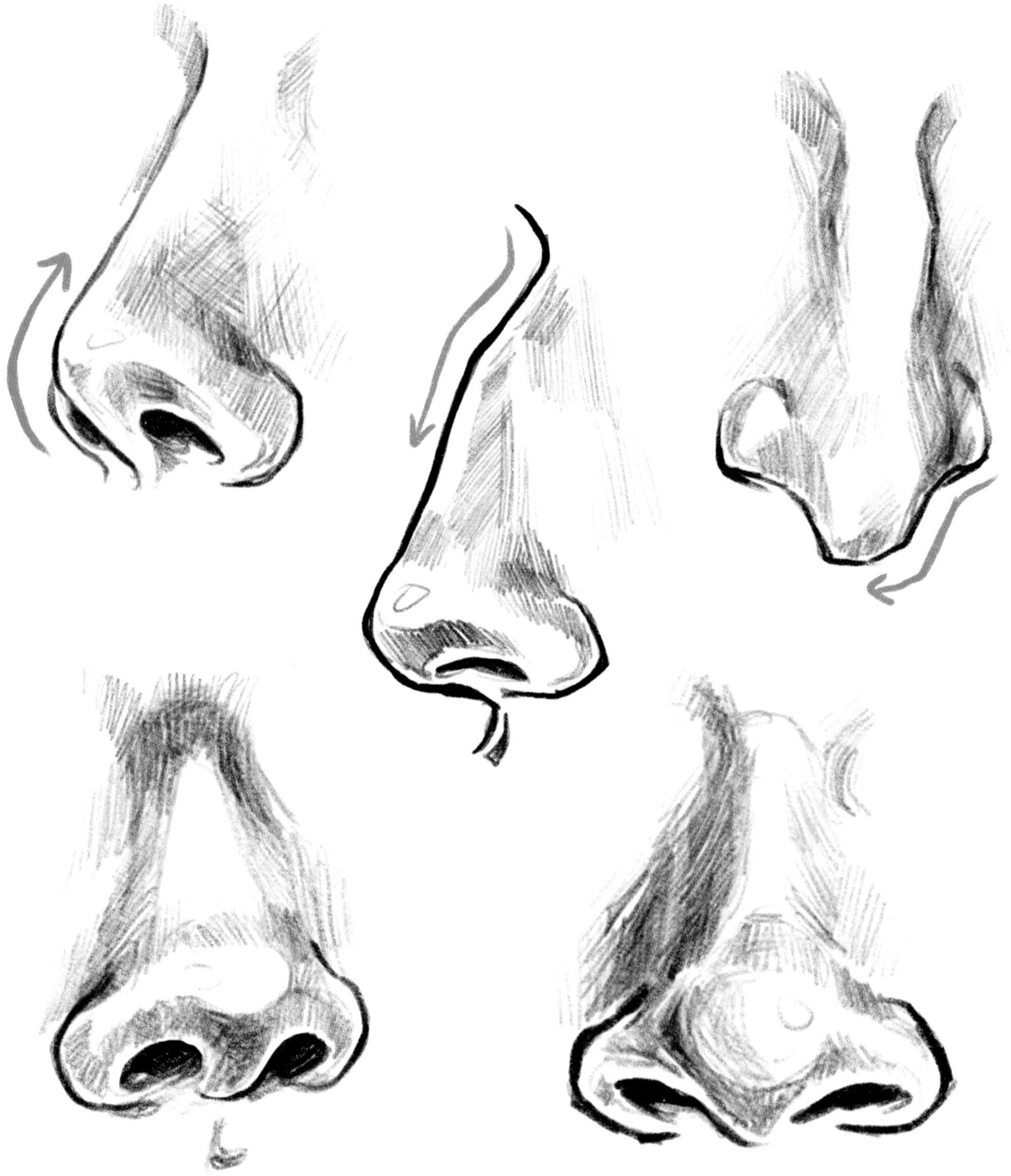

There are droopier noses, squarer noses,
noses where the nostrils are visible, and ones
where they are not. It will depend greatly on the
character or face you are drawing the nose onto.

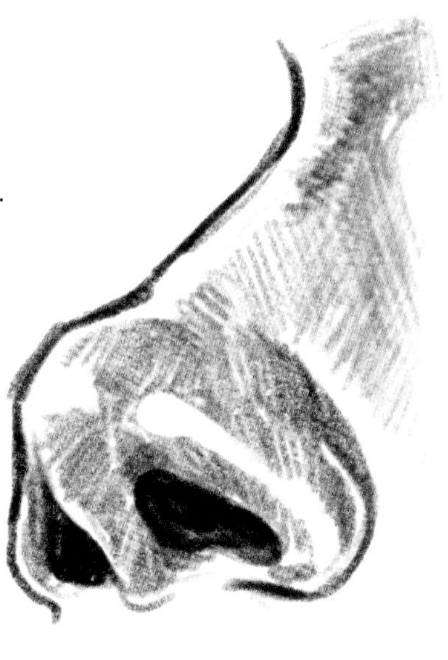

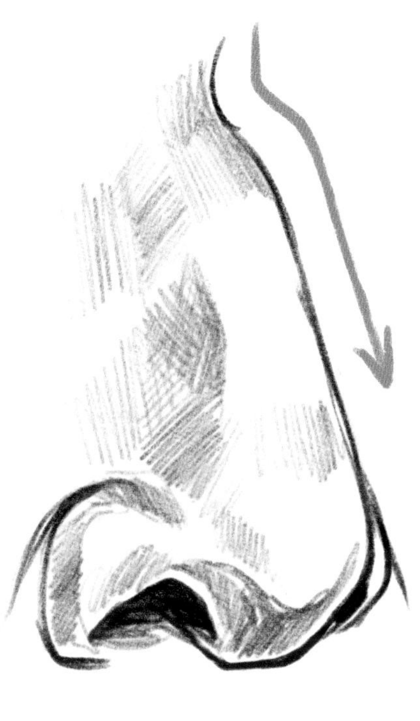

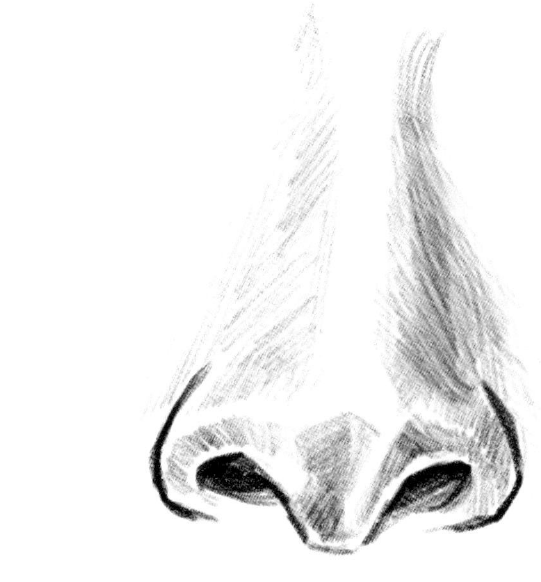

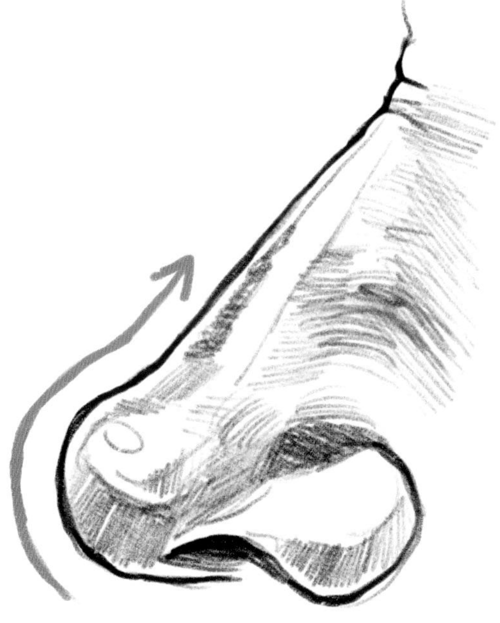

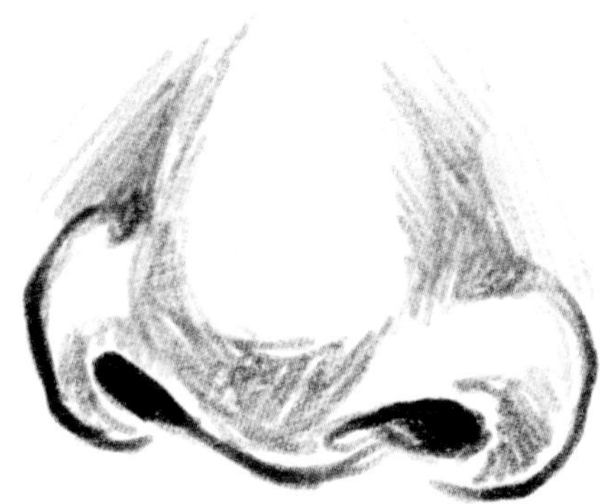

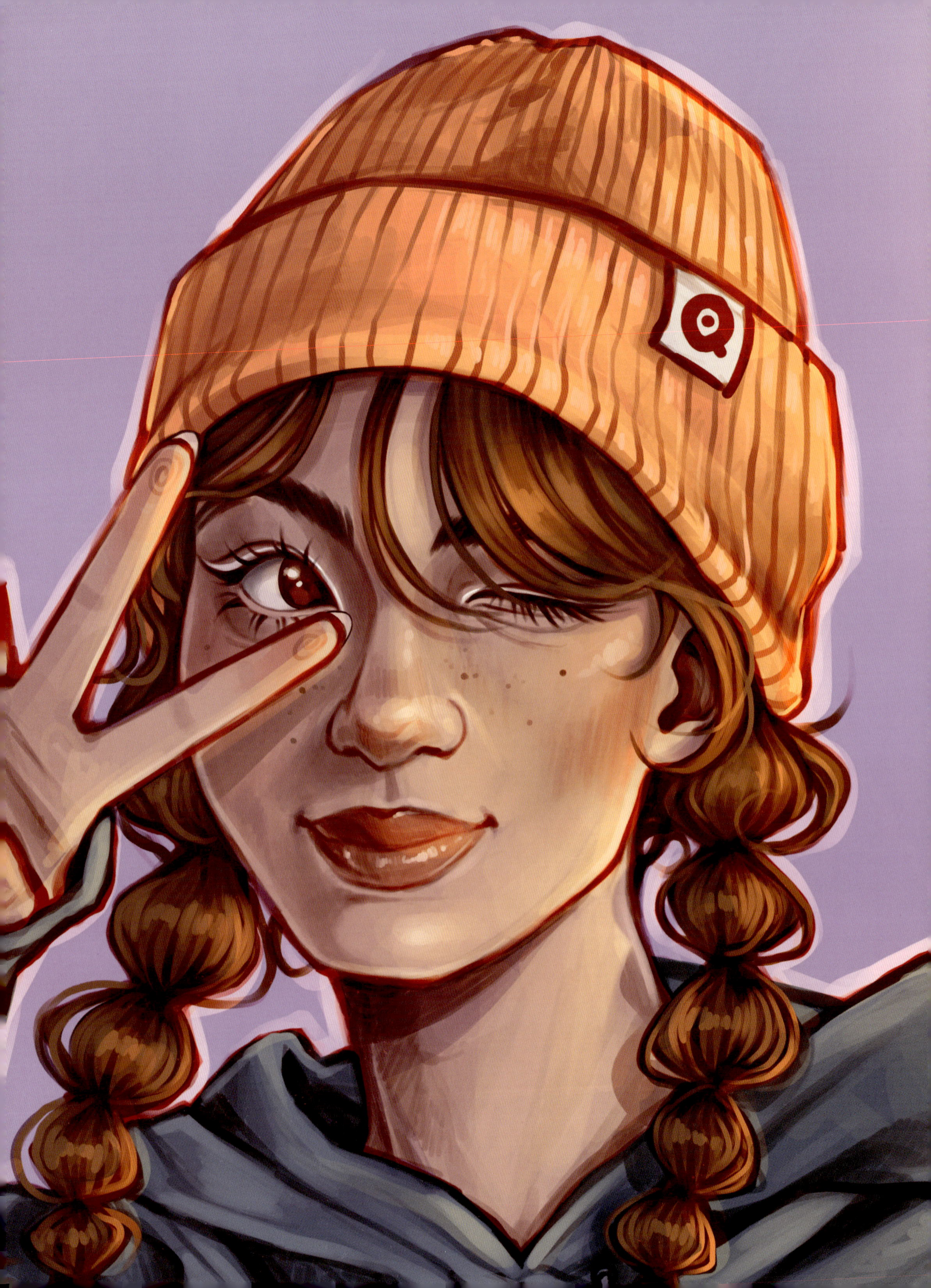

6

DRAWING THE MOUTH

We are making our way through the facial features, and next up, we have the mouth. I like to think that the mouth, much like the eyes, is a beacon of emotion and expression. The mouth has an incredible range of motion, allowing itself to change into all kinds of shapes. So naturally, the mouth and lips can change the portrait you're drawing significantly. Let's dive into the lips, mouth, teeth, and smiles!

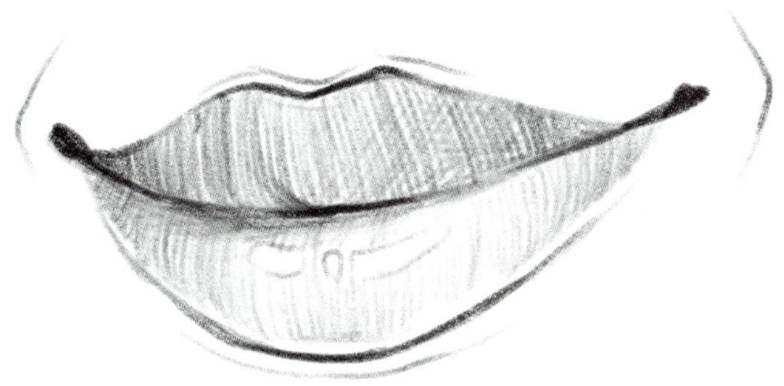

THE SHAPES OF THE MOUTH

The mouth is composed of two lips joined at the corners. But in reality, the mouth is probably the feature of the face that can move into the largest variety of shapes and positions—so that we can talk, for example!

For now let's look at the basic structure of the closed mouth. Once we understand the basics of the lips, we can then venture into different positions and expressions.

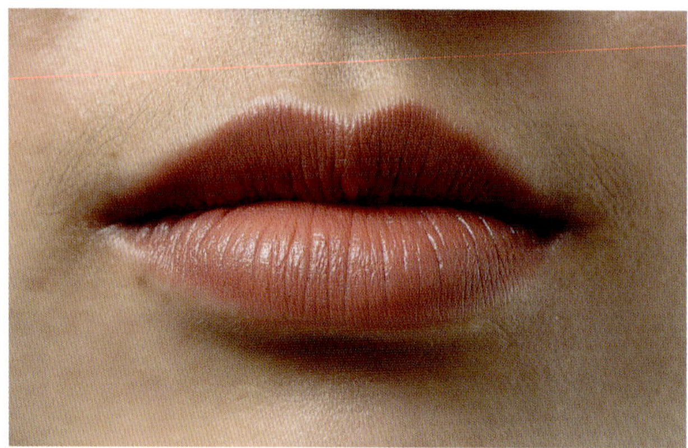

Let's look at this mouth. I always recommend looking at reference images and studying them in order to get a better understanding of anatomy.

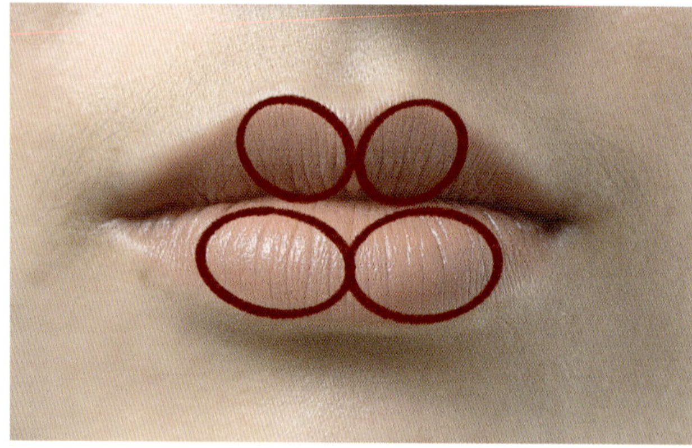

The basic shapes within the mouth are the four circles that create the pillows of the lips: the two smaller ones on the upper lip and two more oval ones on the bottom lip.

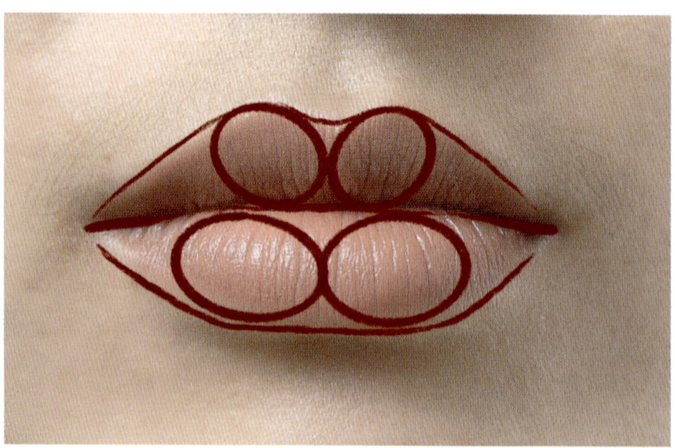

Then, using these circles as guides, you can then create the general shape of the lips by creating a curved line that touches the edges of the circles. The top and bottom line meet at the corners of the mouth, and you can create a little valley between the two upper circles to make a Cupid's bow.

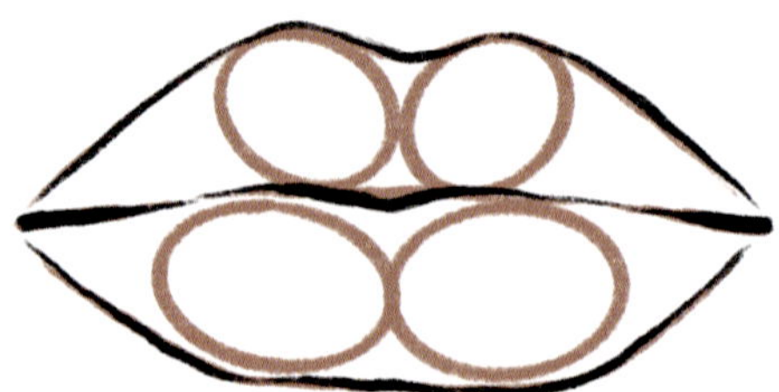

After a bit of cleanup, you can see here how the four circles of the mouth help guide the outline of the lips. The bigger the circles, the fuller the lips. The thinner the circles, the thinner the lips.

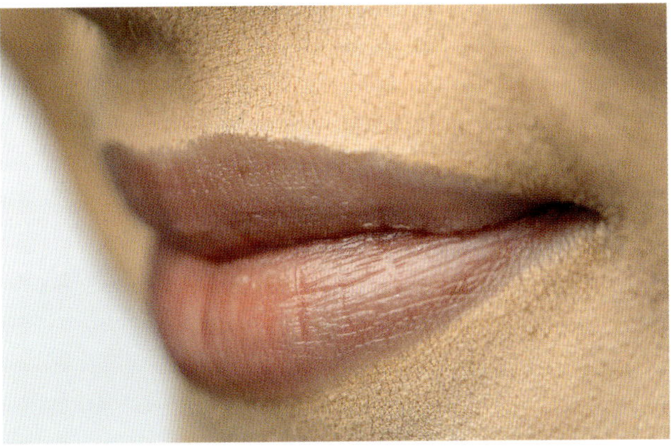

Let's look at this example of the lips at a three-quarter angle.

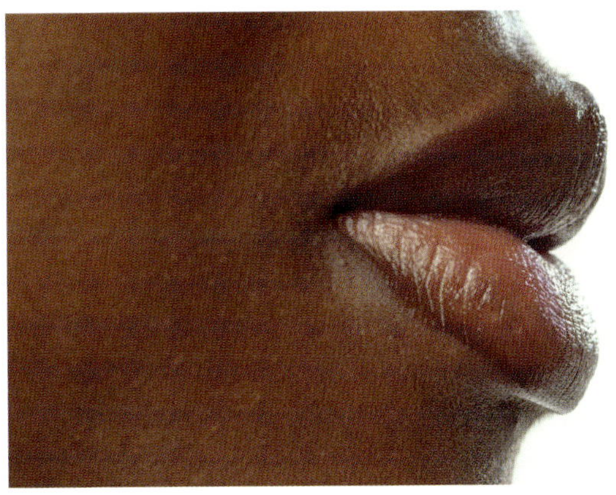

At this angle, the circles actually overlap due to the perspective. But the same rules apply, taking a line from the top of the upper circles and the bottom of the lower circles and connecting them at the corner of the mouth.

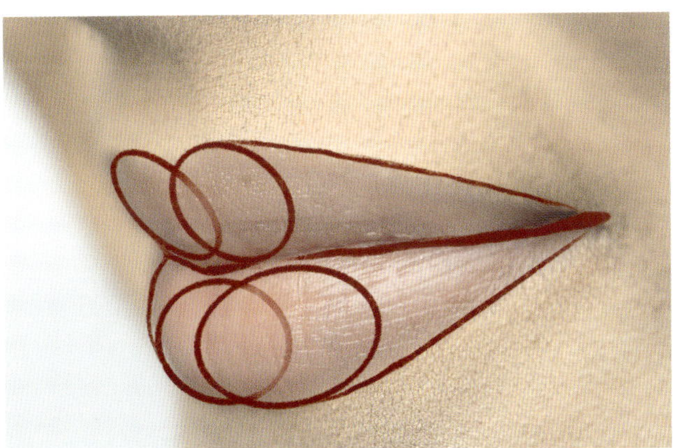

Now let's look at the mouth in profile.

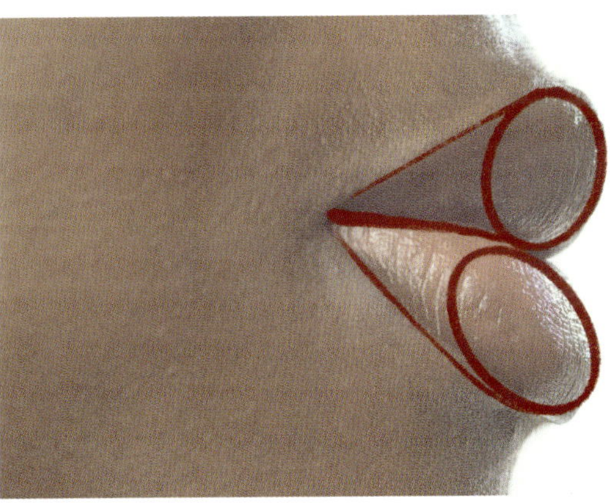

From the side, we can only really see one side of the mouth, and therefore, only one circle on the top and bottom lips. Again, the same rules apply.

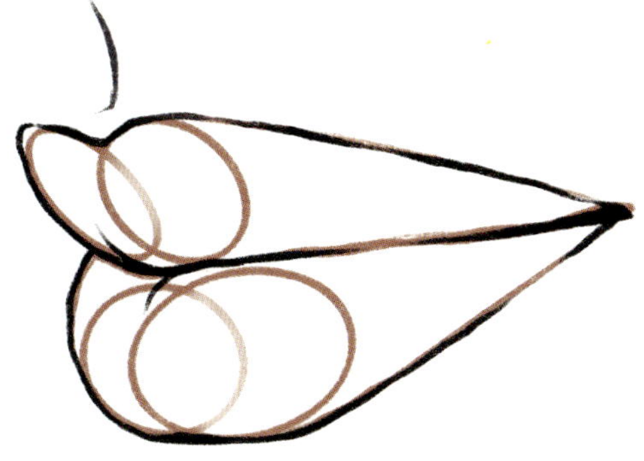

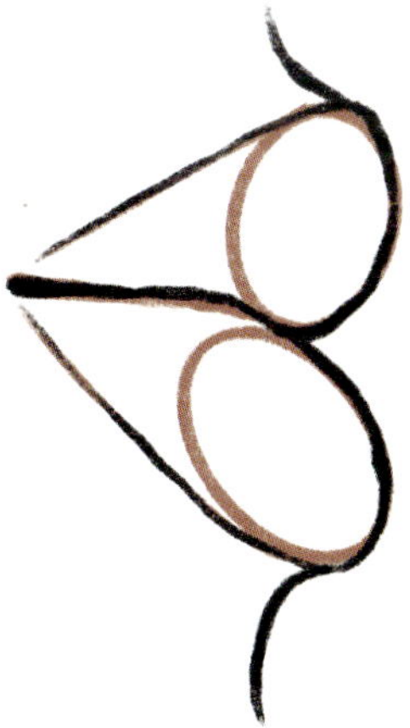

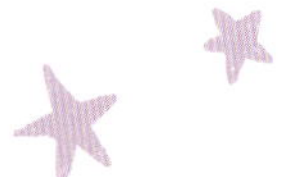

DRAWING THE MOUTH
STEP BY STEP

Now that we have identified the simple shapes of the mouth, it will be a lot easier to draw them.

First, let's learn how to draw a mouth in a relaxed state and then move up in complexity: a grin, a smile, and a fully open-mouthed smile! Taking it step by step like this will allow you to understand the mouth's anatomy and shapes better as you go along.

Scan to watch
a tutorial.

RELAXED MOUTH

1. Start the mouth off with the pillows of the lips. Draw the line across the middle of the mouth for the opening of the mouth. This is usually two circular shapes on the top and two more oval shapes on the bottom. The size of these will dictate the fullness and shape of the lips.

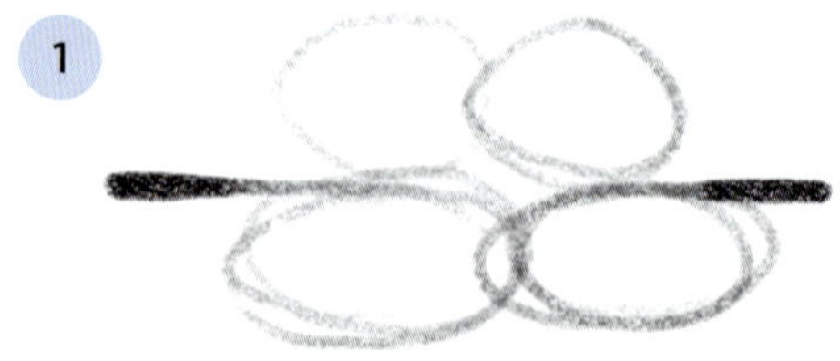

2. Draw the outline of the upper and bottom lips. You can use the valleys between the circles to draw out the Cupid's bow and the shape of the bottom lip. Then you just connect the upper and lower lip lines to the corner of the mouth.

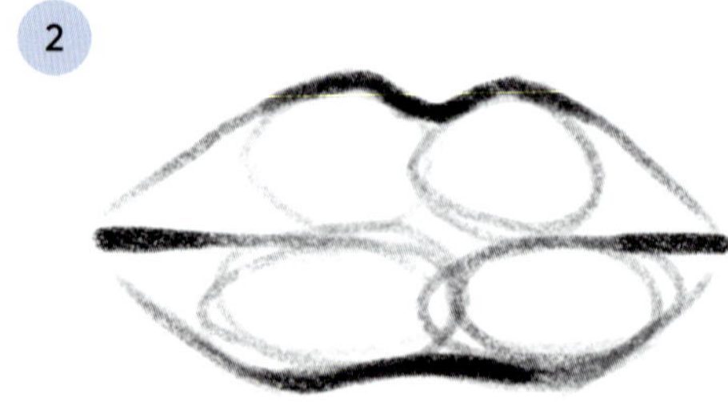

3. You can draw the extra little bump in the middle of the upper lip by following the two bottom ovals as a guideline. Delete the guidelines and initial shapes to see a lovely pair of lips.

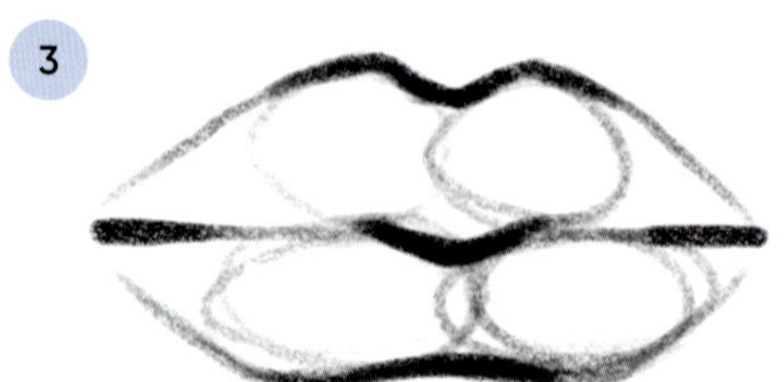

SMILING MOUTH

1. If you'd like to draw a pair of smiling lips, it's not that different. The first step is generally the same, except that the middle line for the mouth opening should stretch out into a smiling curved line. Then you can add in the circles and ovals like before, but slightly flatter.

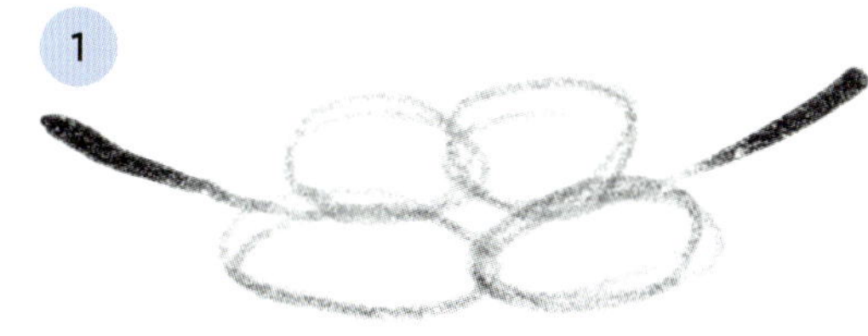

2. When the mouth stretches out into a smile, the skin of the lips stretches too. This makes the lips appear thinner. So when drawing the outline of the lips, make sure to minimize the curvature of the Cupid's bow and smooth out the bottom lip as well.

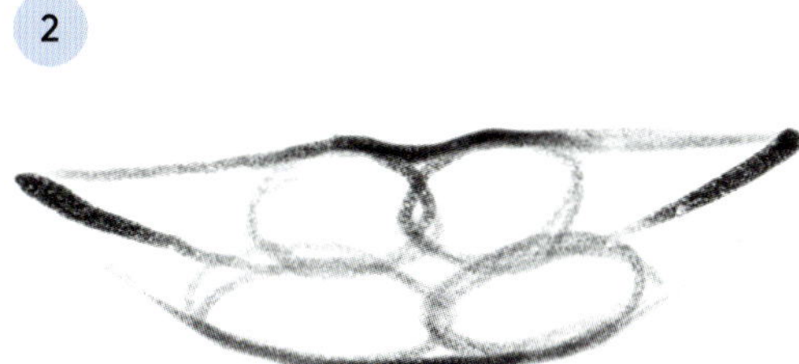

3. When you smile, the corners of the mouth push inward into the cheeks. This creates a dimple in the cheek fat and these smile lines appear. Some smiles can have multiple smile lines and even dimples deep into the cheeks!

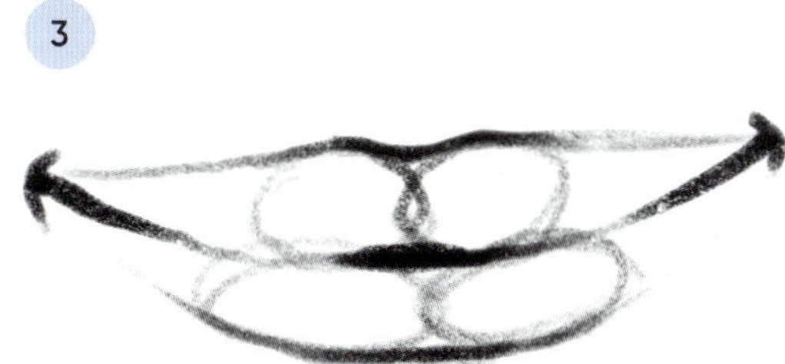

TIP: Use the corner of the mouth as your "pulling point." The directions in which the corners stretch out will give different movements and looks to the lips!

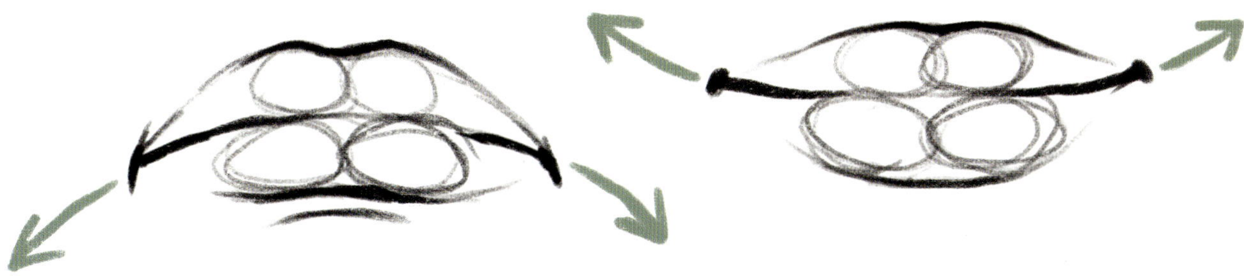

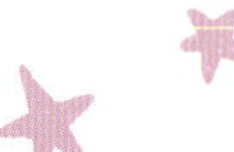 

THE MOUTH AT DIFFERENT ANGLES

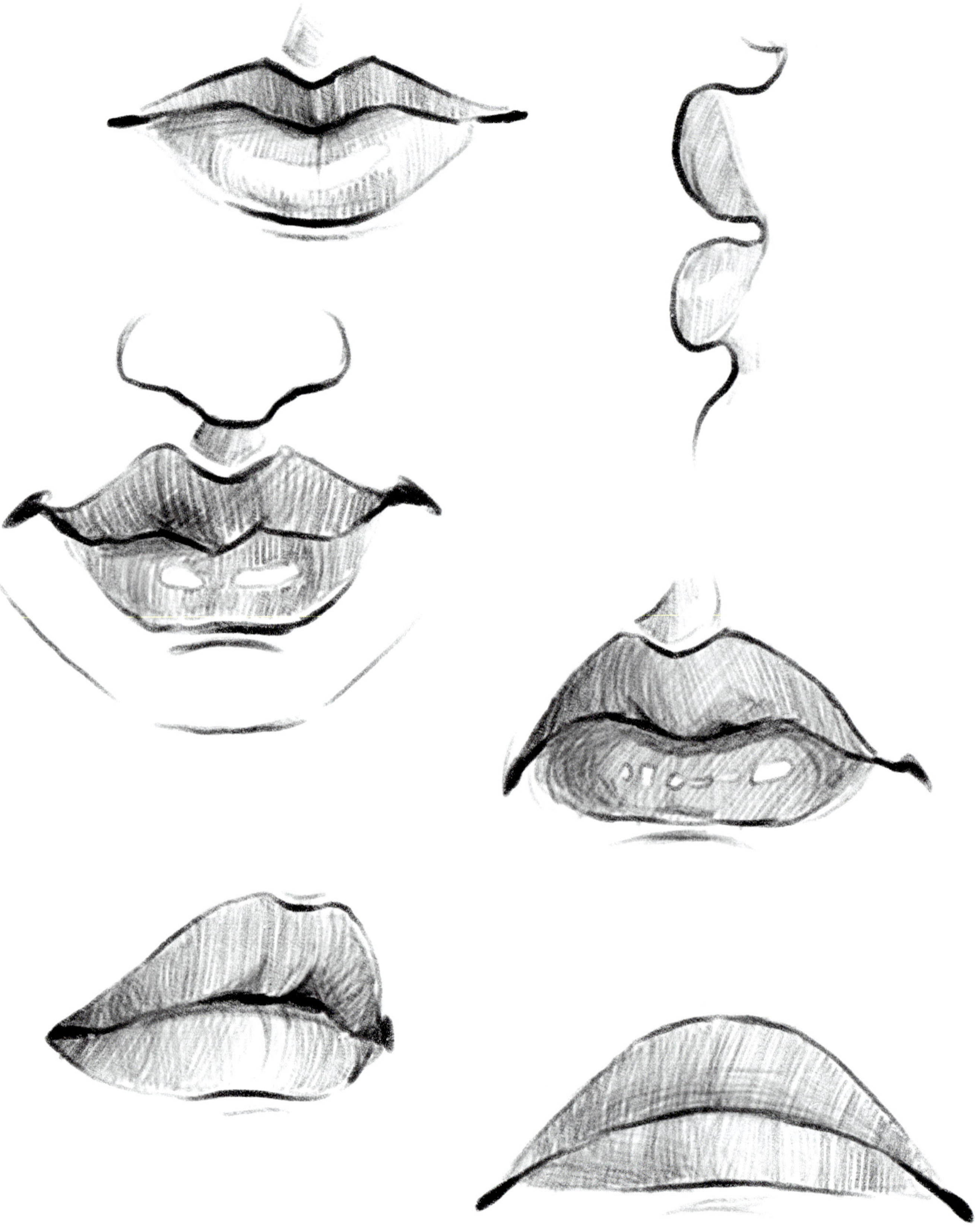

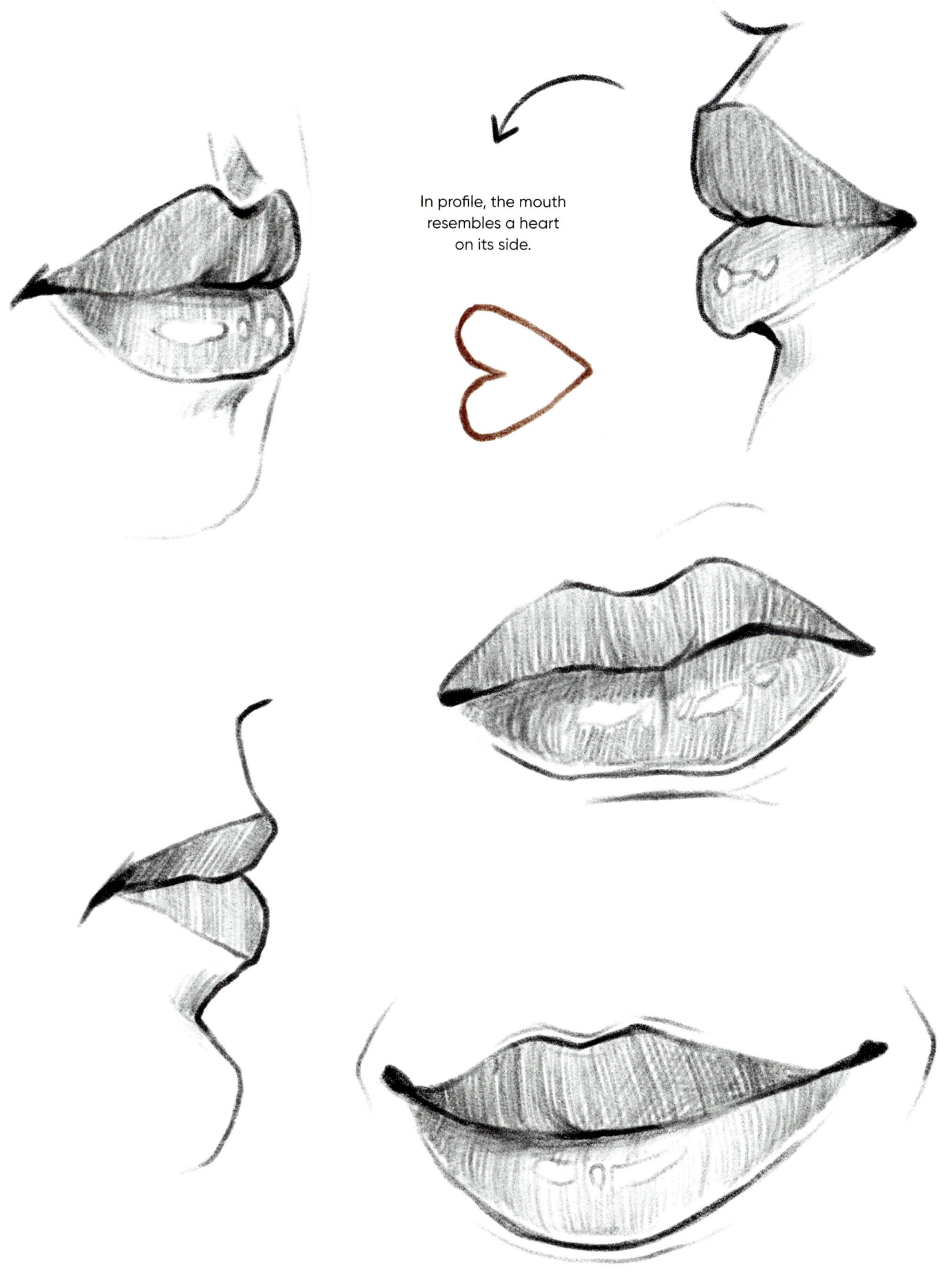

In profile, the mouth
resembles a heart
on its side.

DIVERSITY IN LIPS

It's important to note that people of different ethnicities can have different-looking lips than the ones in the previous examples. Of course, there are many different types and shapes of lips, but when drawing your portrait, keep in mind the ethnicity of your character. Understanding diversity in portraiture is indispensable when learning to draw faces!

For example, people of Black African backgrounds tend to have fuller, rounder lips— sometimes not even having a Cupid's bow at all. Their upper lips also tend to be a darker color than their lower lip.

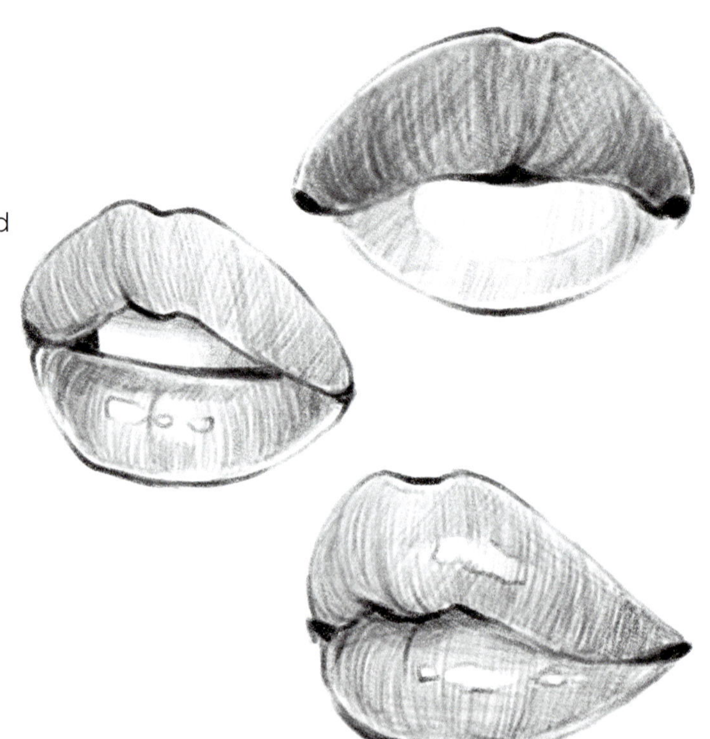

HOW THESE LIPS CHANGE THE PROFILE

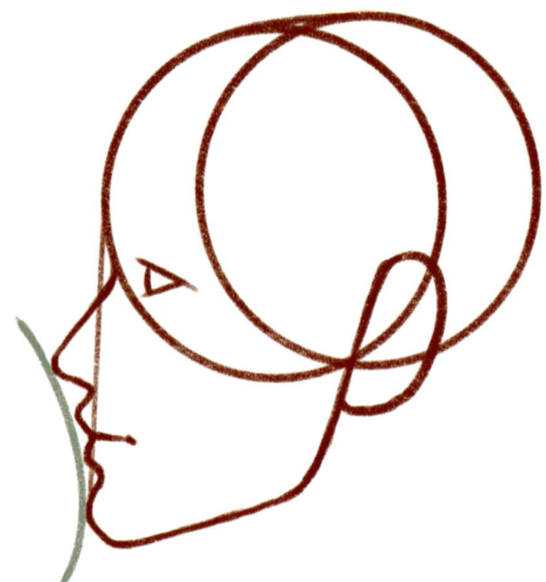 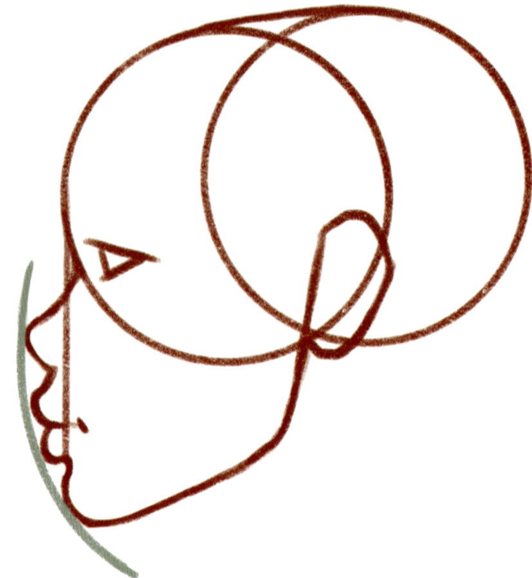

These ethnicity-specific features can make a difference on the overall profile of your portrait too. Using the example again, people of Black African backgrounds will have a profile slightly different from someone of a white ethnic background.

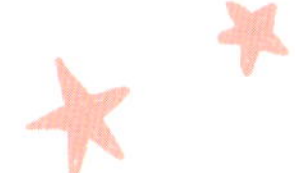 

MOVEMENT OF THE LIPS

As I mentioned this before, the lips and the mouth area have incredibly intricate muscles, allowing the mouth to move into incredible shapes—to help us make different sounds, for example! When drawing mouths for different expressions, keep in mind how the skin and muscles around the mouth move, and then pulling and stretching the lips to create these shapes. This will help you with drawing in any skin folds, wrinkles, and shadows.

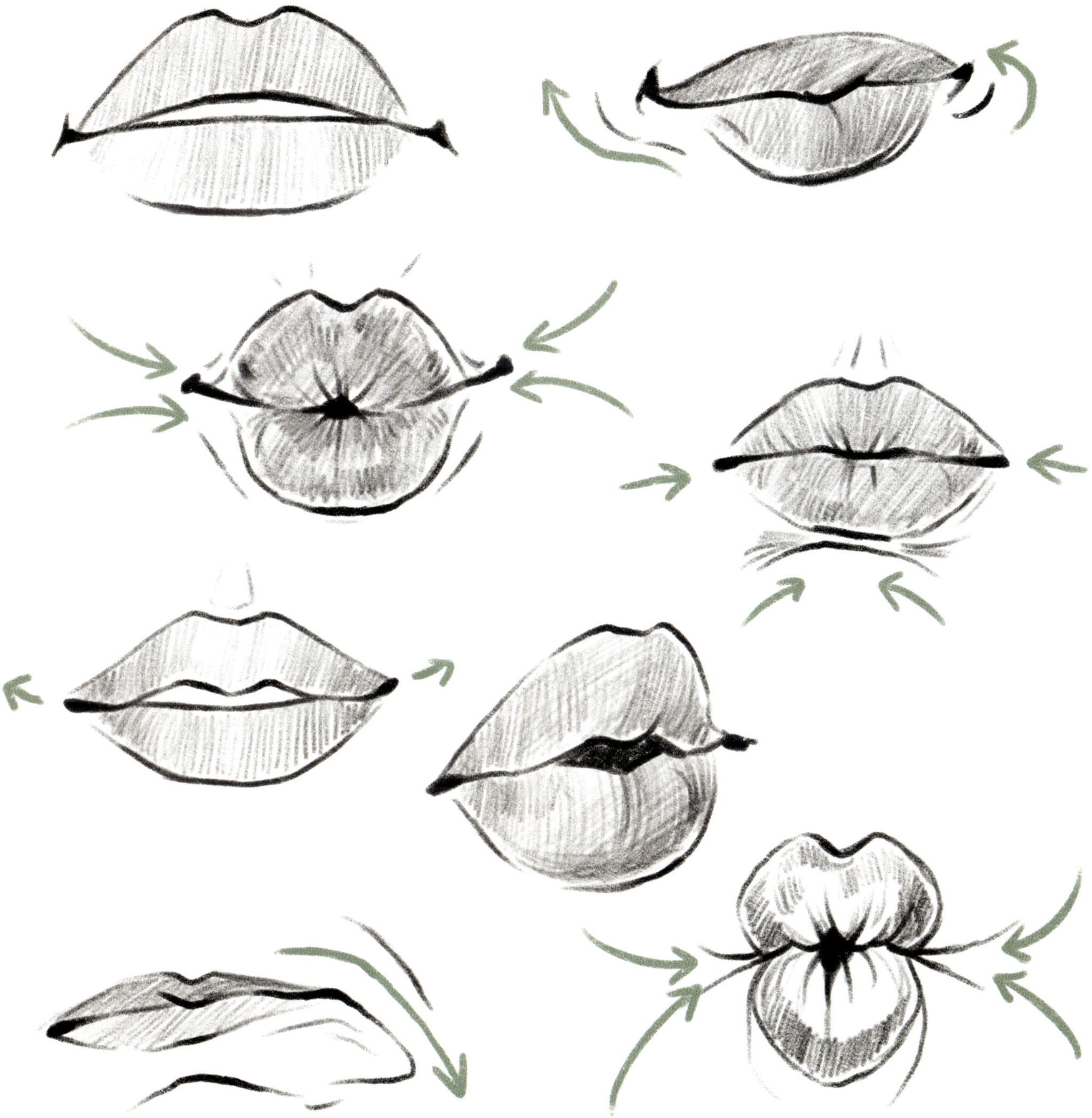

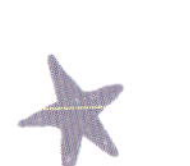
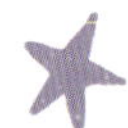

DRAWING TEETH & SMILES

Now that we know how the mouth can stretch and pull in different directions, we can start looking at one of the most basic expressions of the mouth: the smile.

Scan to watch
a tutorial.

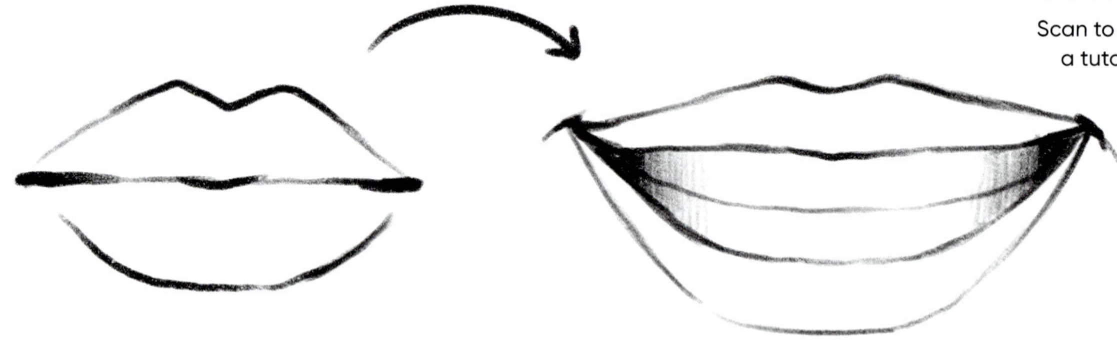

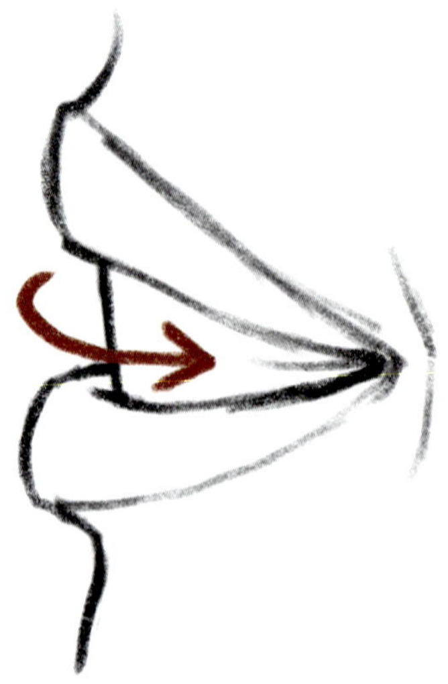

As you can see in the illustration, when the mouth moves into a closed smile, the corners of the mouth stretch out (and slightly upward in some cases). The lips then move apart from each other, revealing the teeth.

We must also consider the three-dimensional space, since the face is squishy in nature! When the corners of the mouth move into a smile, they also push inward into the cheeks. This is due to the curved nature of the skull and teeth.

For example, when you see the smile in profile, you can see how there is a curvature to the teeth wrapping around the face. This causes shadows closer to the corners of the smile and on the teeth closer to the back of the mouth.

Now, as we know, the lips are made of soft, stretchy skin, like the rest of the face—and skin can stretch and pull in order for us to be able to pull all the expressions we do.

So the same pair of lips might look different from a neutral position to a wide, toothy smile. We also have the tongue and inner mouth to think about.

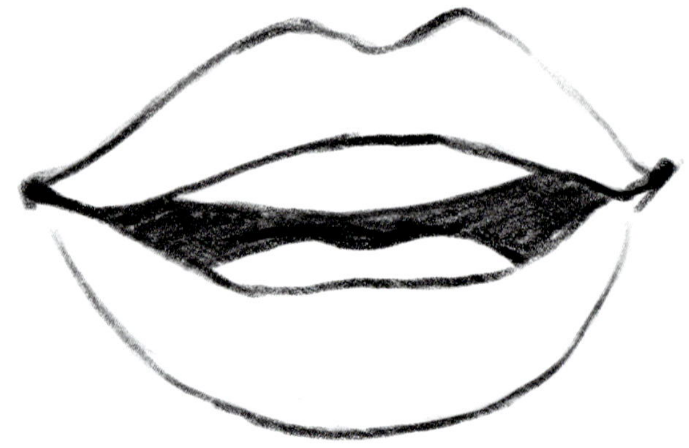

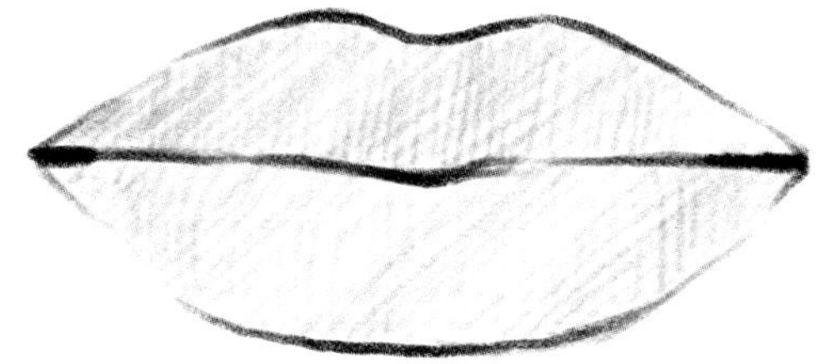

To begin, when the mouth is in its most neutral position, this is where you see the basic structure of the lips: the Cupid's bow, the fullness of the lips, etc.

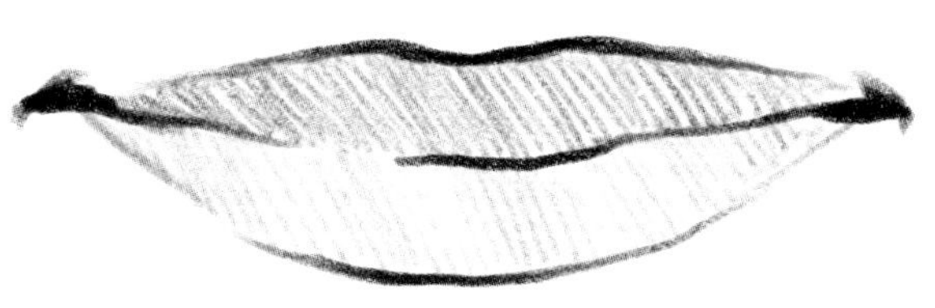

As the mouth stretches into a closed smile or a grin, the lips stretch outward into a thinner shape. So the fuller lips become less full-looking due to the pulling of the corners of the mouth. We also start seeing some smile lines in the corners of the mouth as the lips start poking into the cheeks.

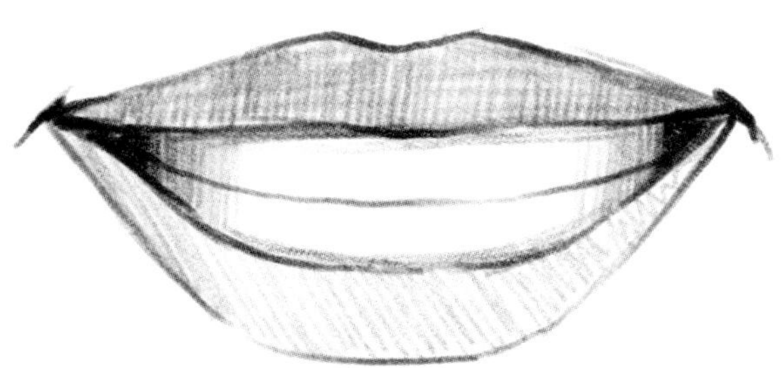

Then, as the mouth opens even wider into a toothy smile, the lips become even thinner and the Cupid's bow will become more and more shallow. The smile lines will become even more pronounced, and we can now see the teeth inside the mouth (more on the teeth soon).

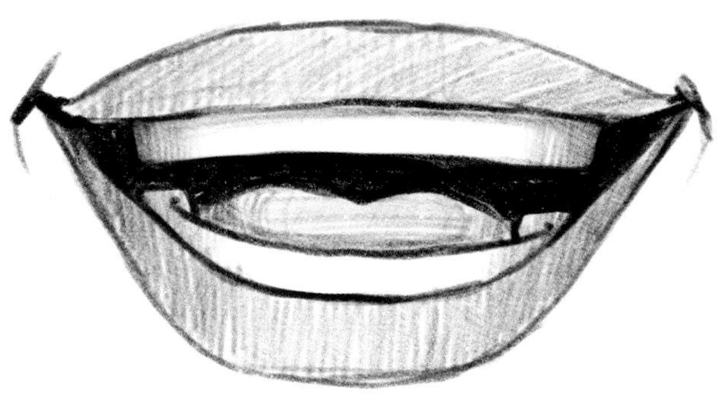

Now we have the big open-mouthed smile. Here the whole mouth opens up and the teeth open to reveal the surface of the tongue. The lips have also stretched out even further, sometimes eliminating the Cupid's bow. The bottom part of the mouth opens down the most, as that is the part of the skull that moves up and down, and the corners of the mouth have now pushed into the cheeks even deeper, creating shadows and a deeper crease in that area.

And just like that, you can turn a simple mouth into an expressive smile of joy.

When we get into the inner structure of the mouth, this is where it can get a little more intimidating. I'm not a personal fan of drawing individual teeth and gum details, but it's important to know how to in case you need to draw a more detailed and realistic portrait.

We are not used to seeing individual teeth drawn out in illustrations and cartoons, so it can seem off-putting when you draw them yourself—which is why a lot of artists simplify them.

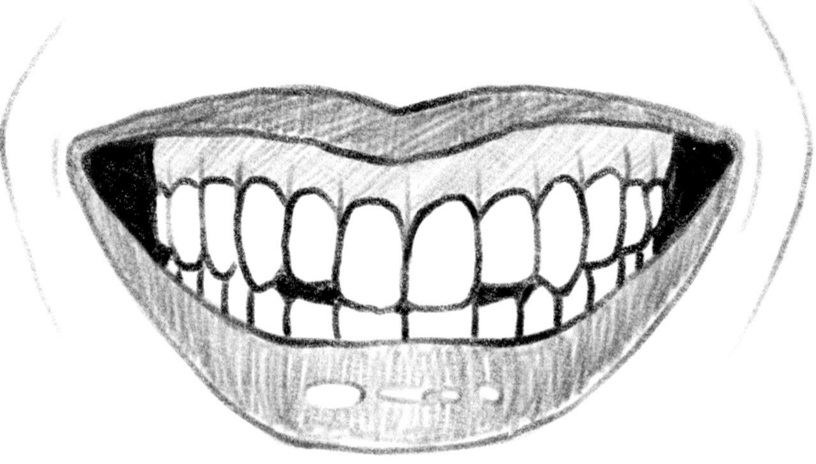

If you think back to the skull, you can study the teeth quite easily from there. Speaking as an artist, and not a dentist, here are some of the things I like to keep in mind when drawing the teeth:

- The upper teeth usually overlap the bottom teeth slightly.

- The twelve teeth at the front are usually taller than the molars at the back.

- The canines are located next to the front eight teeth, and they separate the molars from the front teeth.

If you still do not feel confident enough to add individual teeth and gum details to your mouth, you can always simplify them by drawing the outline of where the teeth sit in the mouth and draw a line separating the upper and lower teeth.

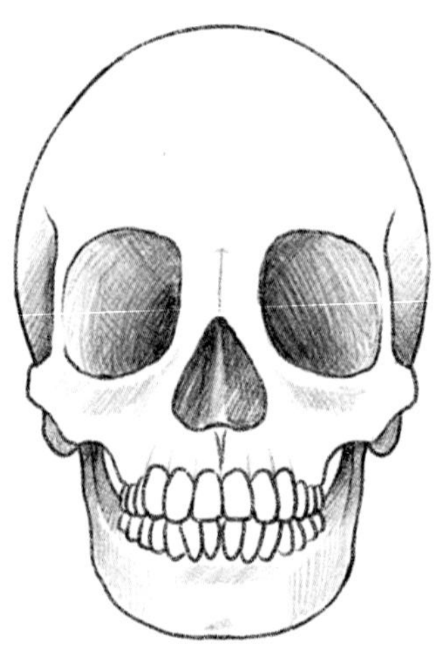

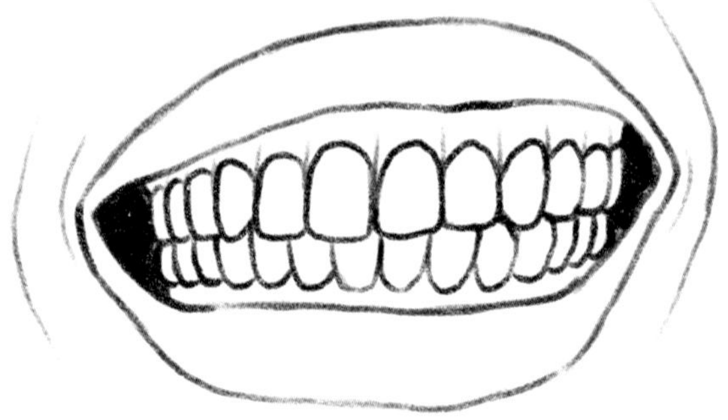

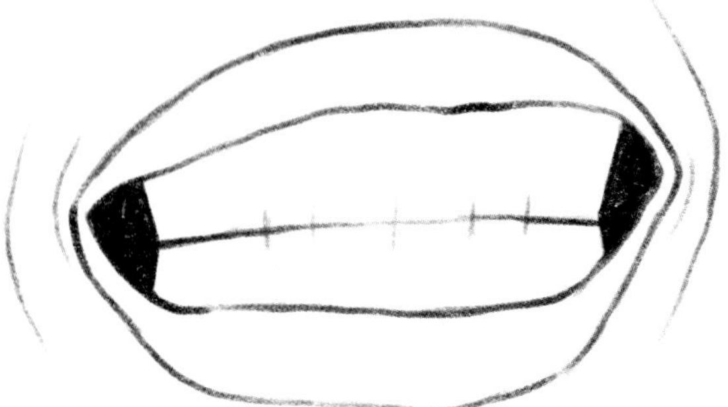

ANGLES OF THE MOUTH

Once again thinking back to the previous page, the mouth and teeth should be thought of as a curve wrapping around the lower part of the face. Thinking of it like this will help you when drawing the mouth in different expressions at different angles.

One thing to keep in mind is that the teeth don't really move; only the bottom teeth move up and down when the mouth opens. So all the work is done by the lips and the area around the mouth. It's so interesting to me how such a small area of skin can create so many emotions by just stretching into different positions.

Here are some examples of the teeth and mouth in some more poses creating different expressions.

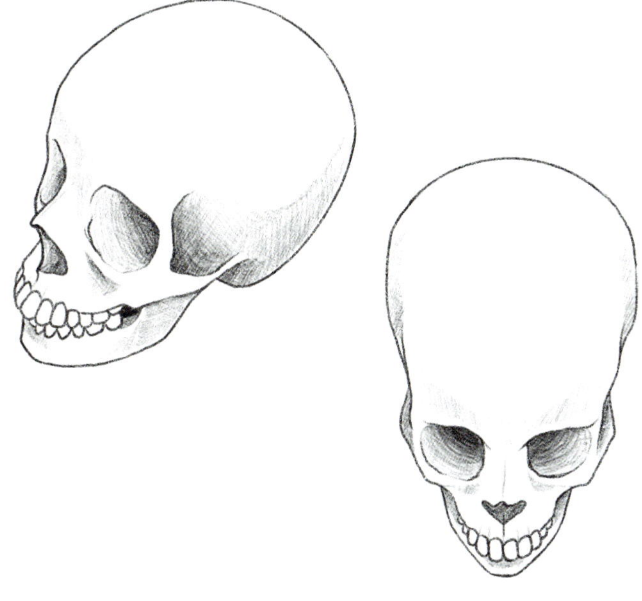

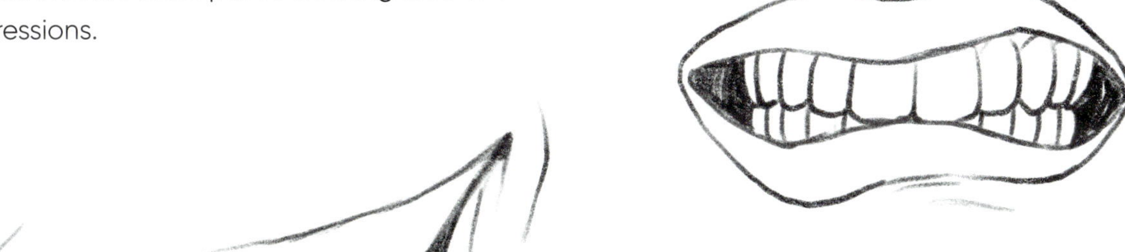

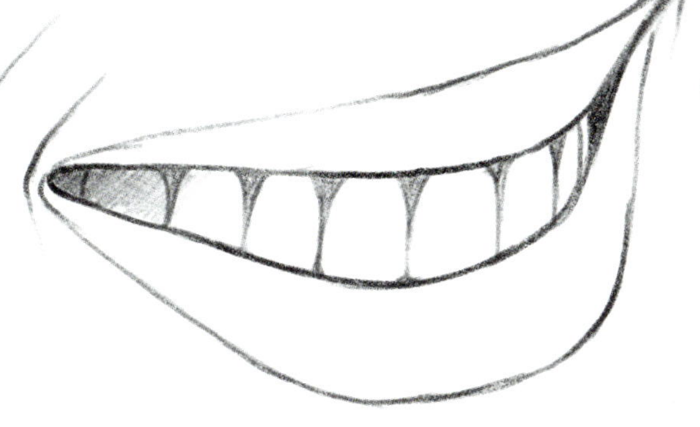

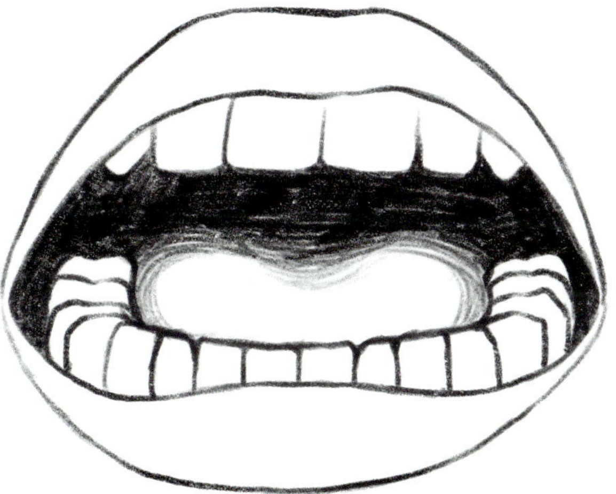

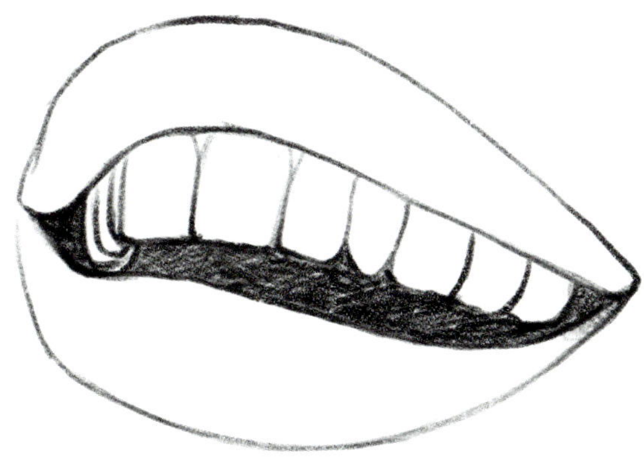

Again, different mouths and people smile in different ways. So keep studying as many reference images as possible to build up your mental reference library.

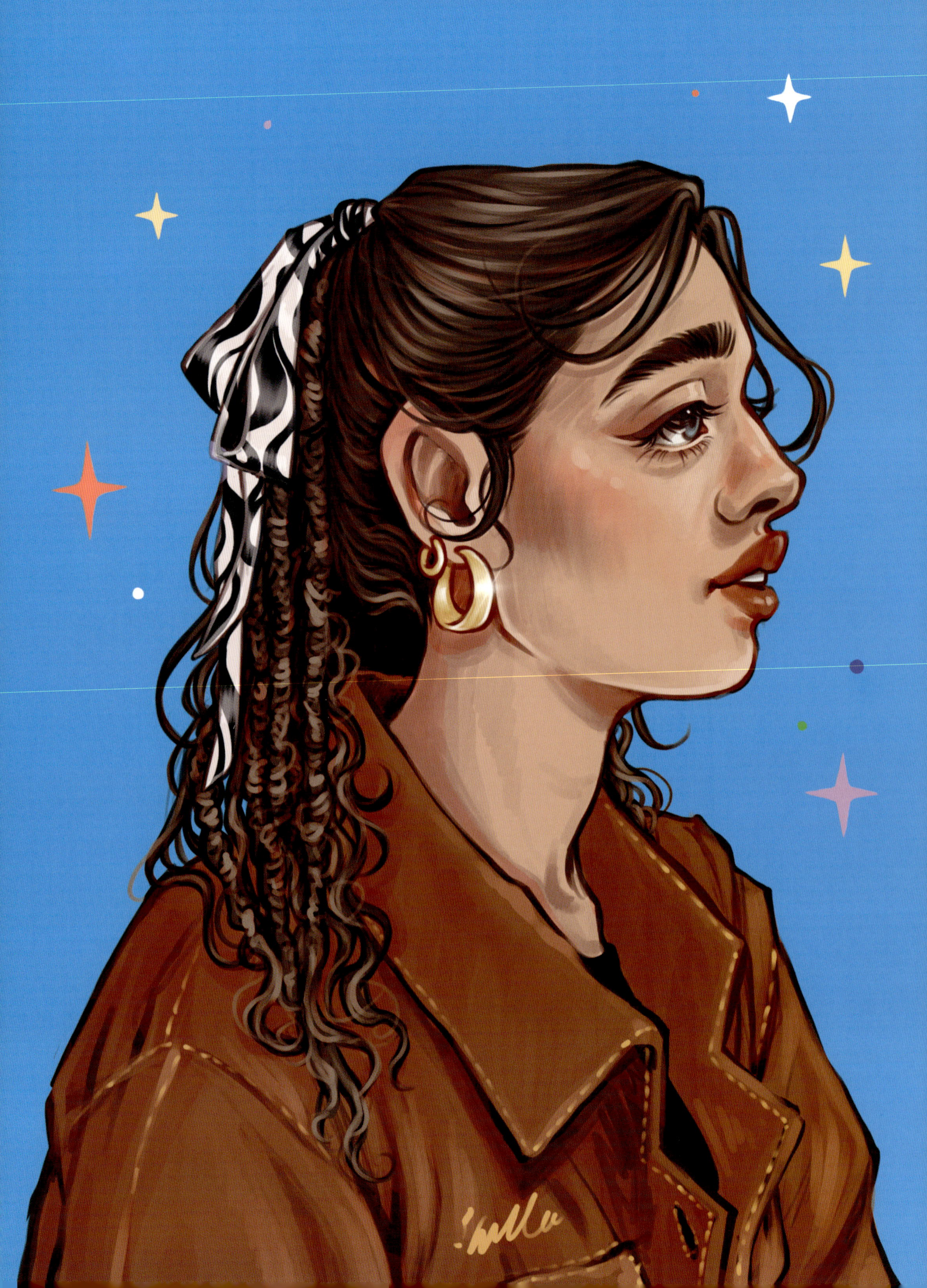

7

DRAWING THE EARS

On the last stretch of the facial features, we have the ears. They often go underlooked and are even covered up by hair most of the time—but they are there nonetheless! The ears thankfully don't add much to the expression game or help the face when emoting. Actually they don't move much at all, so all we have to do is learn how to draw them at different angles.

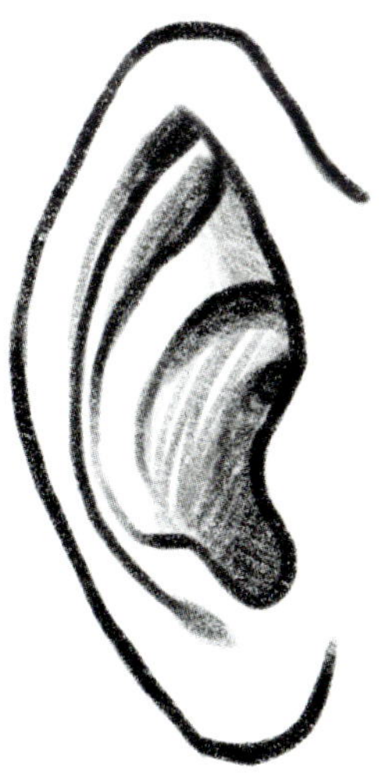

BASIC SHAPES OF
THE EAR IN PROFILE

As per usual, in order to understand the structure of the ears, we should first look into the building blocks and shapes that make it up.

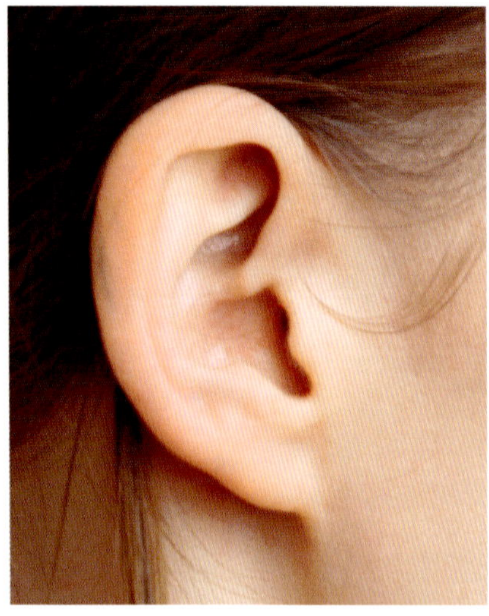

Let's look at the ear in profile first, using a reference image.

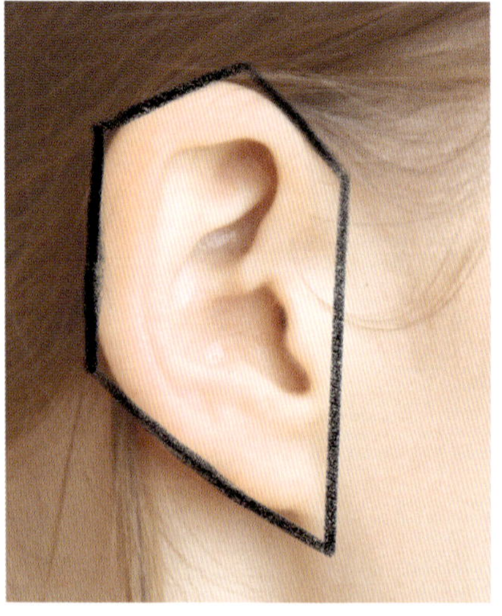

The outer ear is fairly simple. I like to describe it as "half a heart" shape, a semicircle that arches upward.

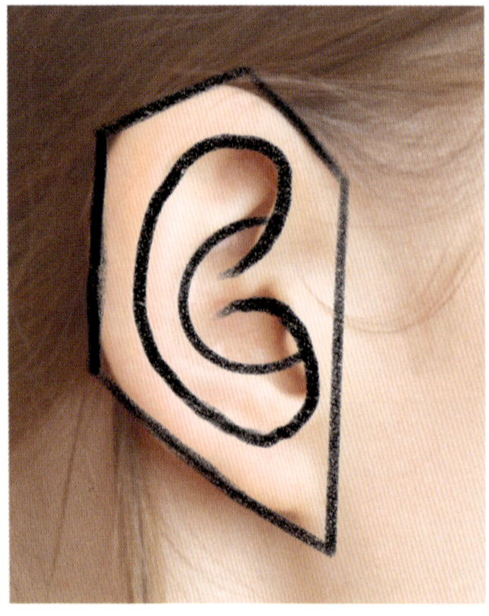

The inner workings of the ear are slightly more confusing. But breaking it down into these two shapes makes it a bit easier to understand: a big curvy C and a smaller C inside.

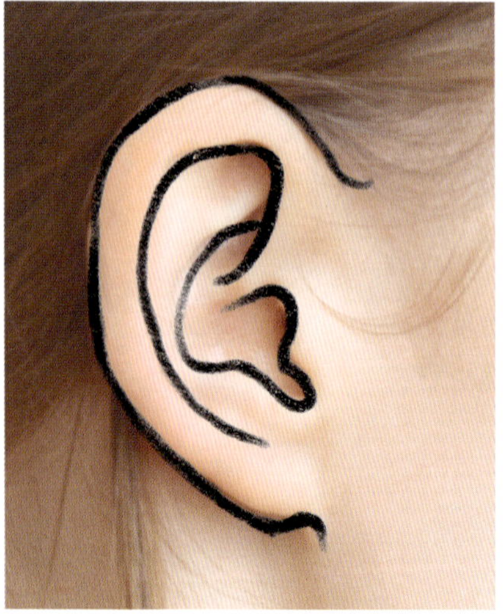

Using those two C shapes, we can then add in the squiggly details of the ear cartilage.

DRAWING THE EAR IN PROFILE STEP BY STEP

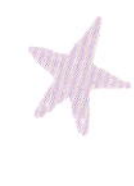

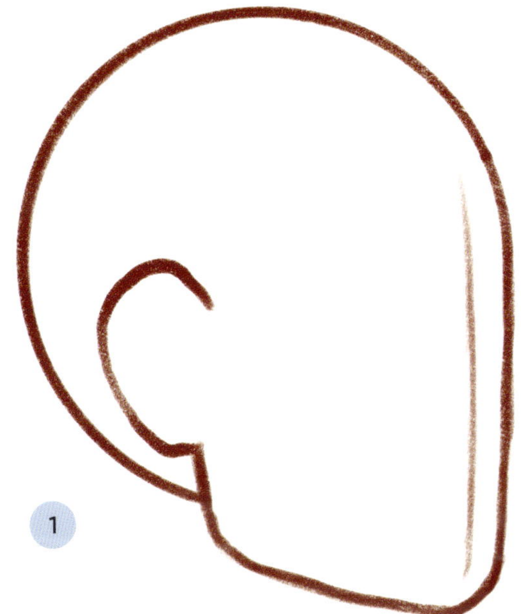

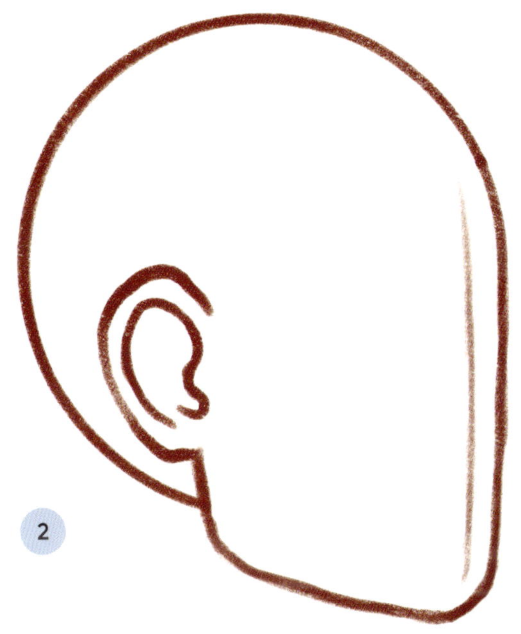

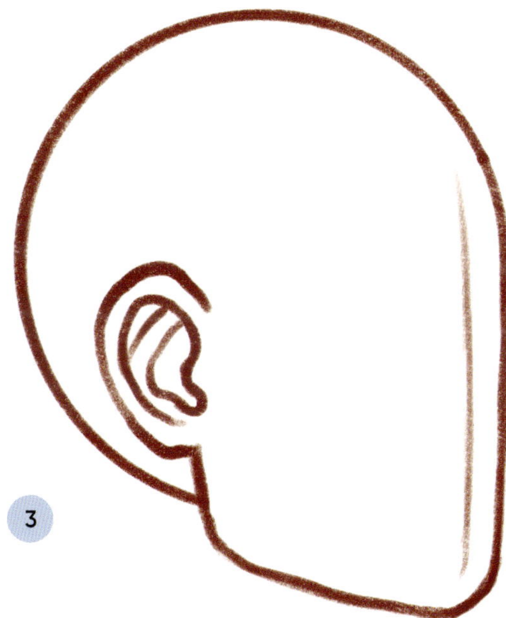

Now for drawing the ear from scratch on your portrait.

1. Start off by drawing the arch of the ear like we learned back on page 24, making sure it connects to the jawline as shown.

2. Draw the ear going inward from the outside. Then draw the line detailing the helix and the little tragus (the little bits of cartilage close to the cheek).

3. Go in further and add in the antihelix (the curved bit of cartilage inside the ear) and connect it to the bottom of the line we did in step 2 (antitragus).

It might all look like a bunch of confusing squiggly lines at first, but once you break down the ear into its basic structures, you will find you'll be drawing the ears out of muscle memory in three quick and easy steps!

THE EAR FROM THE FRONT

When looking at the face head-on, the ears are at an extreme angle, making a lot of structures we just learned look different, or even hidden. So let's learn about the ears at this angle.

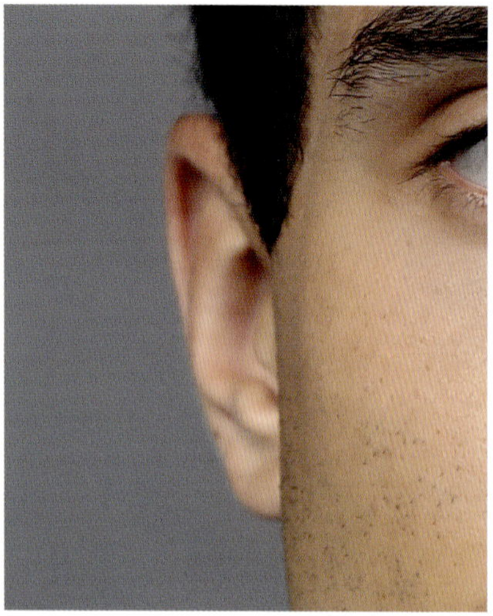

We'll be using this reference image as an example to study the ear from the front.

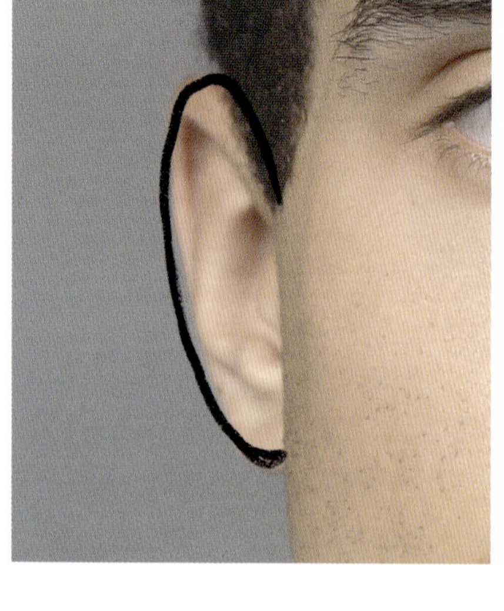

The shape of the outer arch and helix is a lot more squished together at this angle, like you've pushed both sides into each other.

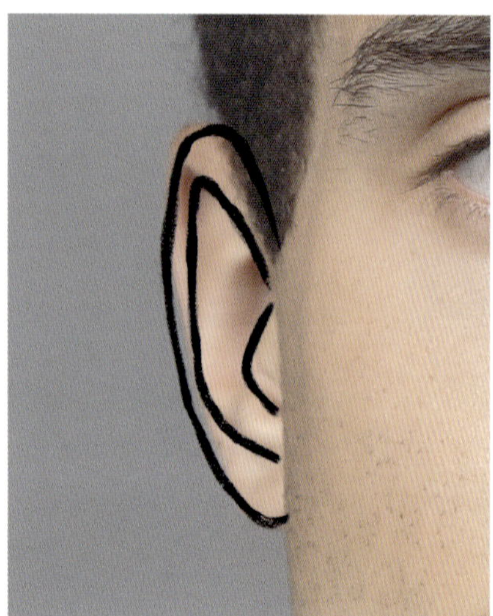

The lines inside the ear follow the same rule, becoming more squished together. The outer big C is more angled and pointier at the top and does not show the curves going back into the ear like before.

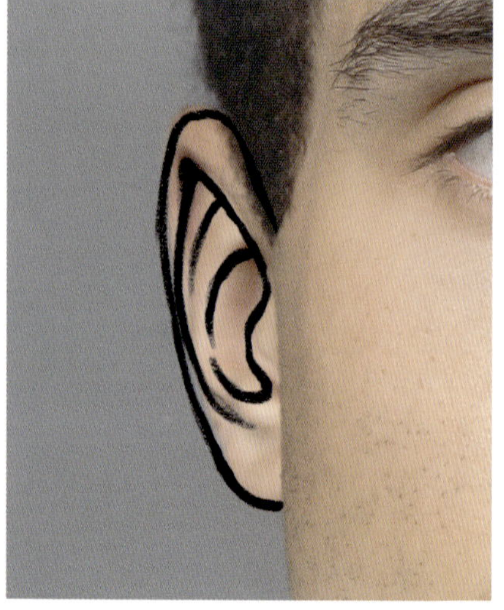

All the cartilage details inside the ear are now much closer together and even overlapping each other, like above.

DRAWING THE EAR FROM THE FRONT STEP BY STEP

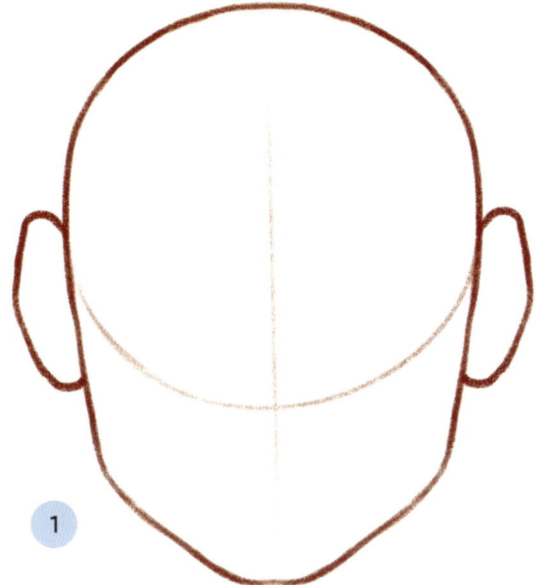

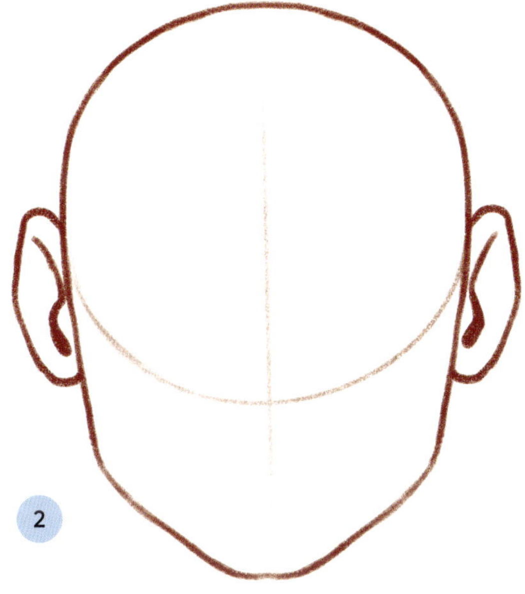

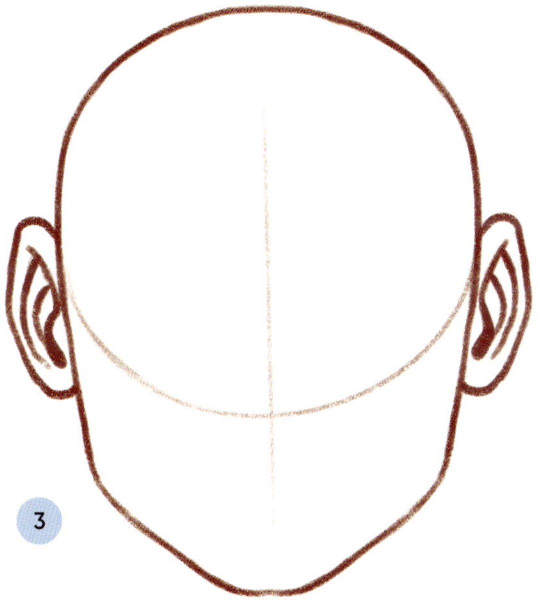

As for drawing the ears on an empty portrait, I find this angle a lot easier!

1. First, draw on the outline of the ears. At this angle, the ears appear to be more pointy toward the top, as opposed to a symmetric semicircle all around.

2. Next draw in a stretched-out S shape close to the inside of the ear, almost touching the side of the face.

3. From this S shape, you can then draw two curves following the curve of the outline of the ear from step 1. The outer curve should be longer and come all the way down to the earlobe. The inner curve should connect to the bottom of the S shape, creating a little dip.

Scan to watch a tutorial.

EXPLORING DIFFERENT EARS

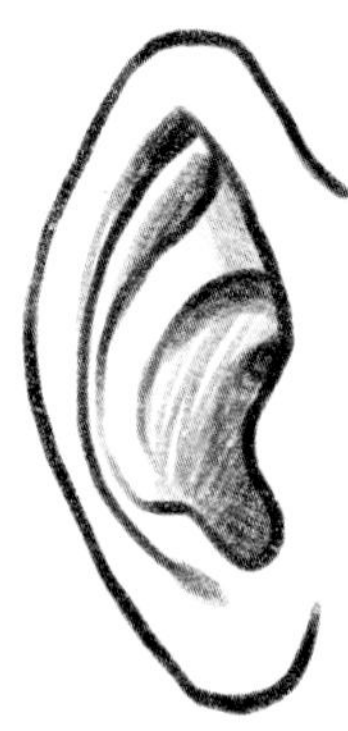 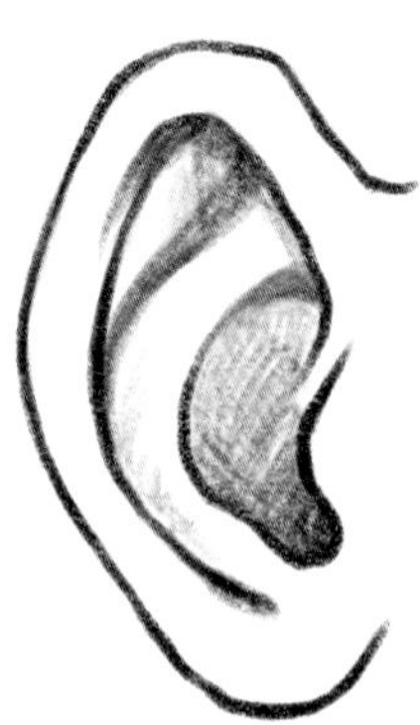 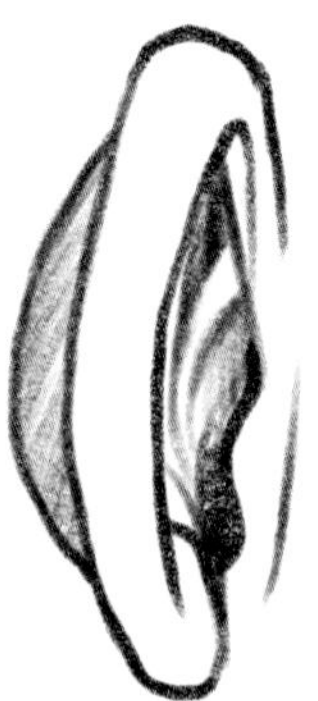 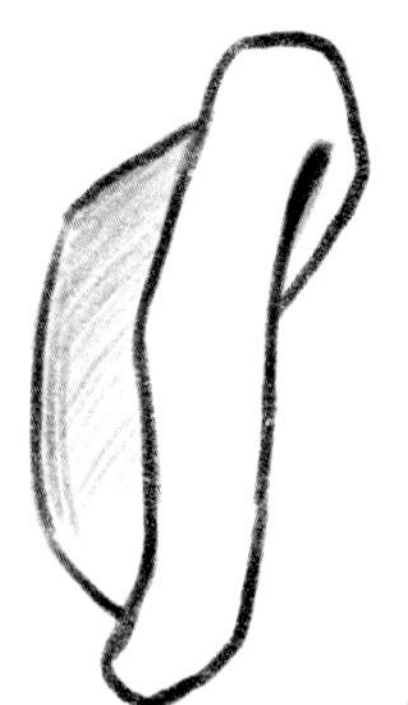 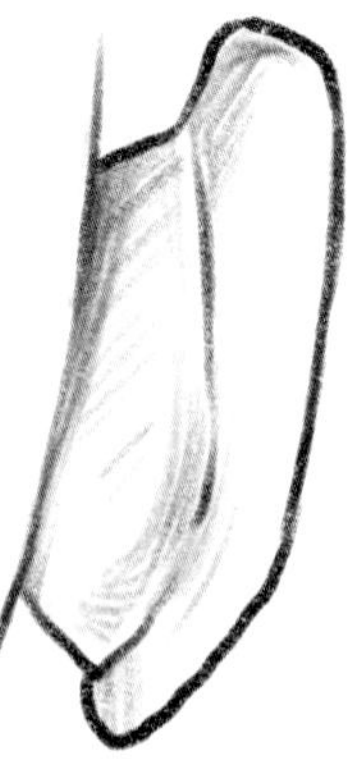

The ear is a very peculiar shape and has many little structures in it that make it look very different at different angles. The best way to think of the ear in your head is as a seashell shape—from the back, you can see the concave shape of the ear as it attaches to the head.

Shown here is a reference sheet for how the ear looks at various angles from the front to the back.

DIFFERENT-SHAPED EARS

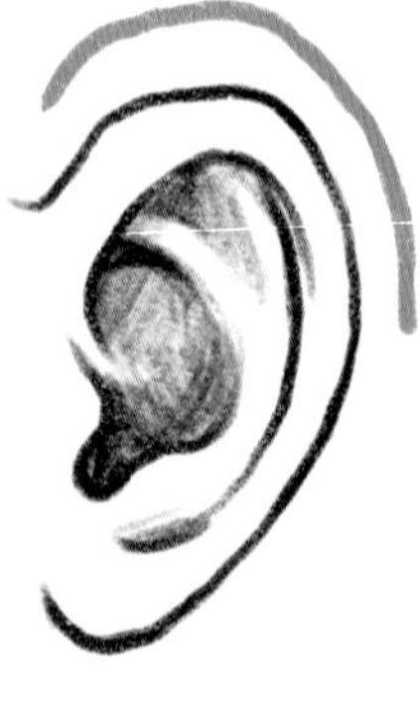 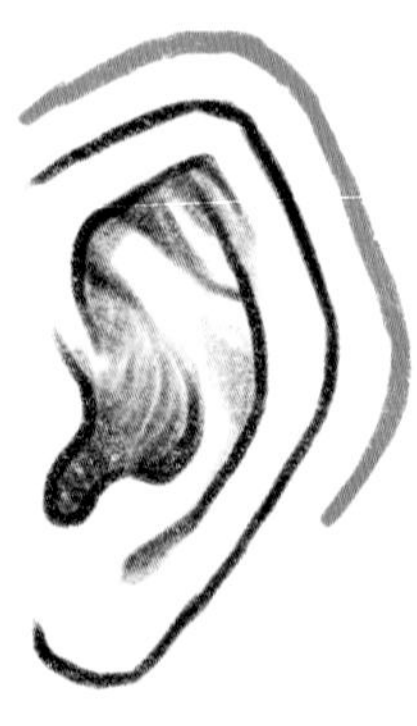 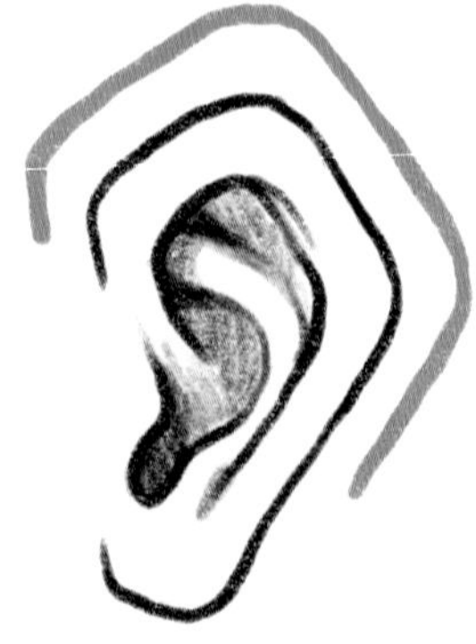 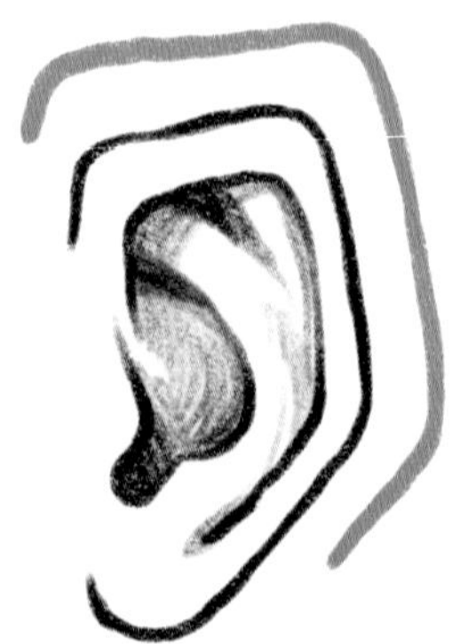

As with everything else in the human figure, the shapes, aesthetics, and looks of people's ears differ from person to person. The two major variables in the anatomy of the ear are the general shape of the ear and the earlobes. Shown here are a few different examples of how you can play around with the shape of the ear, starting with the outline shape and then drawing the inner structures accordingly. The earlobe can be either attached or detached.

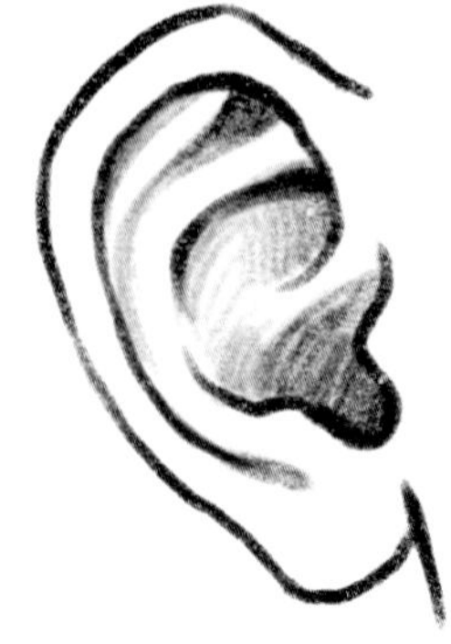 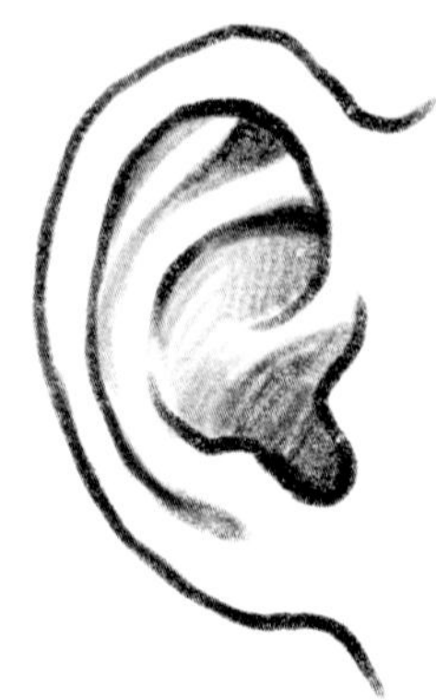

ATTACHED   DETACHED

FANTASY EARS

Why not push it even further and play around in the fantasy world? If you're drawing a portrait of a fantastical being, like an elf or a fairy, the ears will play a huge role in showing your character's fantasy race.

Shown are some examples of ears for different races, such as Drow (dark elf), Elf, Orc, and Tiefling. There are tons of others out there for you to play around with, but these are the most commonly used fantasy ears, I'd say.

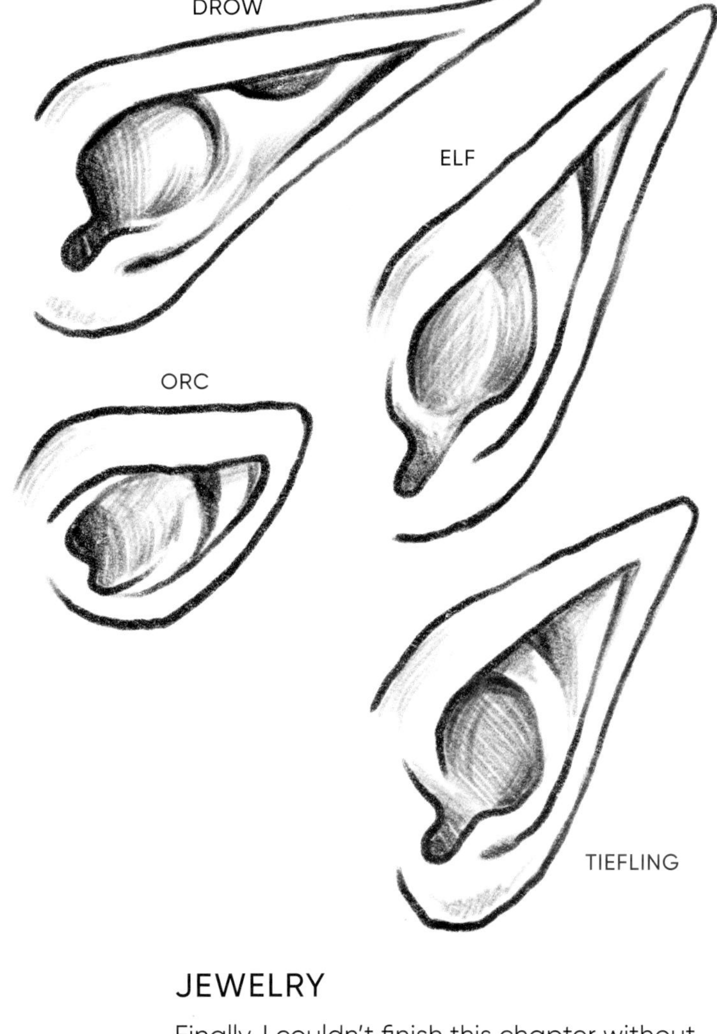

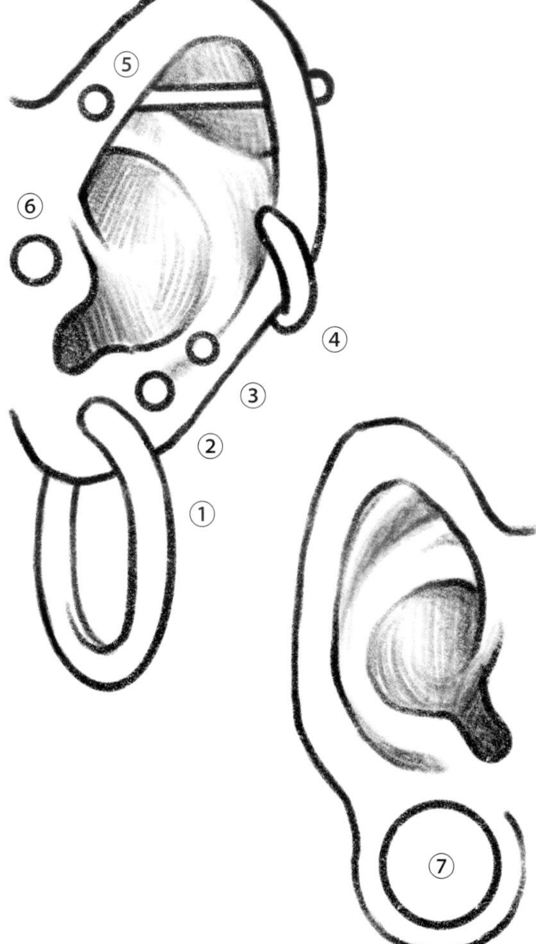

JEWELRY

Finally, I couldn't finish this chapter without mentioning jewelry and earrings. There are, of course, many different piercing types, placements, and shapes.

There are the most common earrings on the earlobe, which can support up to three earrings (①, ②, ③). Piercings on the outer cartilage of the ear ④ can sometimes get obscured depending on the type of ear, so people usually do small hoops in these places.

Then you can start playing around with scaffold piercings ⑤, tragus piercings ⑥, and even ear stretchers ⑦. There are even more piercings and placements that can go on the ear and face—whatever your portrait or character requires!

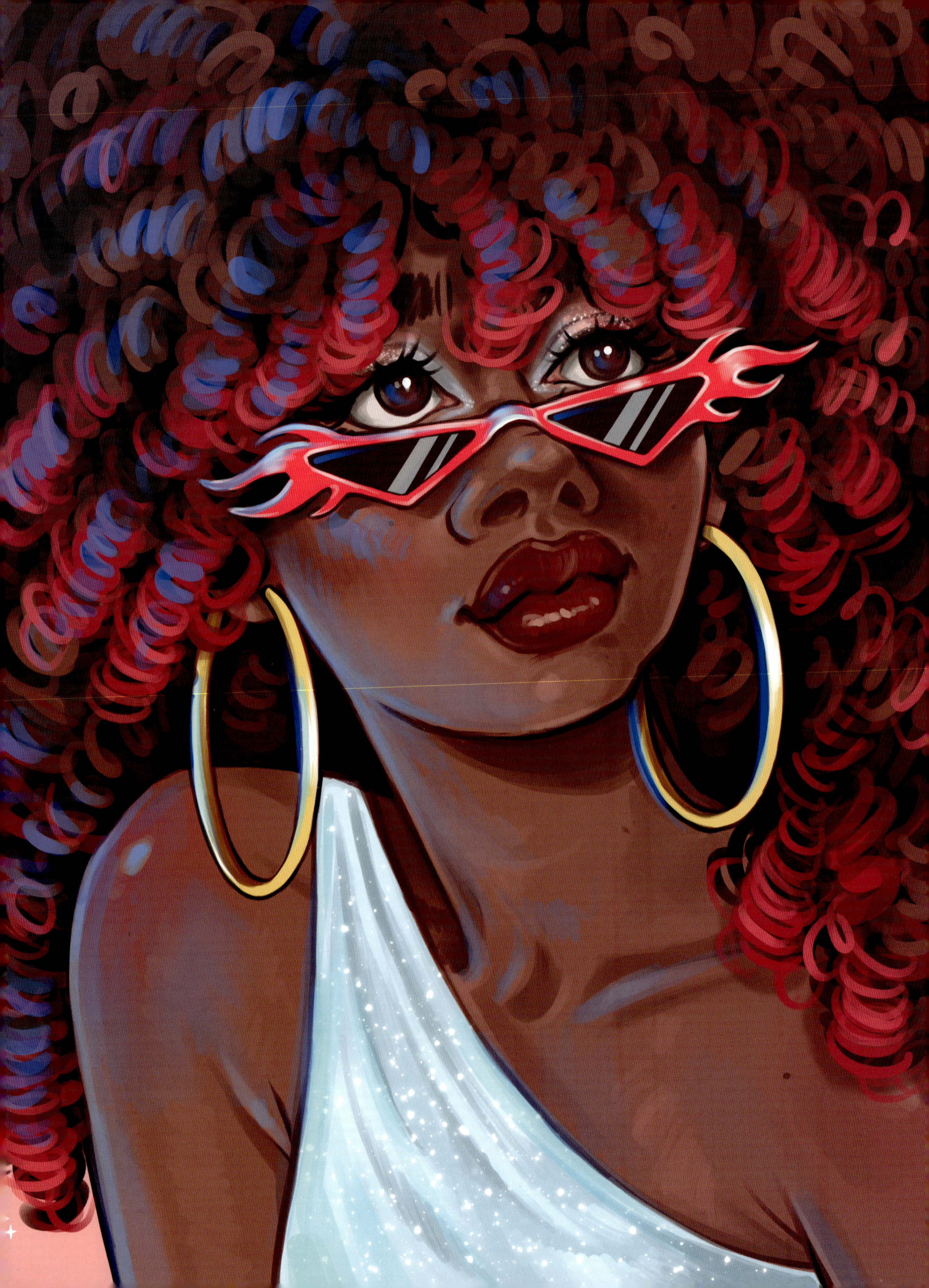

8

DRAWING THE HAIR

We're on to our final puzzle piece to complete a portrait: the hair! Let's learn about all the different types of beautiful hair and how you can draw them. The sky is the limit when it comes to hair! Long hair, short hair, straight hair, coily hair, braids, bobs, buns, protective hairstyles, and so on! There is so much to play around with, and adding hair to your portraits can add even more personality and character to them too.

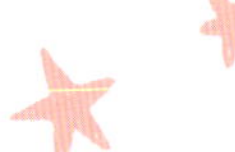

THE FOUR HAIR TYPES

There are many different types, styles, and shapes of hair, and it can feel a little overwhelming getting to know all of them. We can actually separate hair types into four different categories.

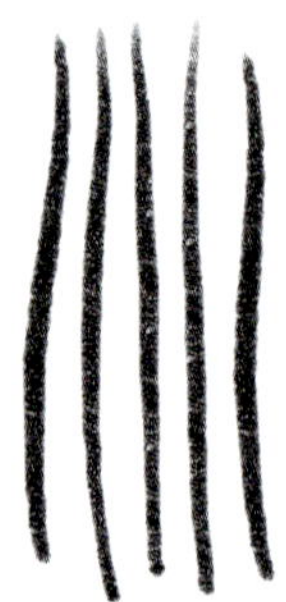

TYPE 1 HAIR

Type 1 hair is the straightest hair. It's also the shiniest, due to it being the most prone to oiliness. It usually refers to stick-straight hair, but Type 1 hair can also have some slight waves.

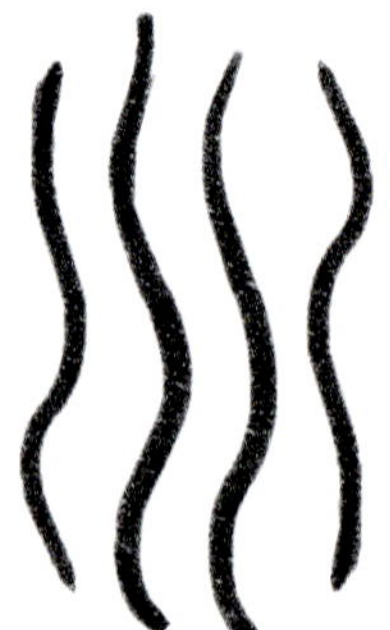

TYPE 2 HAIR

This type of hair is categorized as wavy—in between straight and curly hair. It does not possess any coils but more S-type waves and curls with more volume than straight hair. Due to this, in Type 2 hair we now start seeing something called frizz—dry, stray hairs separating from the main clumps of hair that form.

TYPE 3 HAIR

Moving on to Type 3 hair, the hair strands get more and more curly. In Type 3 hair, the hair forms into coils and clumps of curls that resemble corkscrews. The volume in the hair goes up considerably, and the hair moves out more rather than straight down, creating a round overall shape.

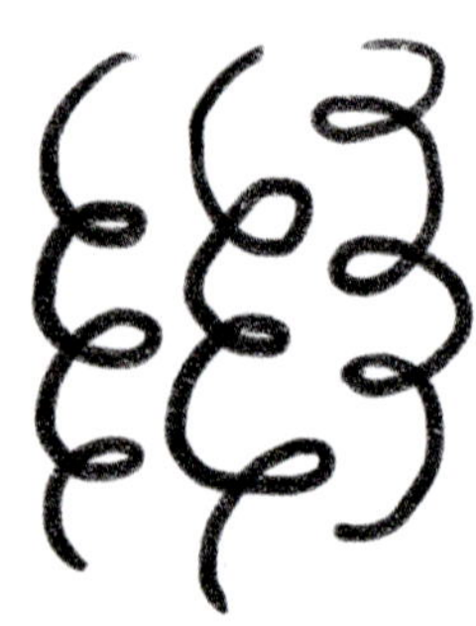

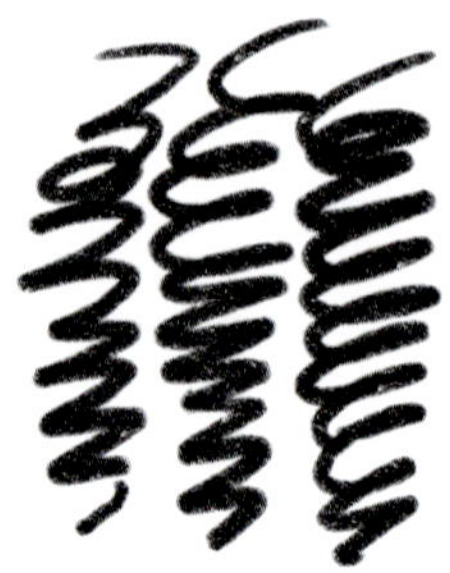

TYPE 4 HAIR

Type 4 hair is so curly that it's actually more kinky/coily than curly. The curls are more Z-shaped than S-shaped, or corkscrew as with Type 3. These curls are tighter and smaller, and the hair shrinks up a lot more than Type 3 hair.

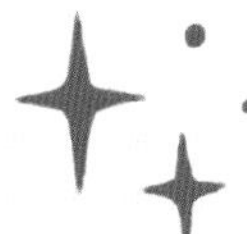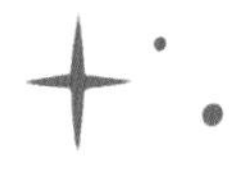

HAIR TYPES CHART

We can even further subcategorize each hair type into three more sections: A, B, and C. Here is an easy reference cheat-sheet chart for you to use:

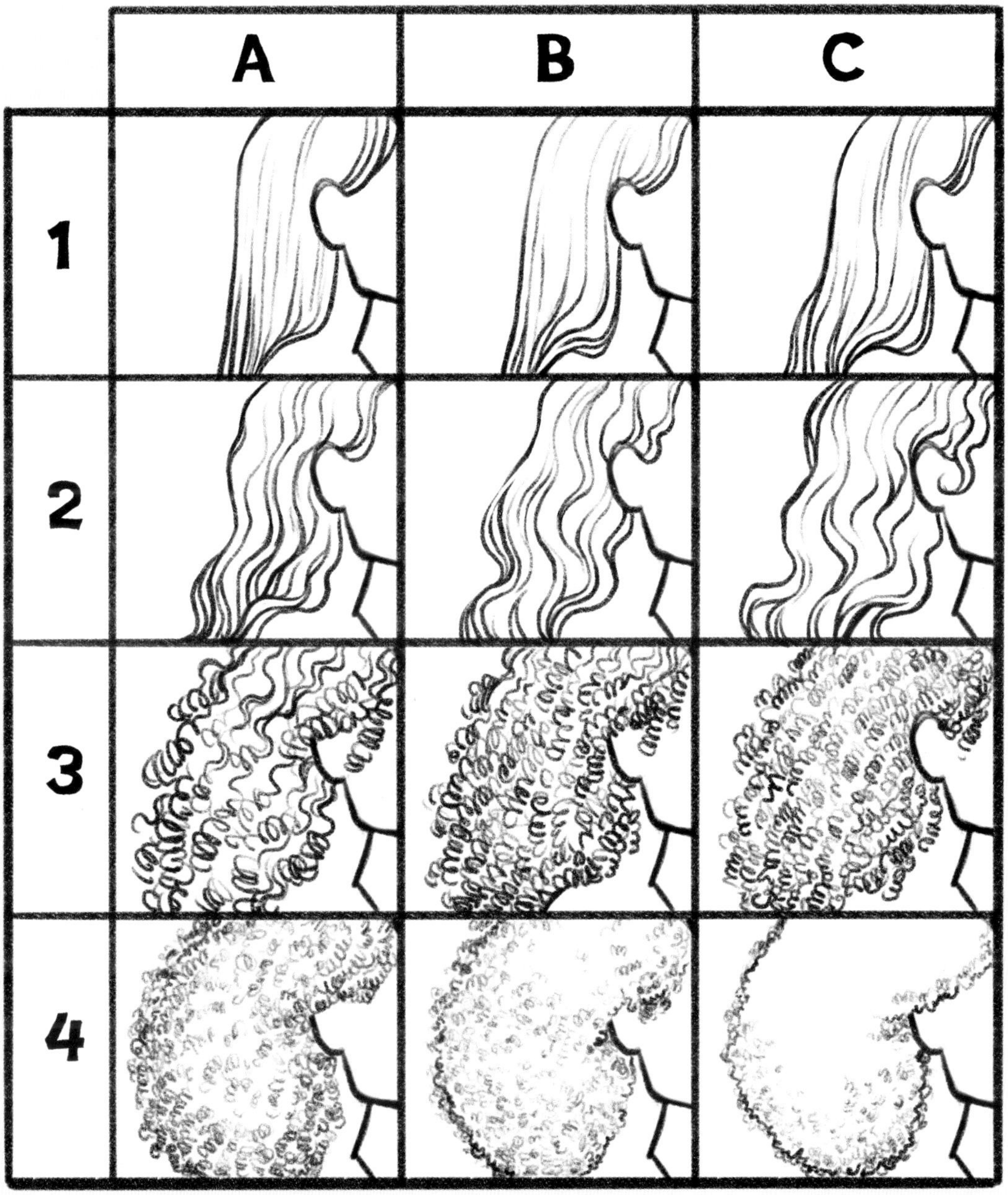

	A	B	C
1			
2			
3			
4			

As you can see, the A, B, and C subsections describe how "intense" the hair looks within its hair type. For example, Type 3A hair has looser, larger curls that get tighter and tighter until you get to Type 3C hair, where the coils are more densely packed and each one is wound tighter. This hair chart is an important resource to have, as sometimes it's easy to get into the habit of drawing one single type of hair. It's important to implement as much diversity and variety as possible in the characters you draw.

STARTING WITH THE OUTLINE

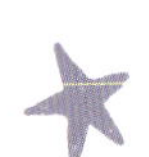
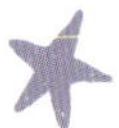

Sketching out the general shape of an object first will allow you to make sure that the size and shape are in proportion with the rest of the drawing. It's a lot easier to tweak a small sketch line than a fully rendered head of hair!

When drawing the hair shape on your portrait, you should usually consider four things: hair type, hair length, parting, and hairstyle/shape. We have already looked at hair type (Types 1A–4C). Hair length is important to decide so you can draw it interacting with the body of your character and around the face. The hair parting is where the hair starts and it will be the starting point for the directionality of the hair strands. Finally, the hair shape/style will determine the general outline shape of the hair: Will it look rounder? Will it have a fringe or layers? Will it have lots of volume or none at all? All these things should be taken into consideration.

We will venture into hairstyles later, but for now let's look at the different hair types and how to draw them out from start to finish.

TYPE 1–2 HAIR

For straighter hair, the parting and the hairstyle is much more important, as straight hair is a lot more "flowy" and will follow the direction of the hairstyle more. The hair does not sit flush to the scalp or the line we've drawn for the head. There will always be a little gap between the line of the top of the head and the hair (and this space increases depending on hair volume, of course). Similarly, the hair will always fall over the top part of the head and either cover the forehead slightly or show the hairline. The hairline is usually more visible on shorter hairstyles.

Once the shape of the hair is down, you can then sketch out some direction arrows showing the way in which the hair flows from the root to the tip (shown in green).

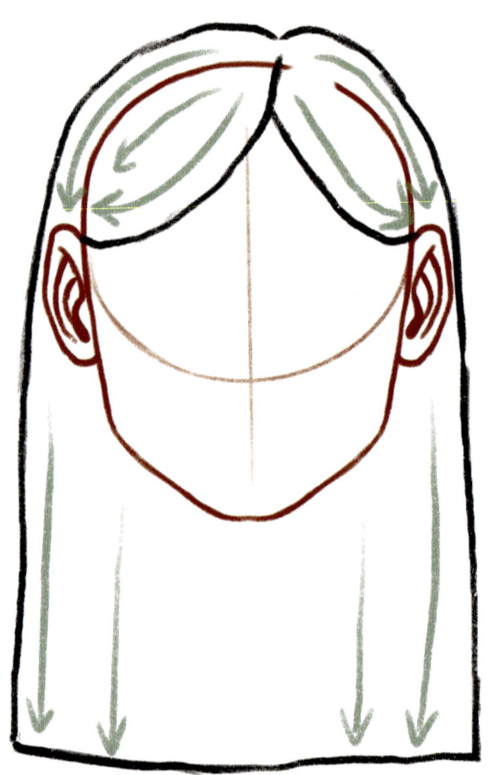

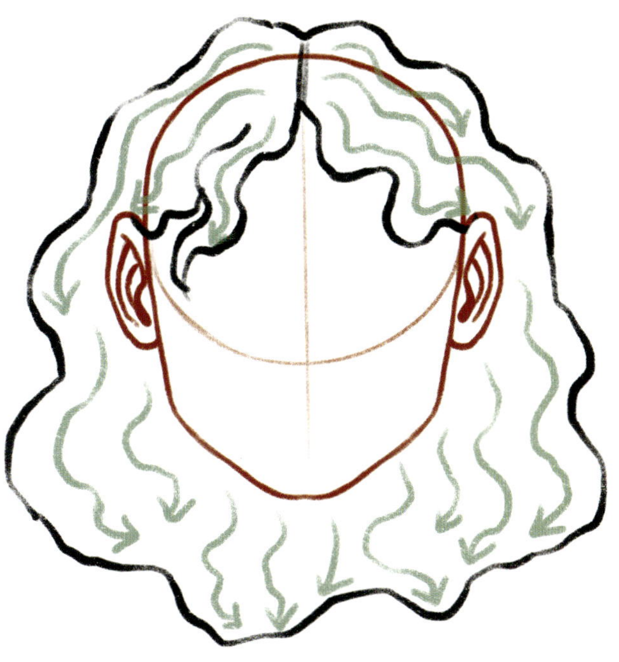

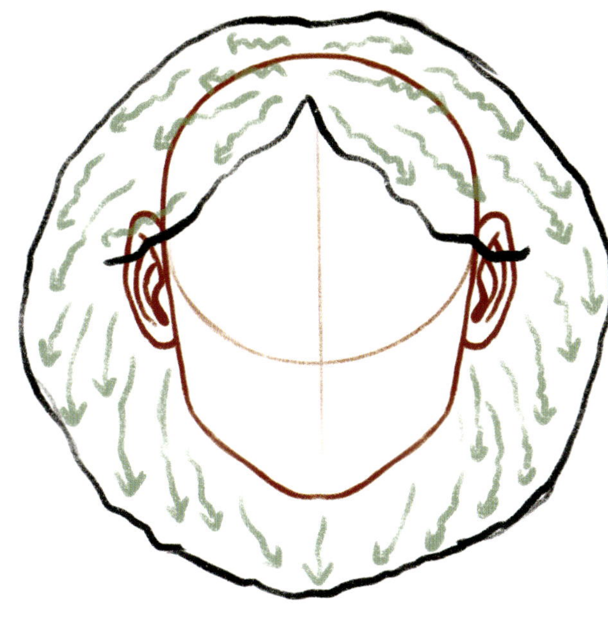

TYPE 2–3 HAIR

For wavy and curly hair, the outline will not be a straight line like for Type 1–2. As the hair becomes curlier, the curves of the hair become tighter and closer together. The same occurs close to the roots at the top of the head. Curly hair typically has more volume at the root as well.

In wavy/curly hair, it's also common to see more stray hairs and stray curls either in the face or on the edges of the hair. I always like to draw a curl or two falling away from the rest.

Now for the direction arrows, these will also not be smooth and straight like with straight hair. Curly hair consists of many different locks of hair, with most of them doing their own thing. Make sure to add in a diverse number of arrows going in slightly different directions, and make sure there are curves and twists in each arrow as well as it reaches the tips.

TYPE 3–4 HAIR

As we get to Type 3–4 hair, the curls and coils of the hair become tighter and smaller. This means they're less and less defined from far away. The volume and density of all these curls also means that these types of hair end up being rounder and flowing out and away from the face. Also, the hair parting is usually less visible or even completely hidden, since the curls are so tight and dense—like an Afro hairstyle, for example.

When drawing this type of hair, I usually create even more distance from the scalp and the hair outline to allow for all that lovely volume. I also tend to draw the hair rounder and avoid drawing the bottom of the hair as a straight line. Each curl is so unique and curls up differently from each other, so the bottom line of the hair is usually curved.

When adding in the direction lines of the hairs, I usually just draw squiggly lines flowing from the face outward and then slightly down. In hair types such as 4A–C, the hair can even point straight up from the scalp!

ADDING IN DETAILS & LOCKS

Once we've drawn out the general outline shape of the hair, we can then refine this shape, adding in extra details for realism, as well as detailing the individual locks of hair.

Scan to watch
a tutorial.

TYPE 1–2 HAIR

Using the general outline shape we drew in step 1, now we can go through it and add some finer details. You can go along the outer edges and create a more organic line; adding some stray hairs and slight curves to the hair will make it look more dynamic and lifelike.

When drawing the tips of the hair, make sure to separate the bottom into "chunks" of hair by adding small gaps here and there. This will add to the realism.

At the roots and areas where the hair is pinched together (like above the ears in this example), you can add some lines and details showing the hair flowing in and out of these areas. Use the directional arrow lines you drew in the first step to help.

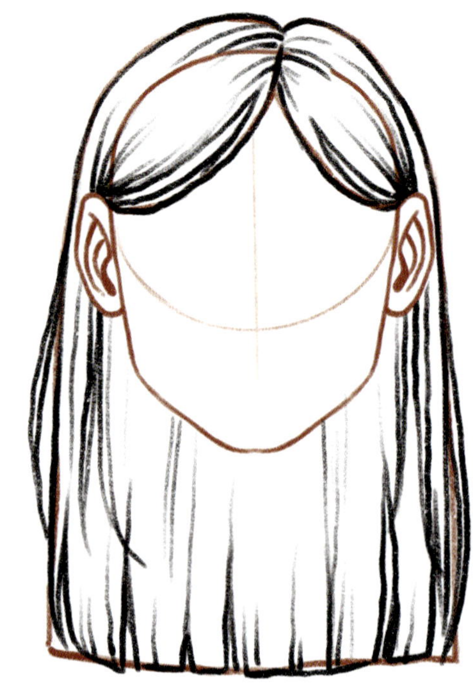

TYPE 2–3 HAIR

For wavy/curly hair, again, go around the sketched outline and add more dynamic waves or curls—don't try to make it look too stiff and perfect! Using the direction lines from step 1, draw out the different curl clumps and locks of hair. I like to make sure the ends of each clump point in alternating directions. This mismatching of curl patterns and direction makes the hair feel more lifelike. There's a lot more going on in curly hair than before, so start off with bigger clumps and work your way into the smaller areas as you go along—it will make it feel less daunting to draw the full head of hair this way.

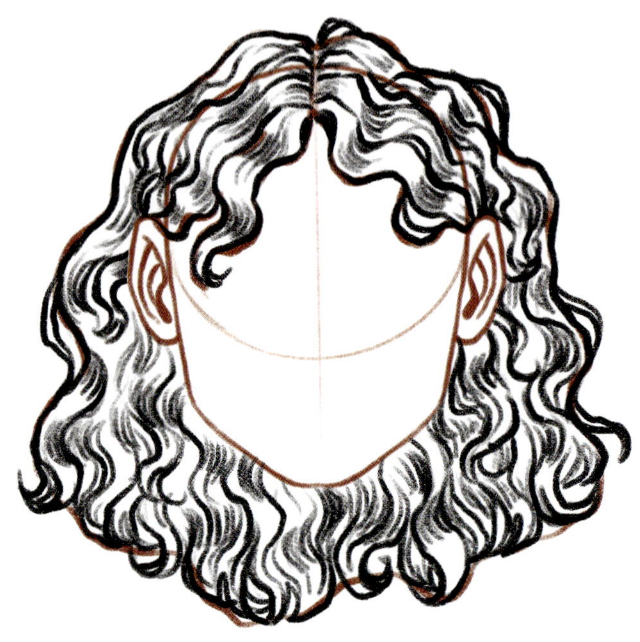

Now's a good time to look at individual curl types up close. Curls will look a little different depending on their curl pattern and hair type. In the illustration you can see some examples of wavy (2B–C) hair next to curlier (3A–B) and coily (3B–C) hair. As you can see, the curl keeps getting tighter and tighter and then into a shape resembling a coil. In Type 4 hair, the curl gets even tighter forming more of a Z coil shape.

A good way of thinking about hair clumps is to think of them like bits of ribbon. Think about how a length of ribbon would curl up and picture each lock of hair behaving like it.

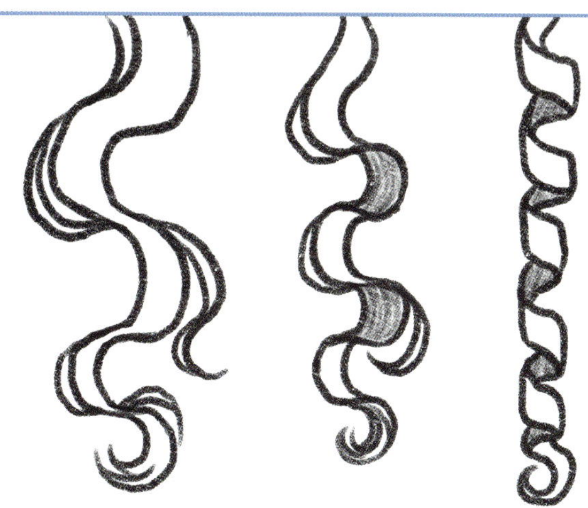

TYPE 3–4 HAIR

Like I said, coily and kinky hair is so densely packed with tiny individual curls that you often don't even see each curl.

In heads of hair such as the example to the left, start off by drawing the textured shape of the outline of the hair. I like to go in with a loose grip on the pencil and vary between small C curved strokes and small coily shapes pointing in different directions.

Keep up these coily shapes and texture lines all over the hair, making sure that the direction of the coils matches your directional arrow lines. I also like to add in lots of extra curls and stray hairs popping out of the edges of the hair for extra movement and randomness in the hair.

If adding in the curl clumps and locks is still too overwhelming from step 1, consider adding a step in between where you sketch out each clump lightly.

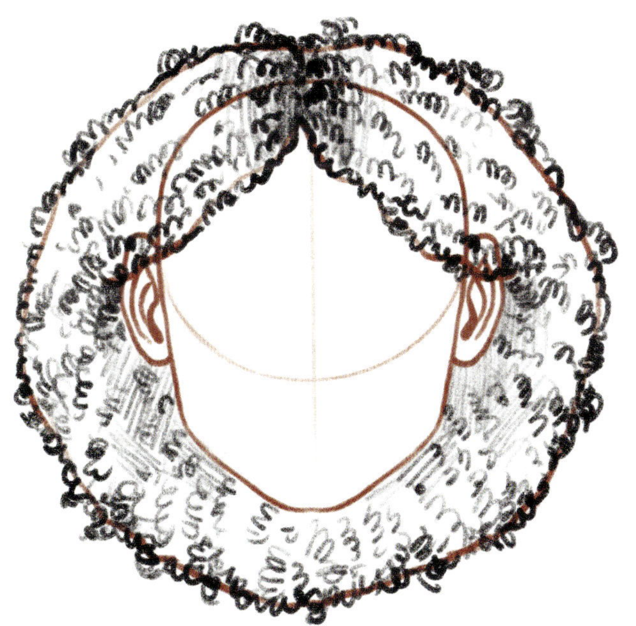

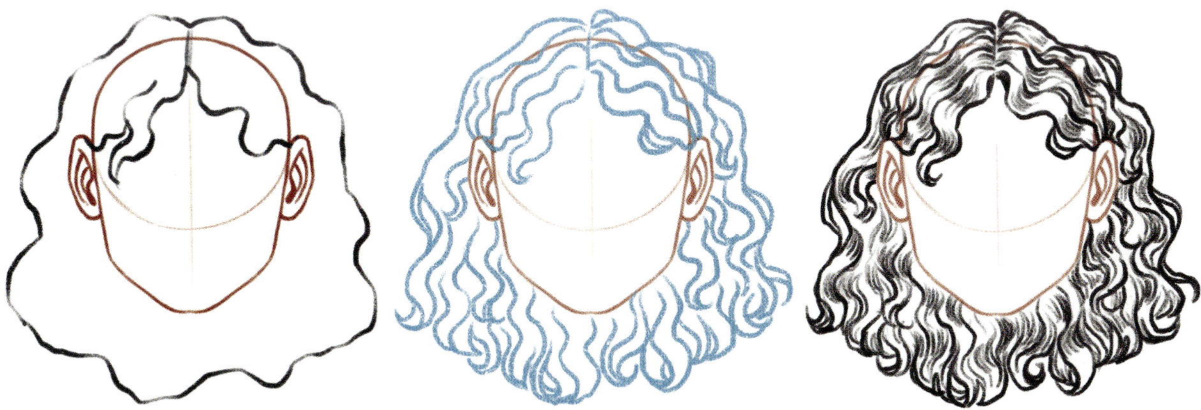

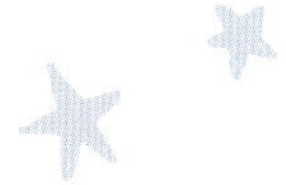

PLAYING AROUND WITH HAIRSTYLES

Now that we know how to draw different types of hair on the head, we can take it one step further and play around with hairstyles!

Using the concept of directional arrow lines from step 1, try positioning the hair in different styles. Like the hair being tied up on the example shown, you can use directional lines to help you visualize how the hair moves from the root to the point of tension where it gets tied up. Knowing the direction in which the hair is moving will also aid you in rendering and shading the hair. If you know the hair is following the curvature of the skull, for example, you will then be able to identify the high points that will have highlights and the darker areas that will have more shadows. This knowledge can also come into play in individual curls and clumps.

CURLS

Shown is a very simplified (ribbonlike) example of a clump of wavy hair. As you can see, the curved areas that bump upward would be hit by light, and the areas curving down would be in shadow. You can use this rule of thumb when shading in any hair type and hair clump to add realistic depth to the hair. See the additional examples of rendered hair.

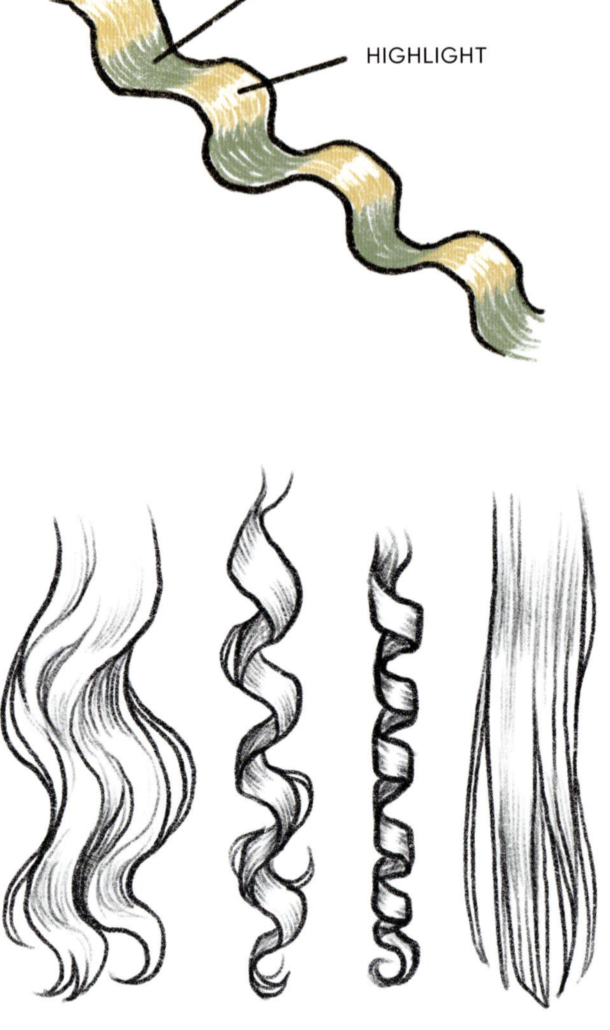

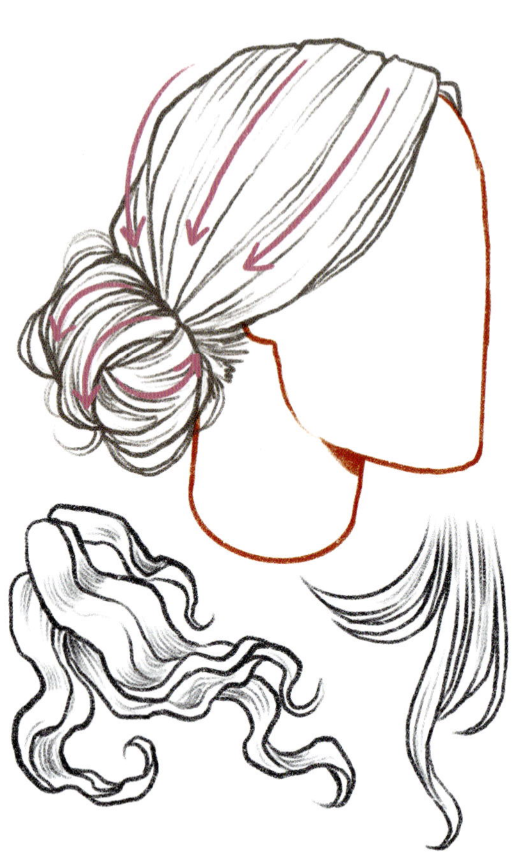

BRAIDS AND BUNS

You can also use these techniques and rules when drawing more complex hairstyles. One that can seem a bit scary to draw is braids, but once you get the pattern down, you just have to keep repeating it all the way down.

As with any hairstyle, you should sketch out the general shape of the hair. This will not only help you with proportions, but it will also help guide your braid pattern as you draw it out. Here you can see how I would draw the general shape of two braids on a portrait.

Then for the braid pattern, it might be easier shown than for me to explain, so make sure to study the breakdown of the pattern shown. I like to draw a wedge-like shape and then draw a flipped wedge and fit it just underneath the first one. Once you join them, they should look like a lopsided V shape with the top edges tapering off. Then you can just recreate that shape over and over again, almost like stacking them under each one.

Add this pattern to the inside of the sketched outline and start making the braid bits smaller as you reach the end of the braid.

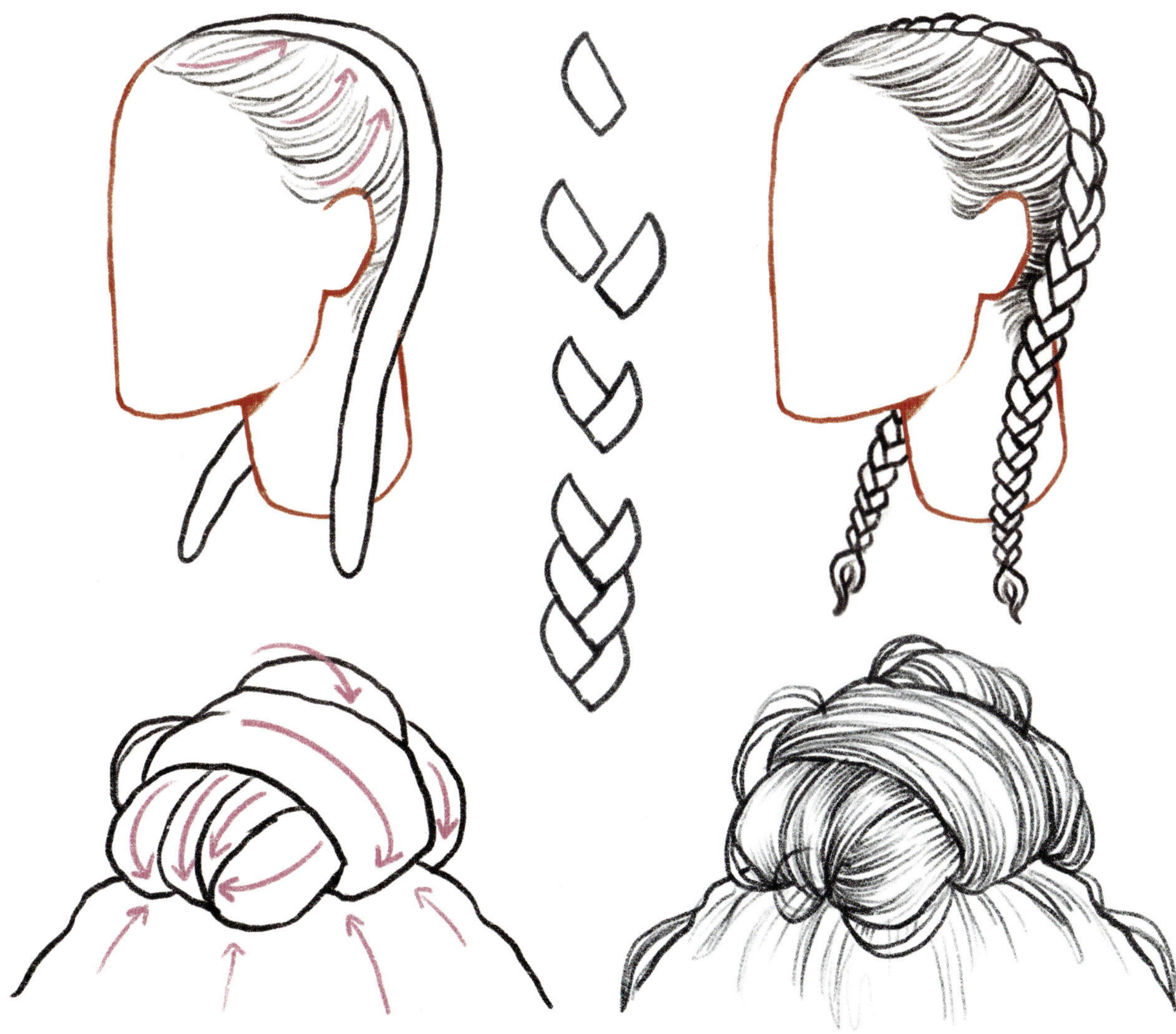

MORE STYLES TO TRY

Here are some more examples of hairstyles you can have fun with. To the right is an example of the Afro curly cut I mentioned earlier. You can see how at the top the curls stack on top of each other and can even curl upward away from the head.

Below is an example of short, wavy hair. You can see how there are still curl clumps and different hair directions all stemming from the roots.

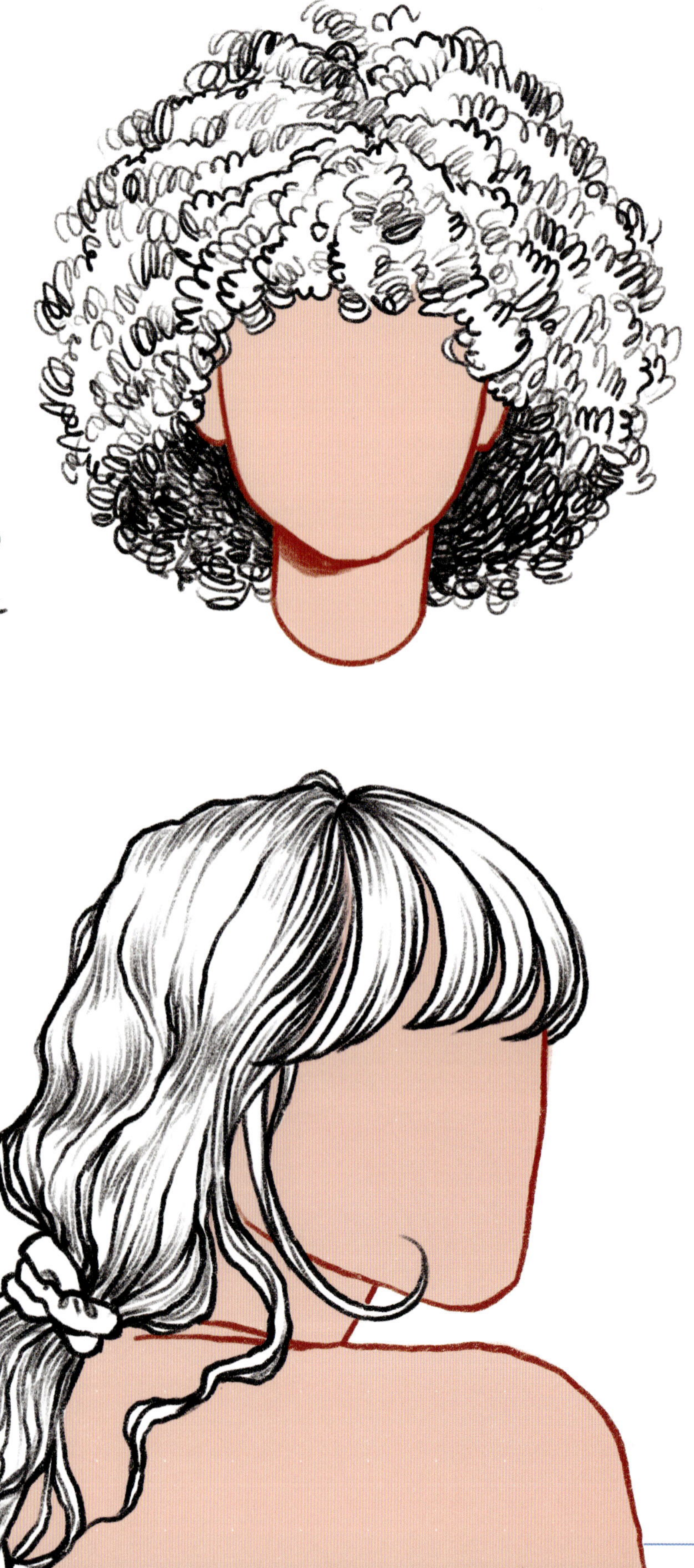

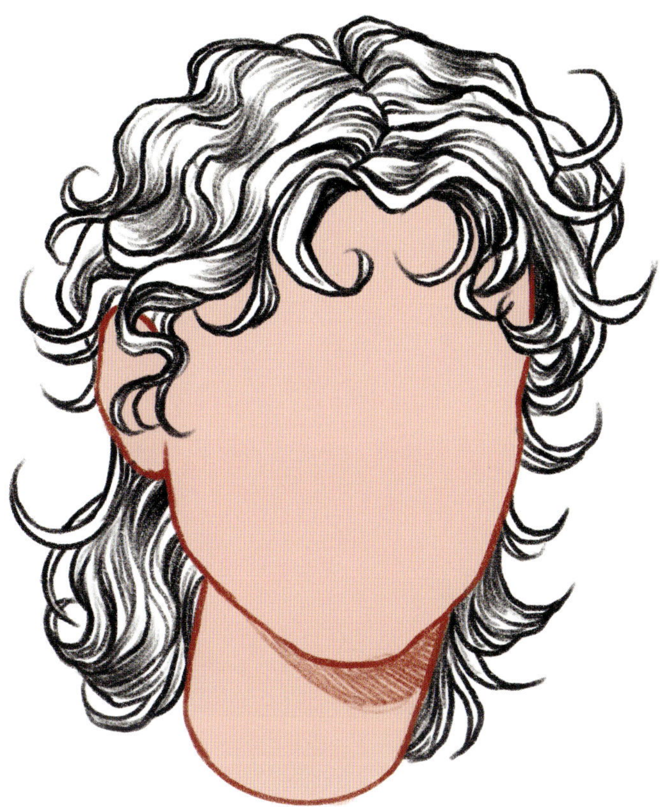

Protective hairstyles are typically worn by people with Type 3–4 hair. They usually consist of the hair being sectioned off into various parts and then braided, knotted, or twisted into small strands. Shown below is an example of cornrows. As the name suggests, the hair is parted into rows and braided into small braids.

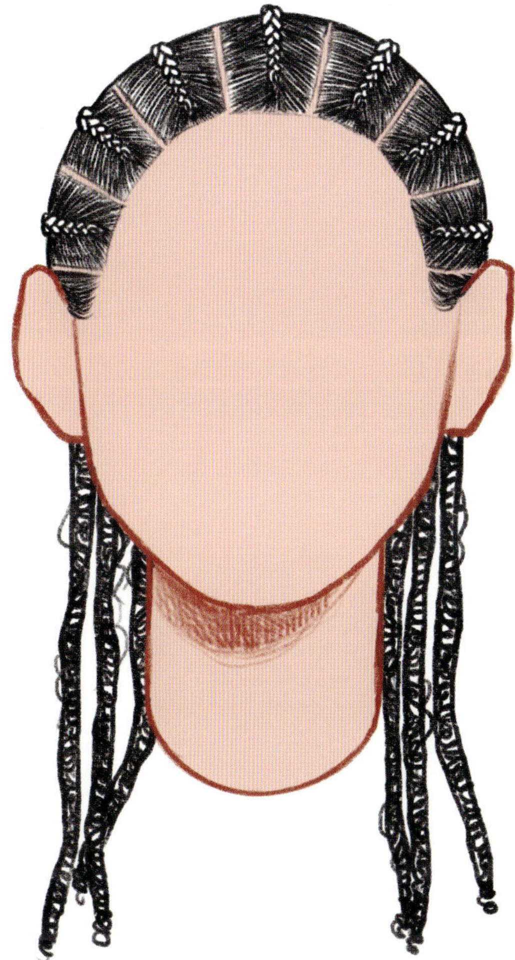

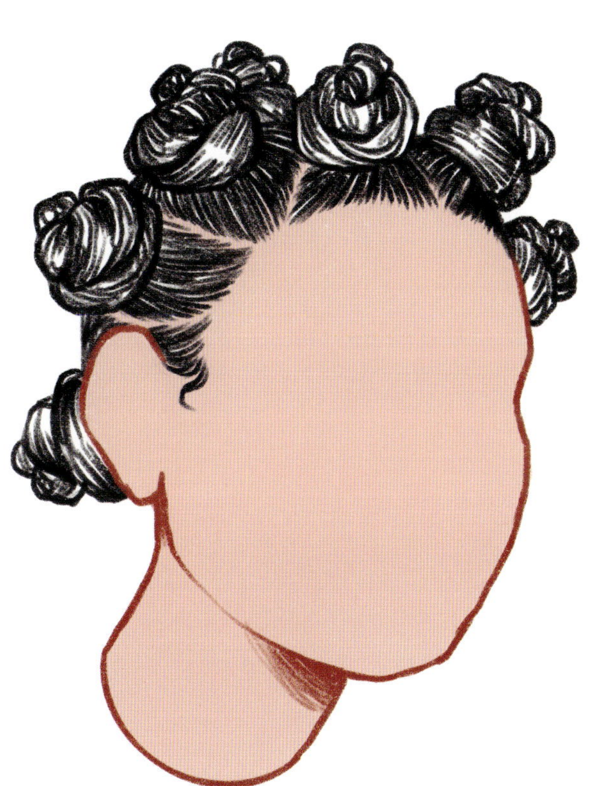

Bantu knots and box braids usually show the hair being parted into square or diamond sections. In Bantu knots these hair sections are made into tiny buns like shown at left, whereas box braids are just small braids coming from each section.

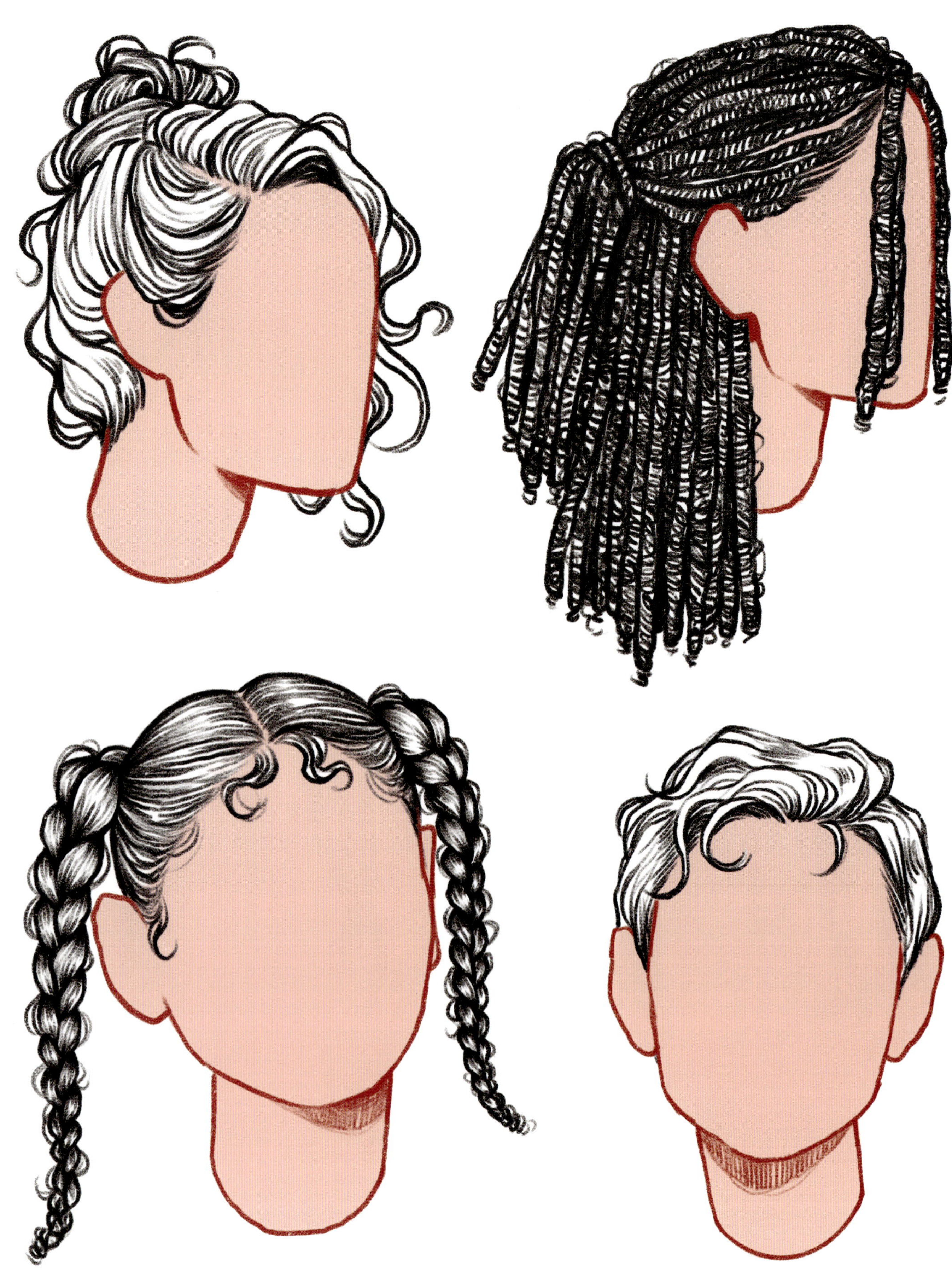

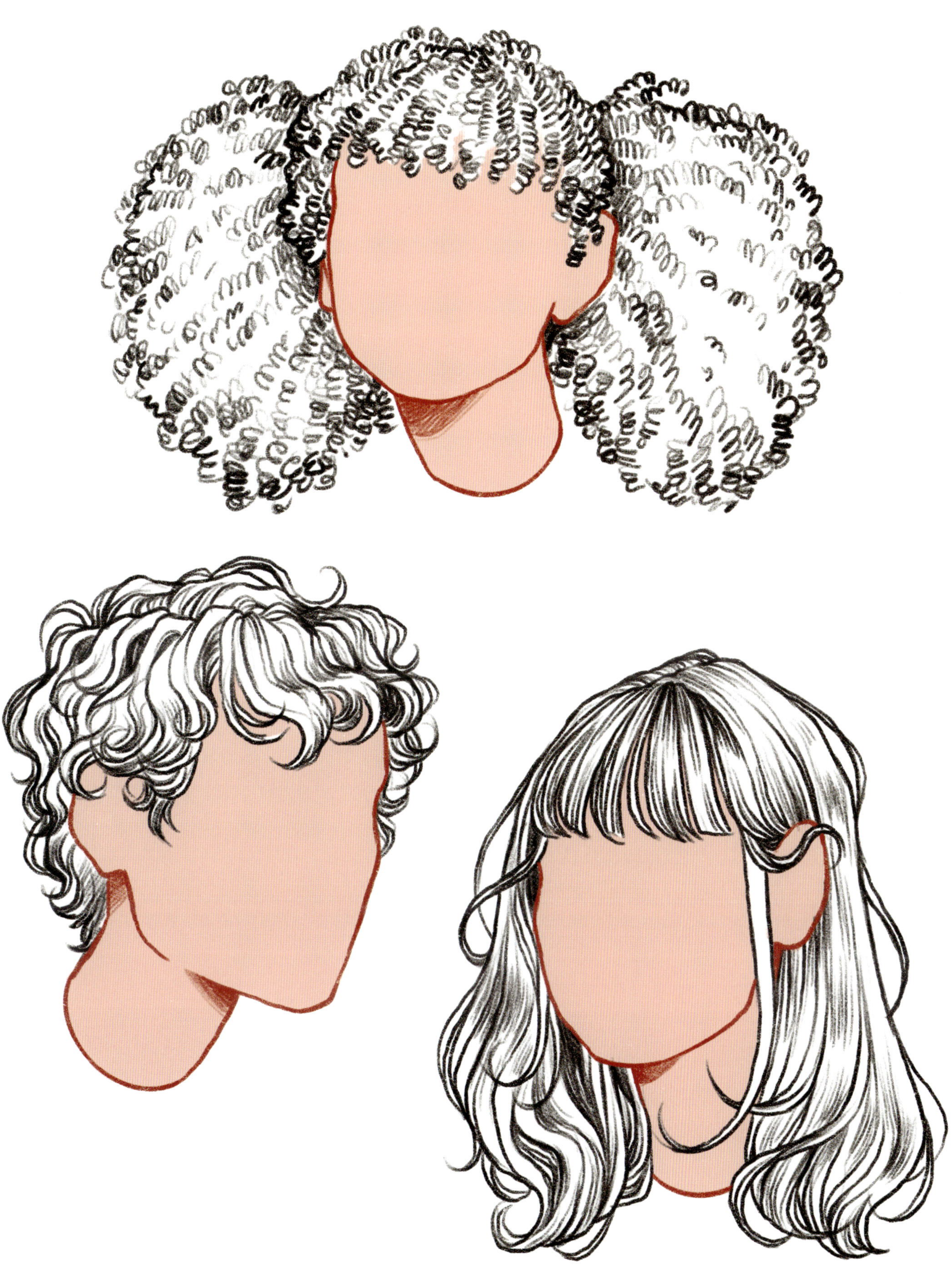

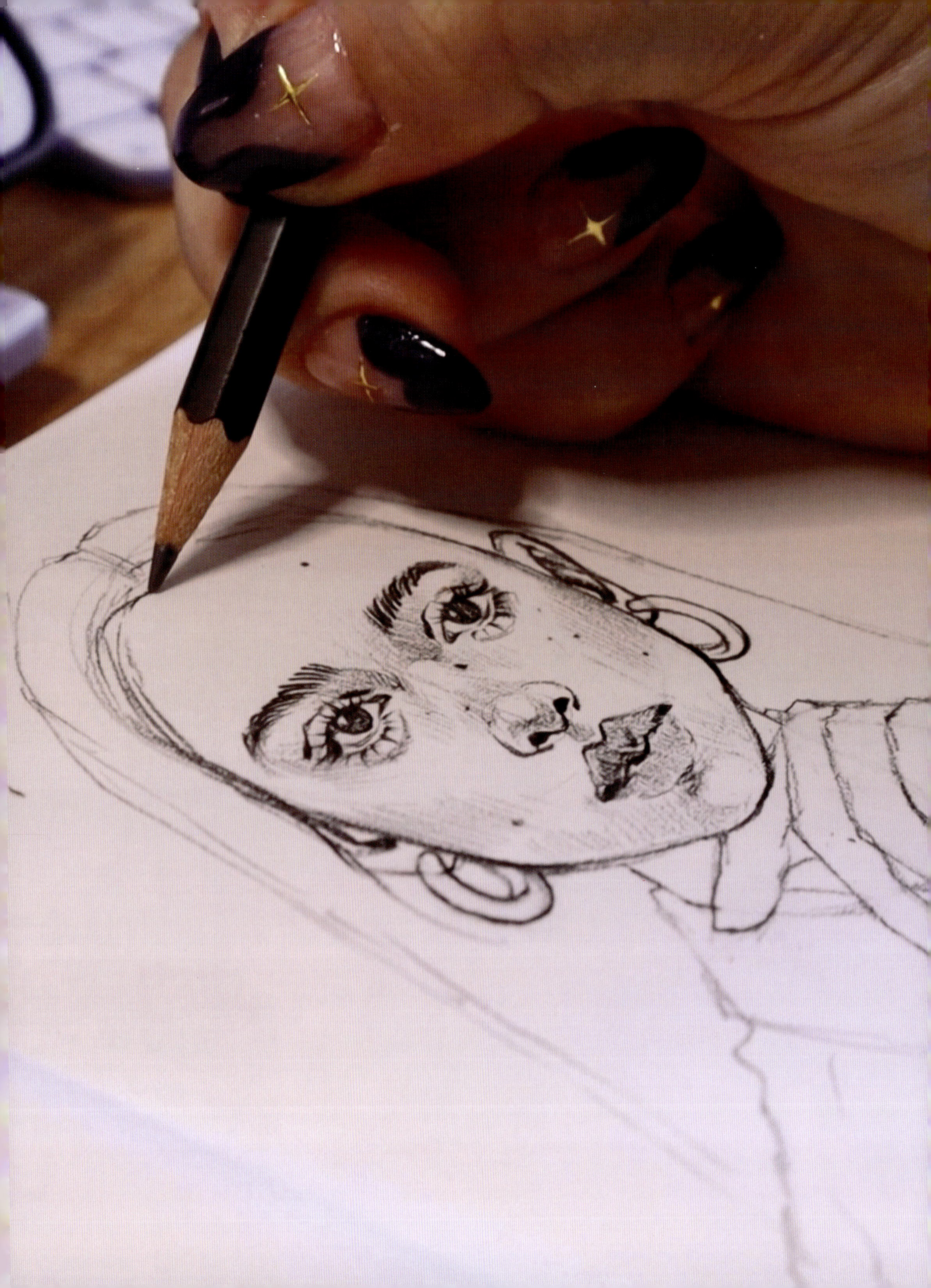

9

PUTTING IT ALL TOGETHER!

Now that we have gone through all the different elements of the face, we can finally draw them all together. We started off by learning where these features go on the face and then saw how to draw each one of them individually. Now, we can see what they all look like in place and fully draw out a portrait from start to finish. We can also add expressions and personality to our drawings to make them totally unique. So, let's take everything we've learned and put it into practice—let's draw a face!

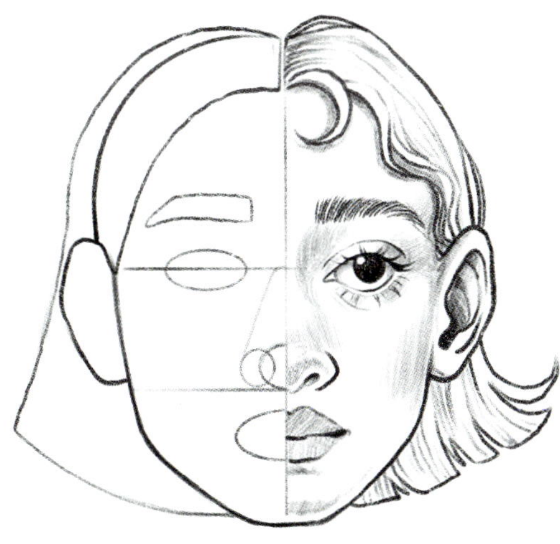

ADDING IN ALL THE FEATURES

Here you can see a breakdown of how to draw a face from start to finish. As you can see, starting off with just the basic shape of the head, then adding in the facial feature shapes makes it a lot easier to focus on each facial feature and render them individually. Then you can erase all the initial guidelines and sketch lines and you have a portrait!

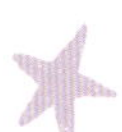

Scan to watch a tutorial.

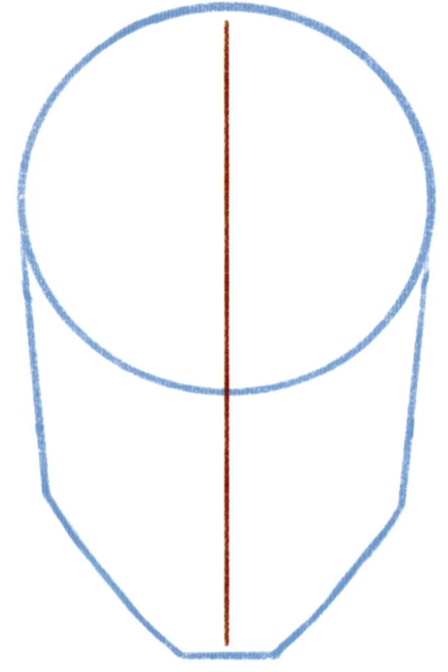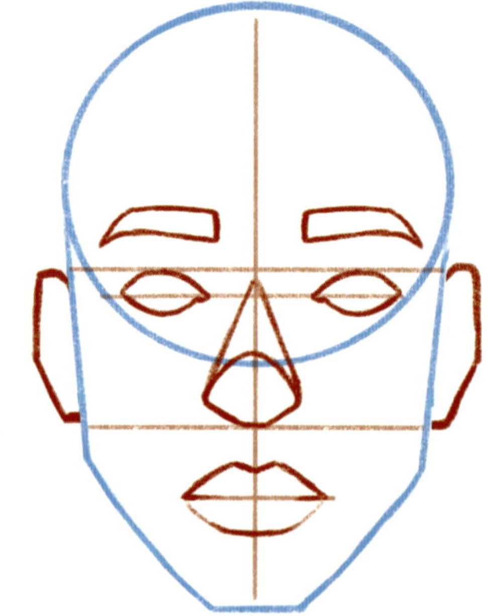

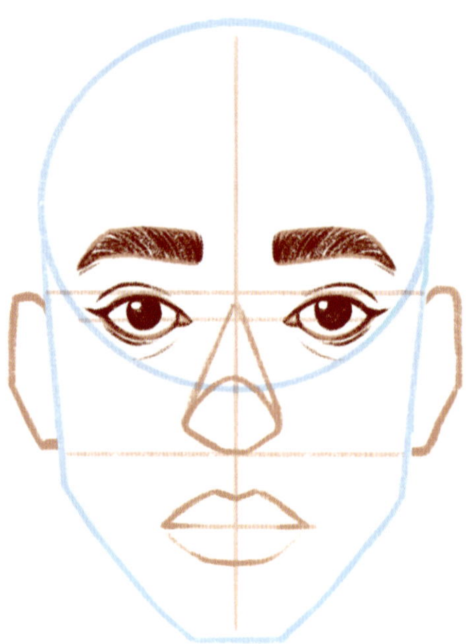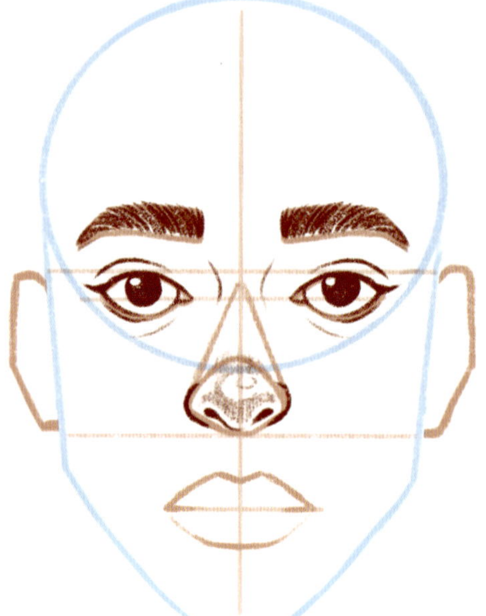

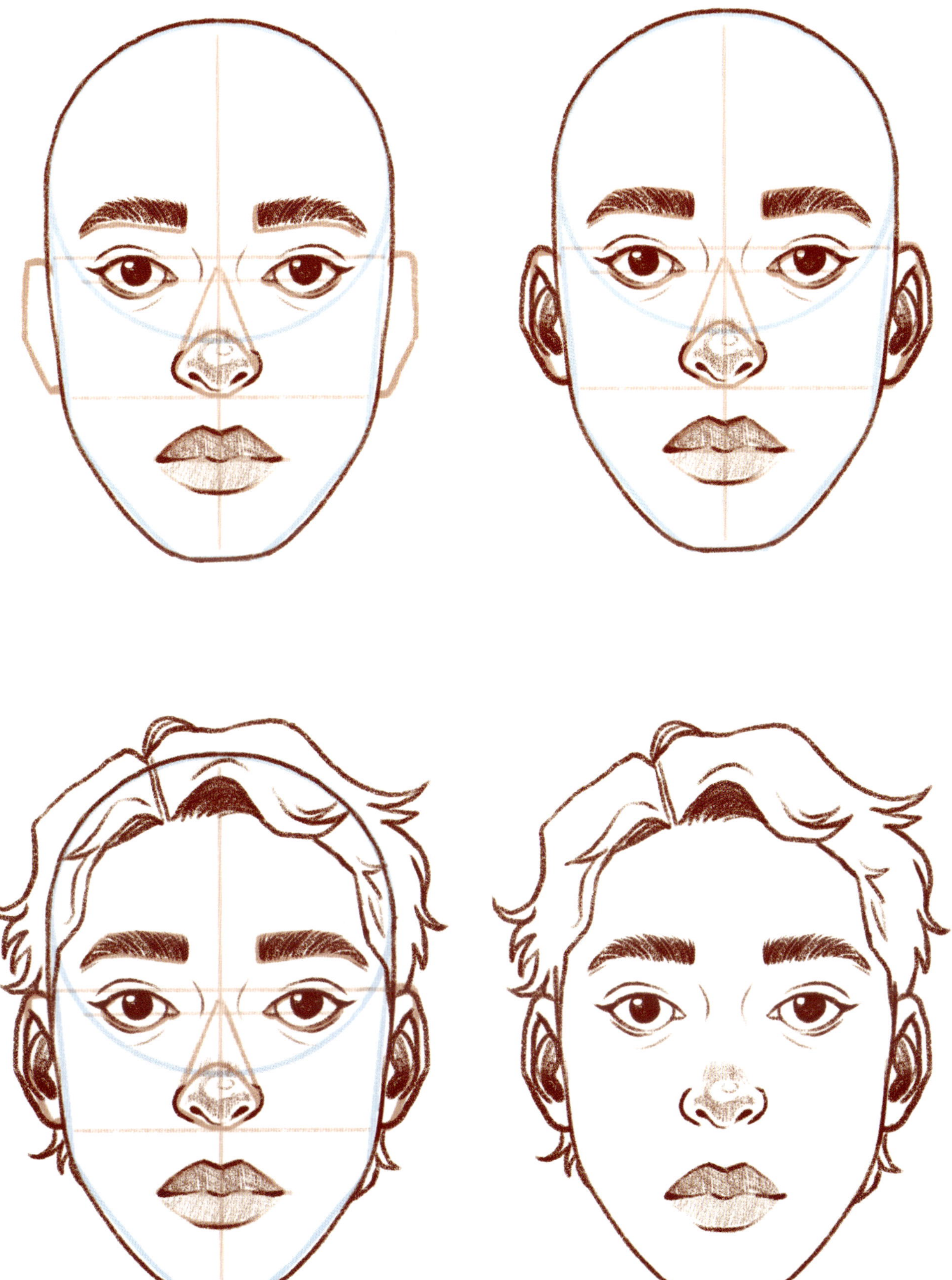

FACE SHAPES: AGE & GENDER

Some other things to consider when drawing your portrait are the shapes of the head and features relating to the age and gender expression of the character. We touched upon this slightly in chapter 1 when showing how proportions change dramatically with age, but with that so does the head shape. Babies and children have rounder, shorter heads, and as they grow up, the head becomes longer and the features shift into their adult proportions.

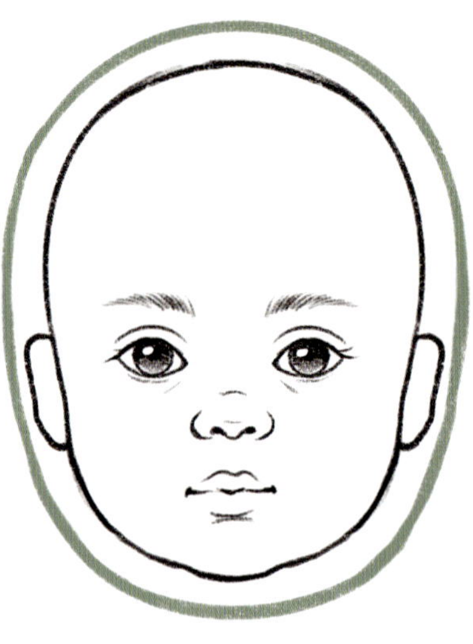

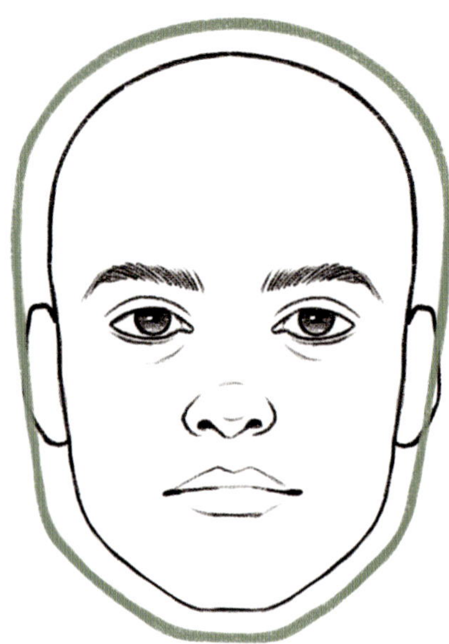

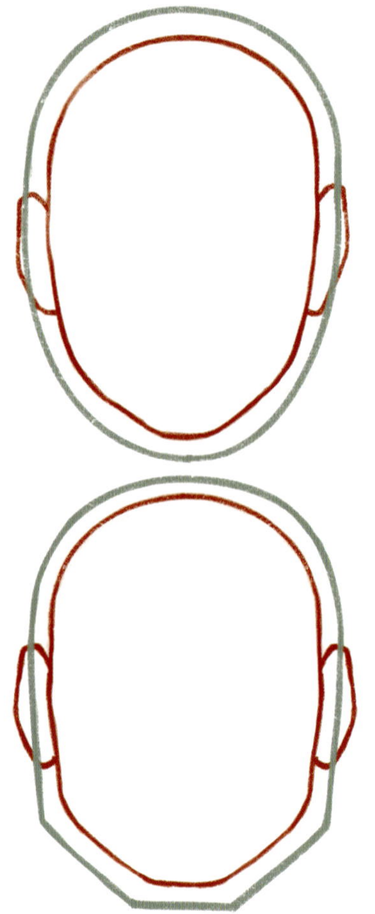

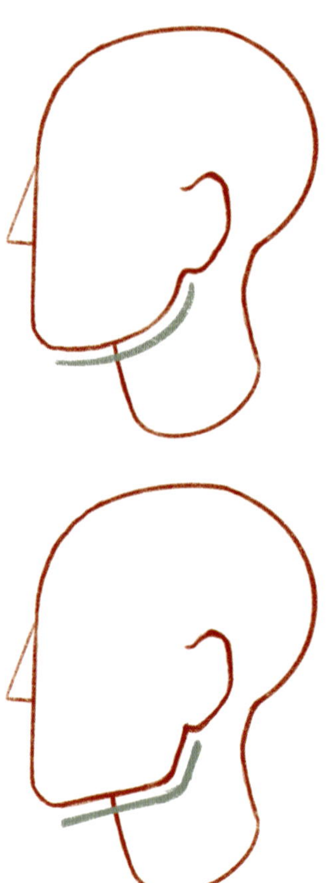

The general rule of thumb is that female features are usually rounder and softer, whereas more masculine features look sharper and have harsher lines.

I generally use this rule mostly when drawing the jawline and the eyes, as that can usually be a good way to make your portrait either more feminine or more masculine.

Keep in mind that this is just a small "rule" that is sometimes used in character design but does not strictly apply to all human beings and their faces!

ADDING FULLNESS

Another thing you might want to customize on your portrait is the fullness of the face, or how chubby it is. The reason why I teach how to draw the face in its "skinny" form is because it's easy to add chubbiness to the face—much like how fat sits on top of the bones and skull, adding fullness. Let's add some fullness to the portrait below. The face we're starting off with is slim and generally the shape of the skull.

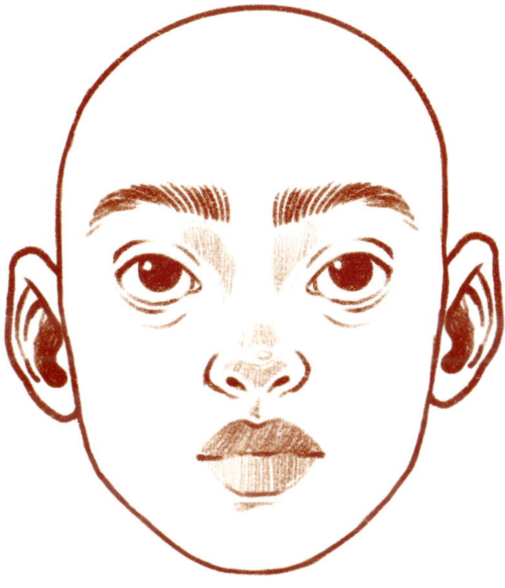

If you take your hand and feel your own face, you can easily identify that the main areas with more muscles and fat are on and around the cheeks, under the chin, and the lips. As you press into your face you will find that those are the areas that are more plump and squishy, whereas areas such as your forehead and bridge of the nose are hard and sturdy. Taking those areas into account, when adding fullness to a face you should add a rounder outline, exaggerating the curves more around the cheeks and under the chin. You should also keep the original line of the chin, as this will add to the realism and illusion of the chin, creating a crease in the double chin, for example.

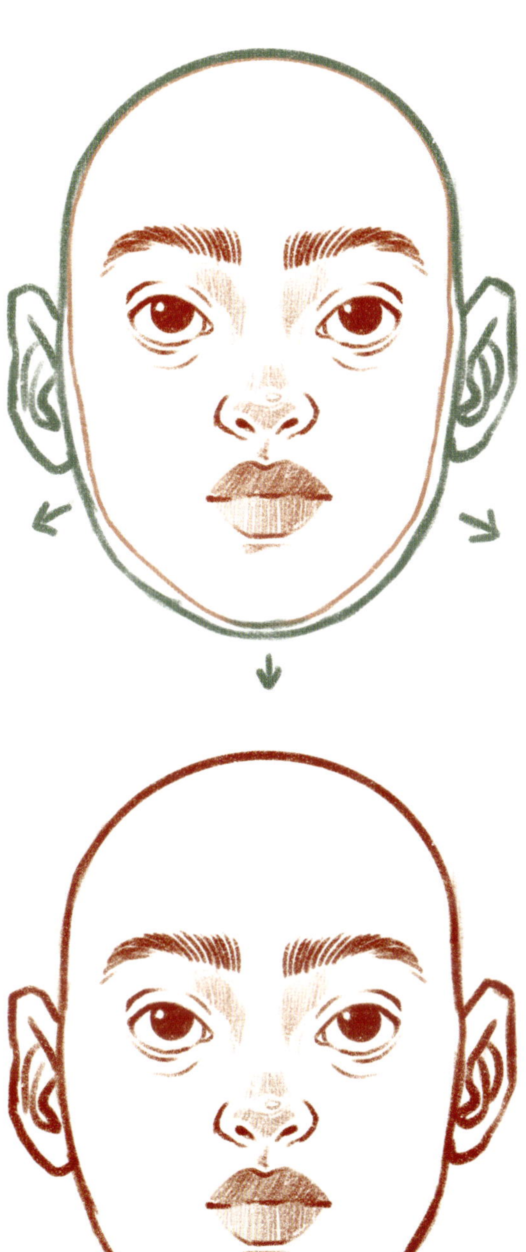

FACIAL EXPRESSIONS

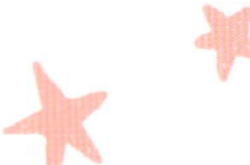

Different expressions affect multiple areas of the face, due to the skin interconnecting everything. So now we must think of the face as a whole, considering the stretch and pull of the features affecting the shapes of each other.

It's easier to take it one step at a time. Think of the main focus of the facial expression you're trying to draw—a smile, for example. Then think of where the skin is being pulled to create the smile, then follow that direction and think of how it could be pressing into and squishing the eyes or the nose. Think about wrinkles and smile lines too.

In the example below, the character is smiling and winking one eye at the same time. As you can see, the action of smiling pulls the corners of the mouth and the adjacent skin outward into the face. However, the winking motion of the eye causes a big squeeze in the eye area, which then pulls that side of the mouth to drift upward. The nose is also forced to a slight tilt sideways, as well as the squeezing and creasing of the nose bridge near that winking eye.

On the other side of the face there is no winking, only a smile, so the eye on that side of the face is simply slightly closed and squinting, due to the pull of the smile.

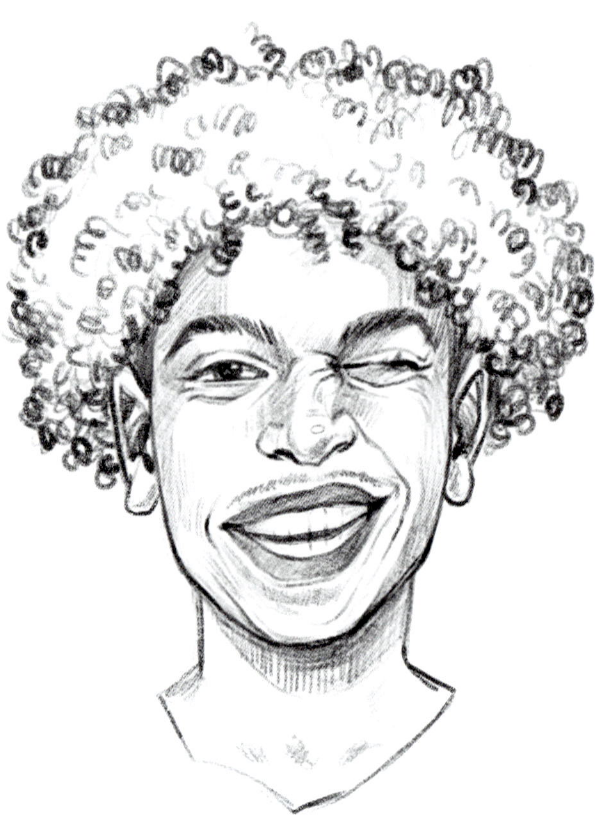

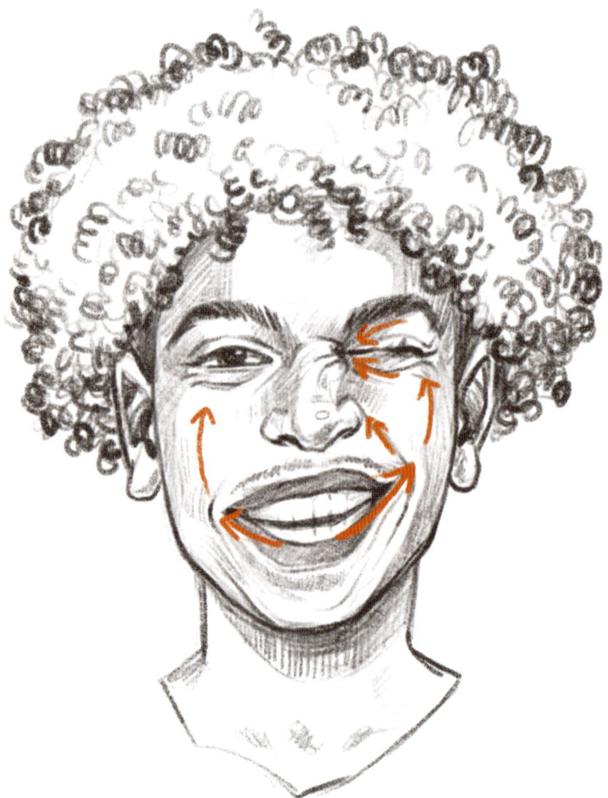

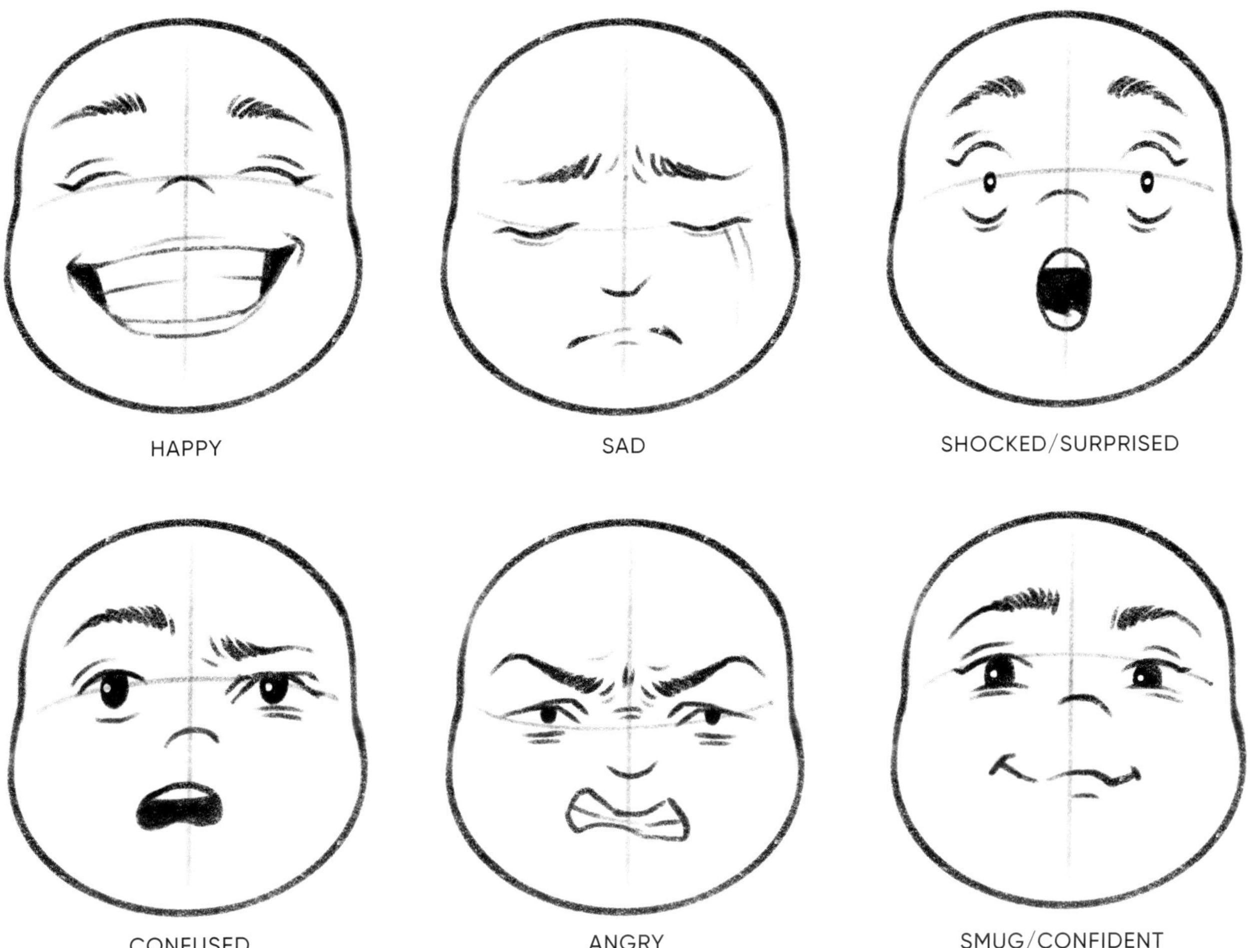

While I always recommend using references for studying anatomy and portraiture, it's good to also build your own way of drawing from your imagination. I like to simplify things to start off.

Drawing facial expressions in a simpler, cartoonish style like the examples shown can be very helpful to work out the basic shapes of an expression. Different emotions and expressions pull the face into different shapes, and so will each feature. Take the surprised face in the example illustration. The eyes and mouth are big, round, and open wide, making the face take up almost the whole head. Now compare that expression to the angry one, where all the features are scrunched up together and the face is all gathered toward the middle of the head.

Think of facial expressions almost like emojis—simple and yet still depicting a very clear emotion. Then, once the simplified facial expression is down, you can then add in the facial features and the rest of the portrait. Then you're free to add as much detail and realism to your portrait as you'd like.

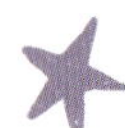

EXPRESSIONS IN PORTRAITS

Let's try using this last tip of drawing the facial expression on a simple head shape and then turn it into a full portrait. Like I said, try thinking of the facial expression first like you would an emoji or a cartoon face.

I like to first draw out the facial expression on a circular head shape with some small curves to depict the cheeks. I am also showing you an example of drawing a facial expression at a three-quarter angle to demonstrate how you can turn a simple face and then add the rest of the portrait around it at any angle.

Don't forget to use guidelines and faint lines to your advantage for blocking in the facial features—you can always erase these later!

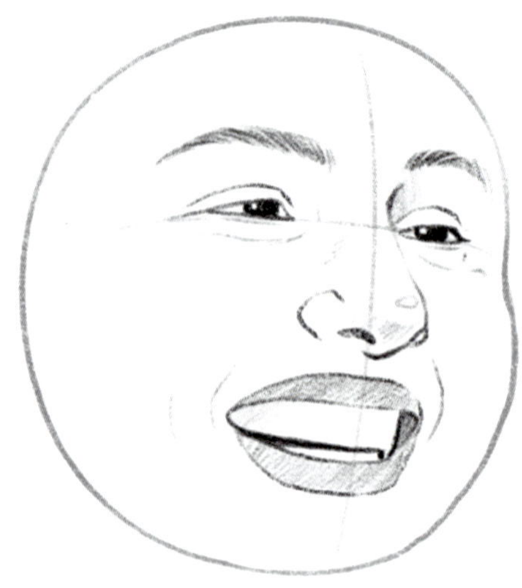

Once you're happy with the proportions and placement of the facial expression, you can then start adding in the rest of the head. You can almost work backward from what we learned in chapter 1 about facial proportions—you can use the nose, eyes, and mouth placements to dictate where your ears and head shape go.

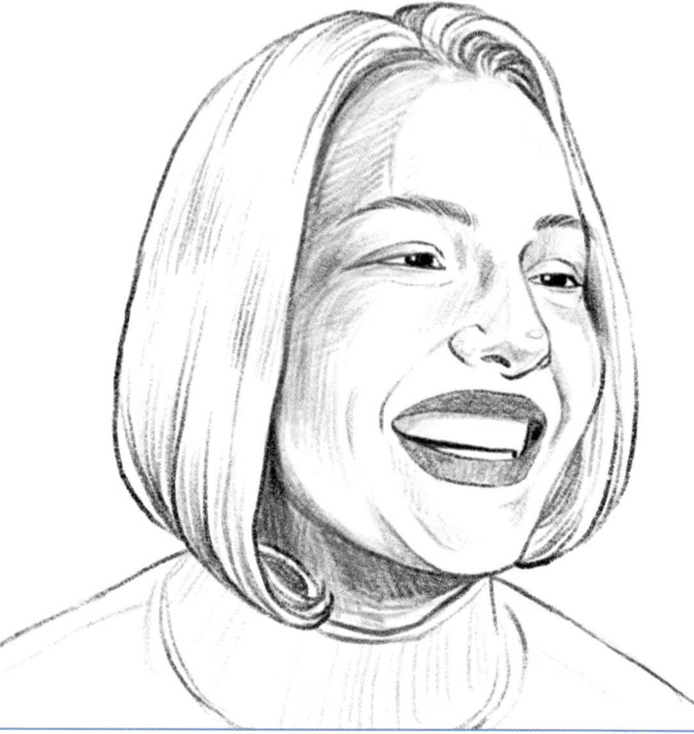

ADDING CHARACTER & PERSONALITY

Once you're comfortable with drawing portraits, you can try showing some of your subject's character to make it more fun and interesting. This can also be very helpful when developing an original character. Instead of drawing your portrait with a neutral expression, try thinking about how that character is feeling, what their personality is like. Maybe your character is a little playful and curious and maybe a little cheeky. You can then give them a little smirk and an inquisitive eyebrow. It seems like a very small change, but it can make a world of a difference to your portrait!

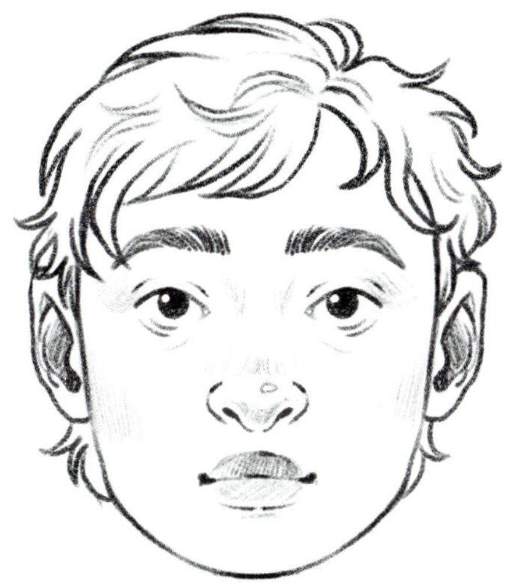
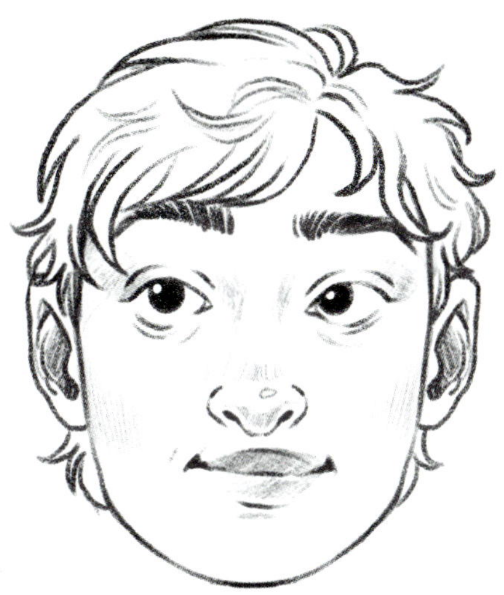

You can even venture into the world of caricature to further push your character's uniqueness, or use these exaggerations to enhance perspective. For example, making the chin and lips much bigger while making the top of the head smaller pushes the perspective that you're looking at the portrait from below. Making the forehead, eyes, and eyebrows very big and narrowing down the bottom of the face gives the opposite effect.

There is so much to play around with when it comes to facial features and proportions, so don't be afraid to experiment!

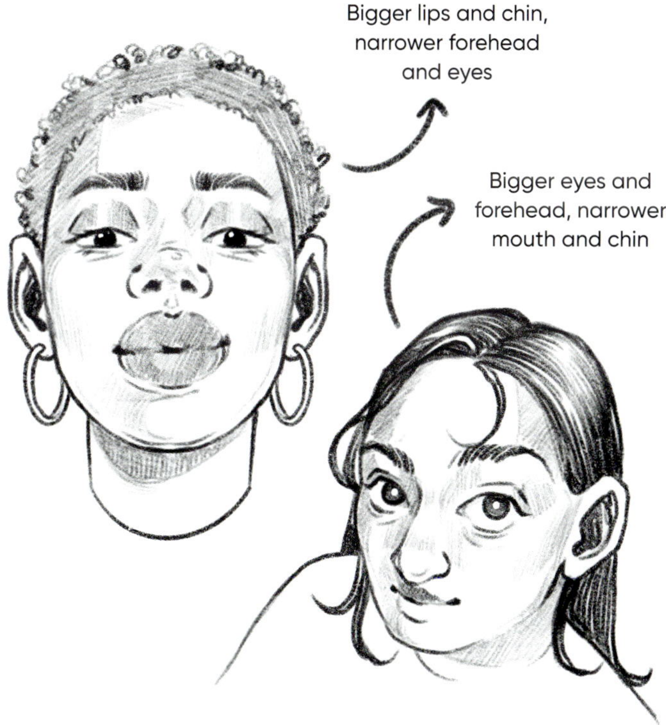

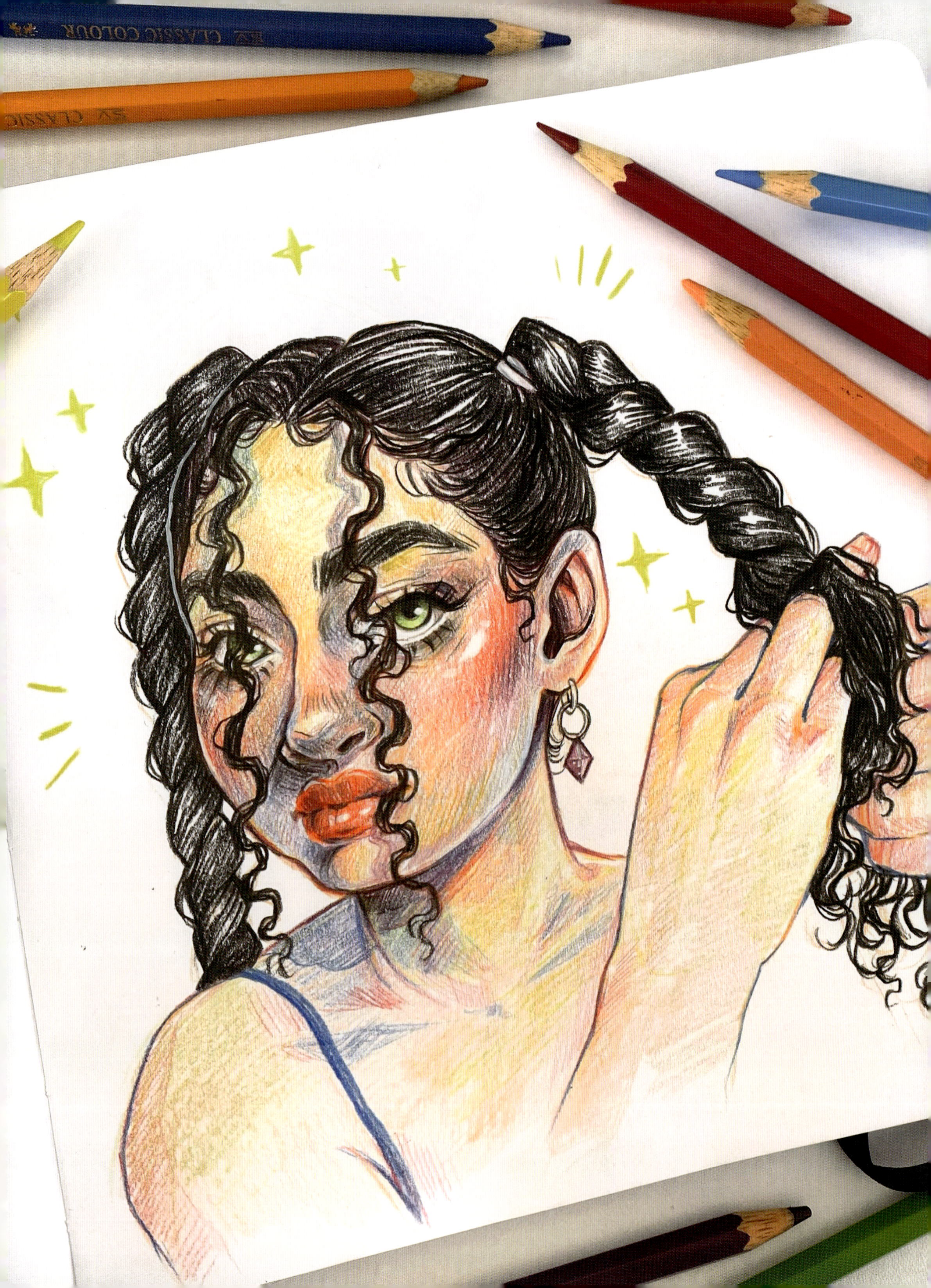

10

FACES IN COLOR

The next step in our portrait drawing journey is one of the most fun—adding color! People and faces have all kinds of colors throughout the face; things like blush, skin thickness, and even blemishes and scars all give the skin a different color compared to the rest of the face. So let's dive into the world of color and find out more about how it can be used to bring your portrait to life.

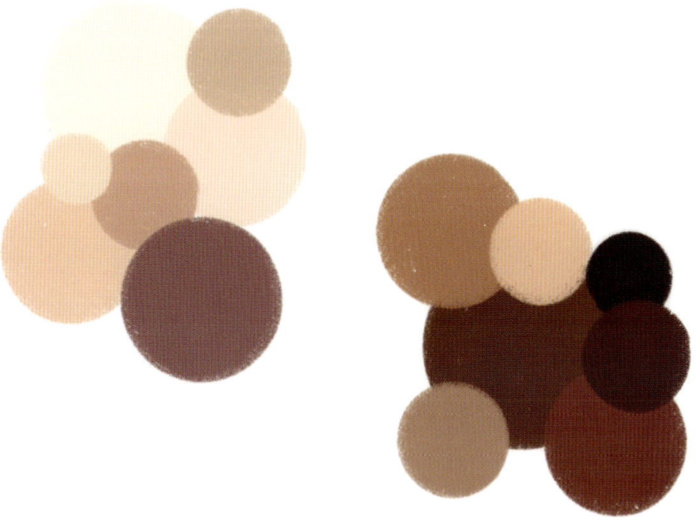

A BIT OF COLOR THEORY

There are three main terms you should know and think about when adding color to your art: Hue, Saturation, and Value.

You can also use a color wheel like the one here to pick out colors that go well together—we call these *complementary colors*. You can pick these out by simply picking colors on opposite sides of the wheel. This is a simple way to pick colors for your art and will make your pieces look cohesive.

HUE

Hue is just the different colors around the color spectrum. Different colors, like blue and pink, are different hues.

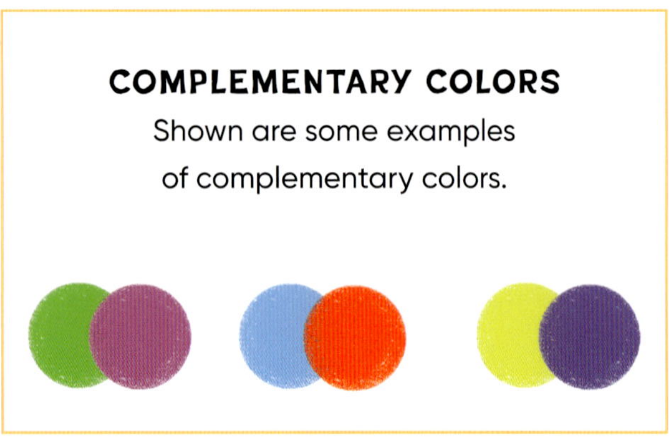

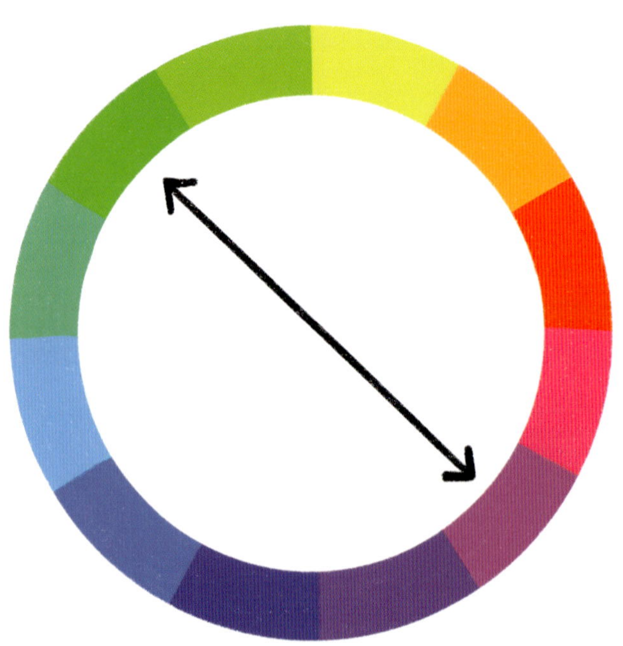

SATURATION

Saturation refers to how strong the color is. The saturation spectrum for any color goes from an almost neon shade all the way down to pure gray. An unsaturated color is described as muted or dull.

VALUE

Value refers to how light or dark the color is. Again, the spectrum for any color or shade will go from a very light, almost white shade of that hue, down to a very dark, deep shade of that color.

SKIN TONES

Skin varies massively not only in shade from person to person but also on each individual face itself. Every portrait and face will have a combination of colors ranging from warm tones, blush tones, cool tones, and light and dark colors for highlights and shadows. So when picking a skin tone for your portrait, you actually want to pick out multiple colors—a color palette.

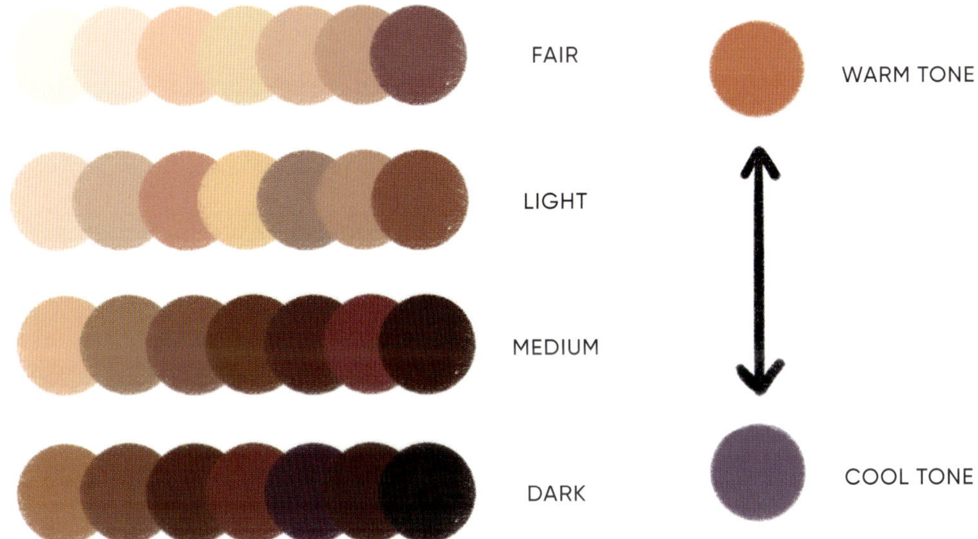

When I mention warm and cool tones, that refers to whether they're on the more orange, red, and pink side of the color wheel (warm) or on the more blue, green, and purple side (cool).

When picking out colors to render a portrait, I always like to make sure I check off the following:

- One midtone (the general skin tone)

- One highlight color

- Two deep tones (one for light shadows and one for the darkest)

- A blush tone

- A cool tone

With this basic checklist, you should have all the colors you'll need to render a realistic portrait (bar the eyes and hair, of course).

You should consider whether your character is more warm-toned or cool-toned, and has olive, dark, or fair skin. The skin tone spectrum is enormously varied and is not limited to the examples shown.

You might also be wondering where you'll be using your warm and cool tones on the face. The general rule of thumb is that the face colors are yellower at the top, warmer in the middle, and cooler the further down you go. This rule is used a lot, since light usually comes from above and hits the forehead, and we have a higher concentration of blood in the middle of the face—like when we blush! Finally, the further away from the light you go (down), the cooler the colors you get.

"

LIGHT SKIN TONES

Here I start off with an overall base color of the midtone color, adding in some blushing to the lips, cheeks, nose, and ears, as these areas are usually where the skin flushes.

I then add in shadows, keeping my light source in mind. I also add in some highlights to the areas of the face being hit by the light.

Finally, I blend the colors in between highlights and shadows by lightly using the midtone between the two. At the end I like to add an even sharper highlight to the highest points of the face, as well as some darker blush color to the face.

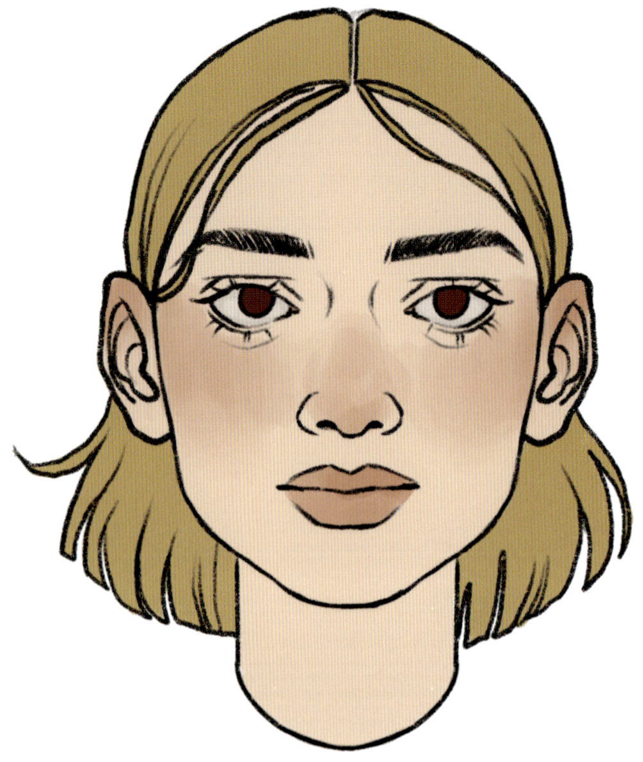

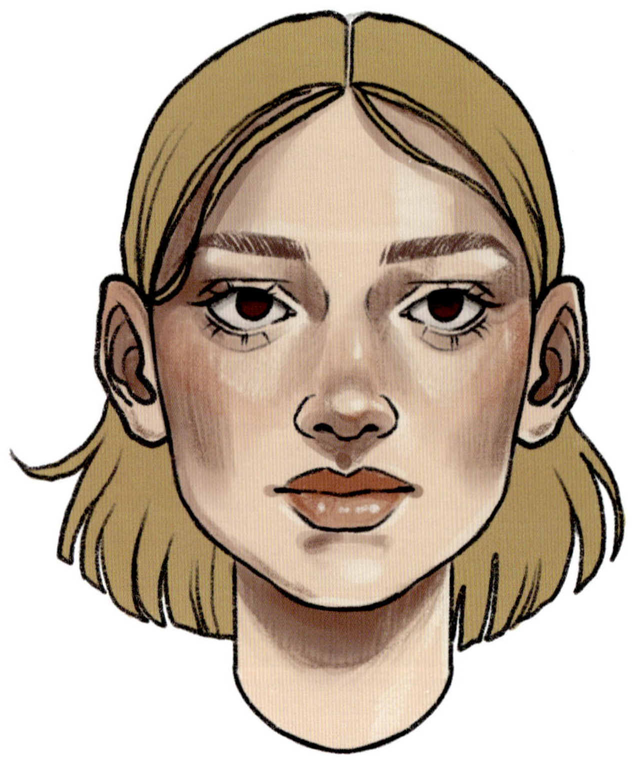

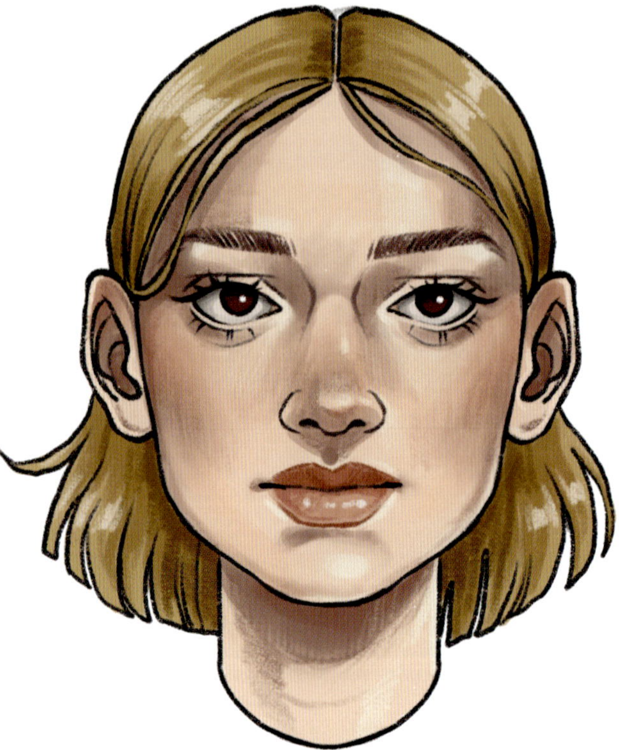

DARK SKIN TONES

Here is an example of how I do the same process when coloring in a darker skin tone on a portrait. I start off the same, using the midtone to color in the whole face and adding in some blush. For the lips, I keep in mind that the upper lip is darker than the lower lip, and I add some more dimension to the lips using highlights.

I then follow the same steps as before, adding in shadows and highlights where needed, making sure to use warm colors so as to not make the skin look ashy or unsaturated. To balance out the yellowish highlights I add some cooler dark purple for the deepest shadows.

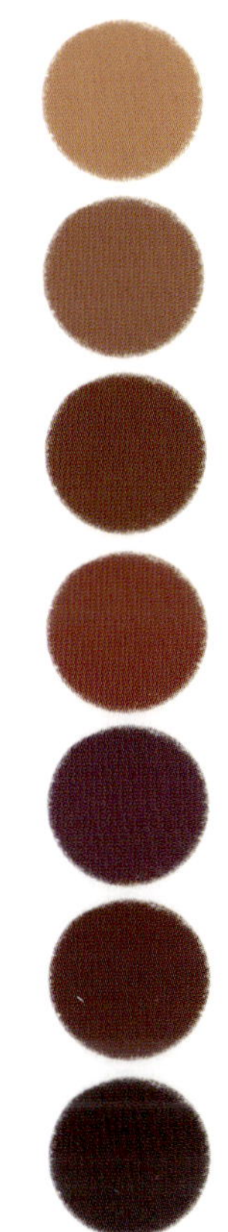

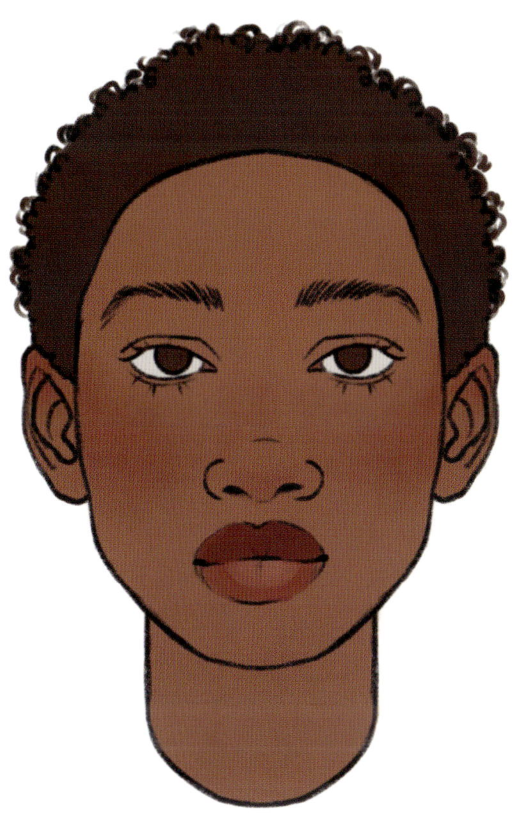

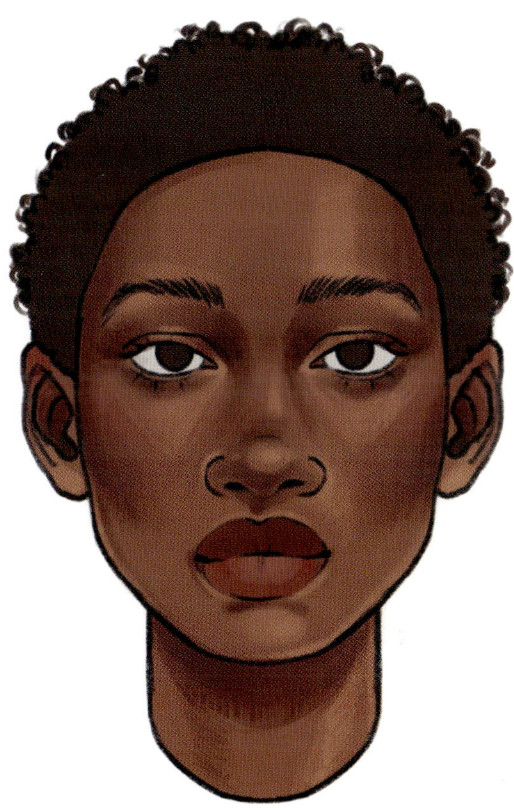

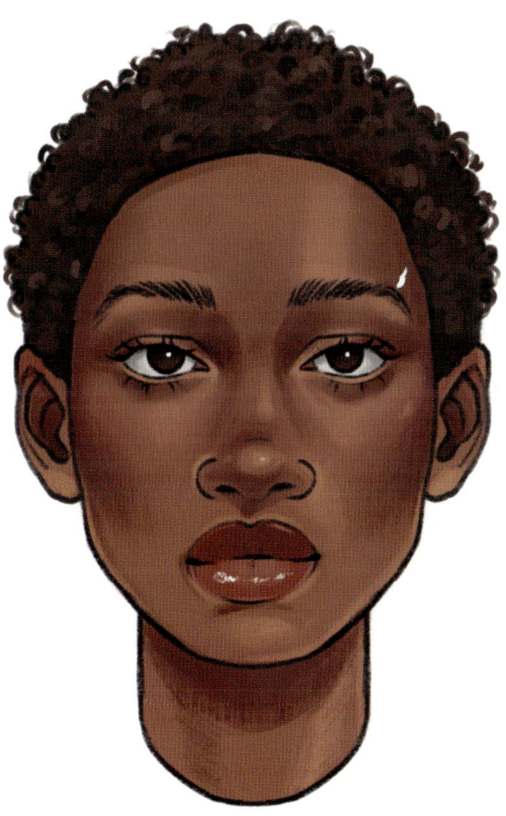

RENDERING THE FACE IN DIFFERENT MEDIUMS

There are an astonishing number of different mediums and art materials for you to explore out there, so don't just settle for one! Experimenting with different mediums and allowing yourself to learn to use new materials is part of the creative process and will open up new avenues for your portrait art.

PENCILS

Removing the element of color allows you to focus on shadow and highlight placement, making sure you are maintaining a good amount of contrast in your drawings to give them depth.

You can use a set of graphite pencils with different graphite hardness. In a set you get a small selection of pencils that will probably range from HB to 6B. HB is the average pencil hardness you get at school, and the higher you go in the Bs, the darker the pencil is (the softer the lead, the darker it is).

Remember, always start off light and slowly add darker shadows as you go!

MARKERS

Markers are a great mess-free option for adding color onto the page, but they take a little more getting used to than pencils.

Markers can be used with a layering technique too, starting off with lighter colors and layering them on top of each other to create shadows and overlays. They can be, however, a little tricky to use. Markers can bleed into each other and need some time to dry in between layers. I recommend testing your colors on a separate piece of paper before using them on your drawing so you know exactly what shade you're using and how dark it comes out.

I also love to mix mediums and go over the top of markers with pencils and other markers!

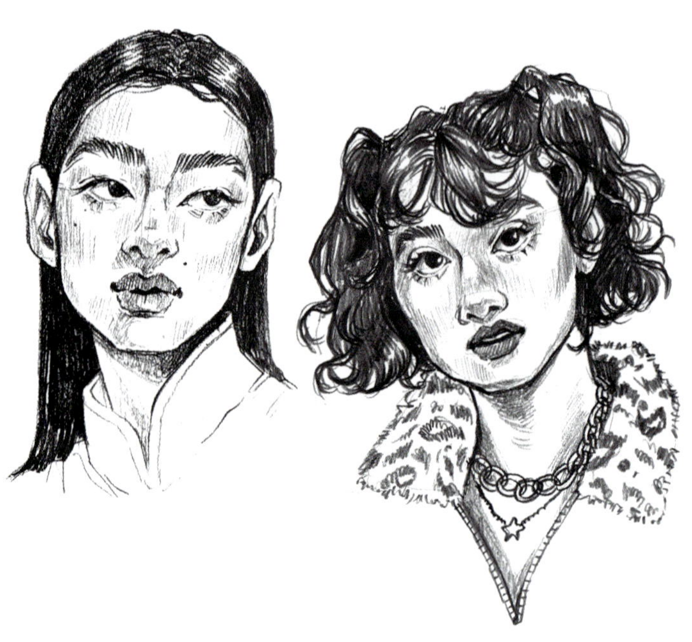

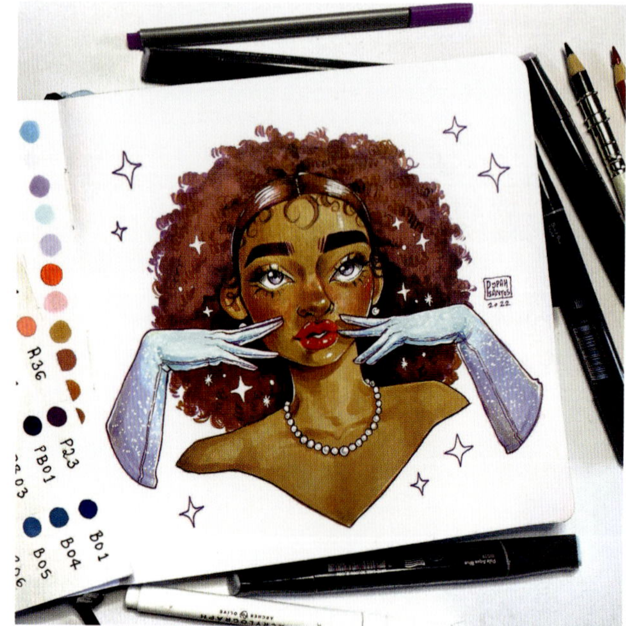

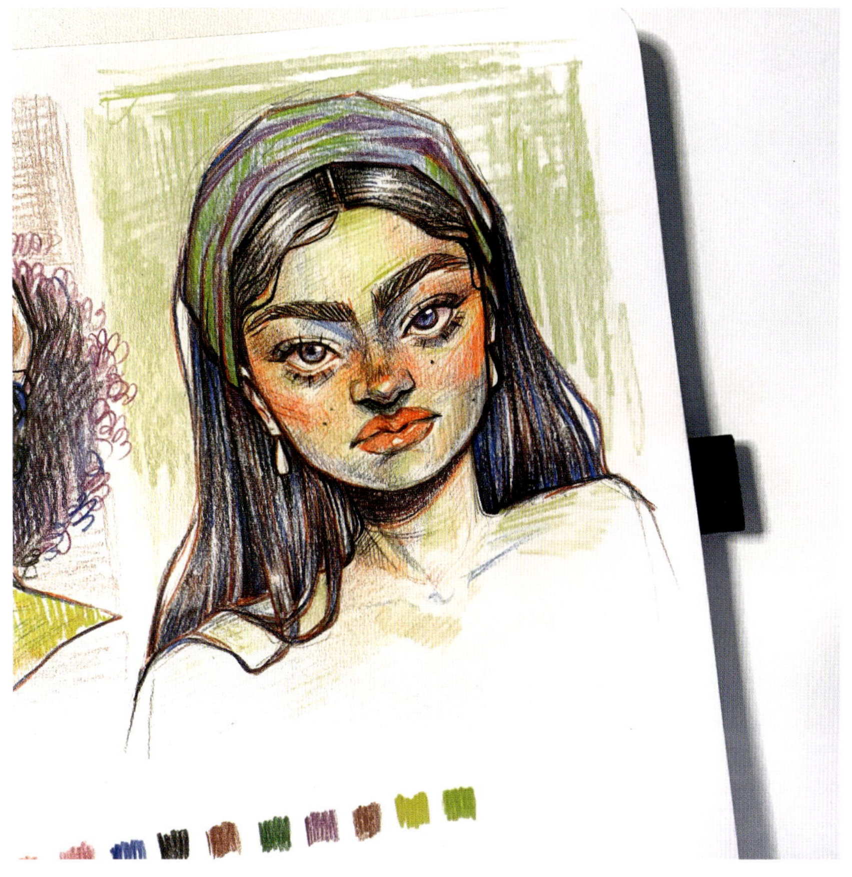

COLORED PENCILS

My favorite way to draw with colored pencils is much like I draw with other materials—by layering colors over each other. This process makes it easier to slowly add color and look at how the drawing is coming out, seeing how the colors interact with each other, and making decisions accordingly.

Another thing you can start playing around with is mixing colors with pencils and using overlays. This mostly entails using a more limited selection of colored pencils and using this layering technique to mix colors; for example, using blue pencils on top of a layer of red or pink to make a purple tone. This is very helpful when you want to change the tone of the drawing or the warmth of a certain area of color. You can keep referencing the color wheel from earlier on to check which colors are complementary and which are cooler and warmer.

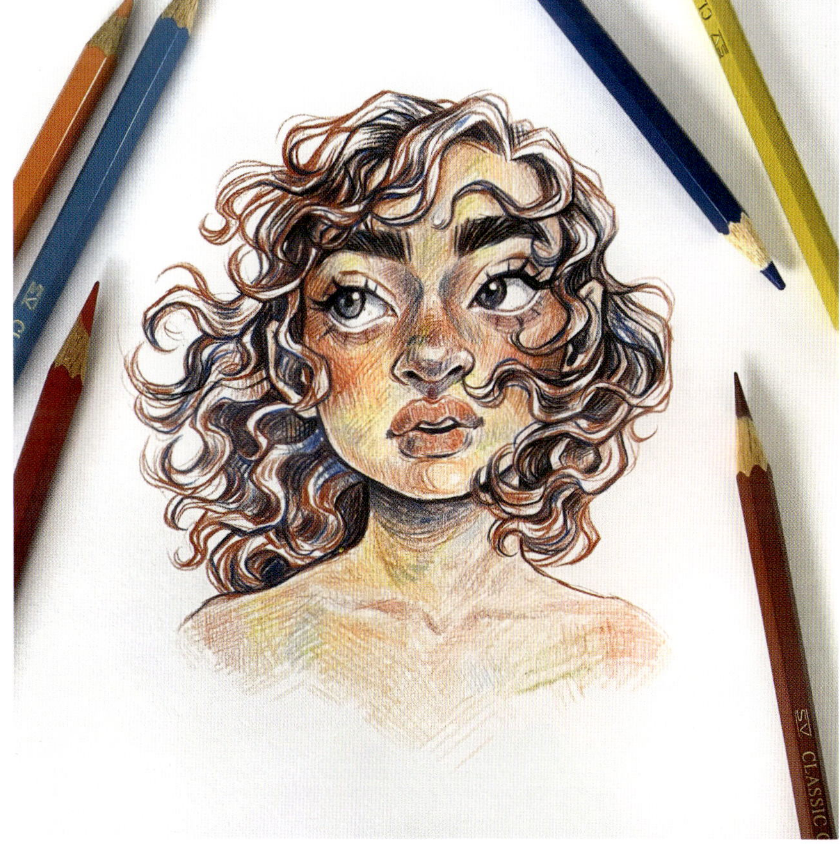

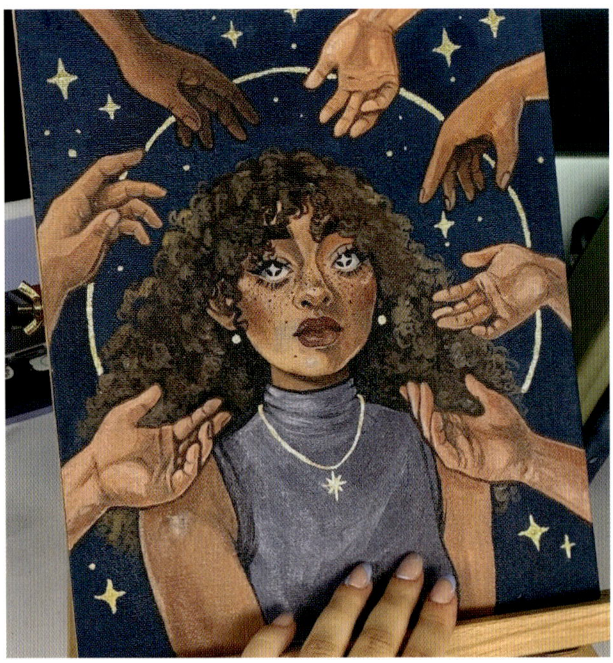

ACRYLIC

Working with paints can be so incredibly therapeutic and soothing! Waiting for the paint to dry also forces you to take your time and keep looking back at your painting with fresh eyes.

Acrylic paints are great if you're impatient, as they dry very fast. They can also be very versatile, as you can add as much water to them as you'd like to change the consistency of the paints. I love to use acrylic paint when I want to put bright, bold colors onto a canvas and know that I can keep going over certain areas as many times as I want.

WATERCOLOR & INKS

Another great medium I love is watercolors and water-based inks. This type of paint takes the longest amount of time to dry (except for oil paints), and they're very watery.

Watercolors allow me to work in a layering process, much like I do with markers or pencils. Because these paints tend to be more sheer, they're great for working in layers and adding pigments on top of each other to build up color.

Much like with acrylics, you can manipulate the opacity and consistency of the paint with how much water you add to it—meaning you can use it in a more watery form, mixing wet colors with wet colors (wet-on-wet) or using it on top of dried layers of paint (wet-on-dry).

Inks work in a very similar fashion to watercolors, except inks tend to be more pigmented, and the layers of ink don't bleed into each other as watercolors tend to. I like using inks for creating overlays and layering different colors, since I know they won't mix with colors on the layers below.

Watercolors can be very lovely for rendering portraits when you get the hang of them, as they can create very seamless soft blends between colors, adding to the realism of the drawing, if that's what you're after.

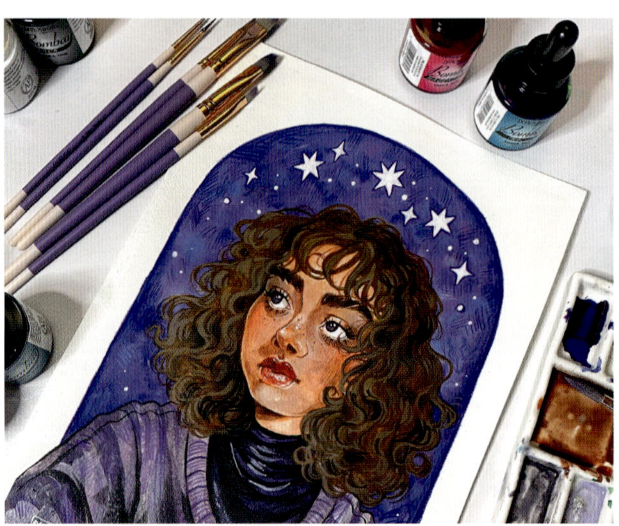

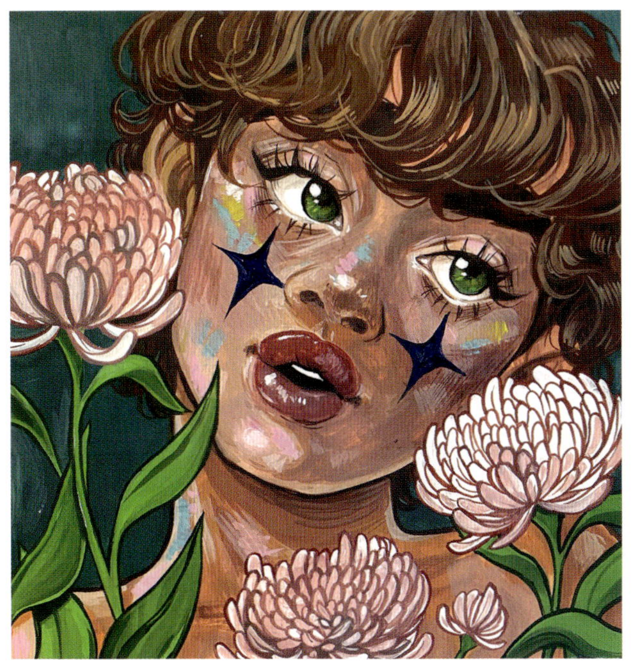

DIGITAL

Digital drawing is becoming more and more common in the art community, as it's so portable and easy to make art anywhere. I use an iPad and Procreate to make all of my digital artworks. I find it's great for experimenting with color, sketching down ideas, and taking it on the go.

Digital art does end up lacking in that pencil-to-paper feeling that keeps bringing artists back to traditional mediums. I don't think digital art will ever be as satisfying to make as traditional art, but it does create a lot of incredible shortcuts.

GOUACHE

If you're indecisive about which paint to go with, might I recommend gouache? Gouache is the most versatile type of paint! It dries quite quickly and is thicker in consistency when less water is used but can simultaneously mimic the effect of watercolor when it is more diluted. It is a great paint to try practicing different painting techniques, and you can achieve different styles and textures with just this one medium.

Gouache reacts with water. This means that you can go back in and blend two dry layers of color with a wet paintbrush.

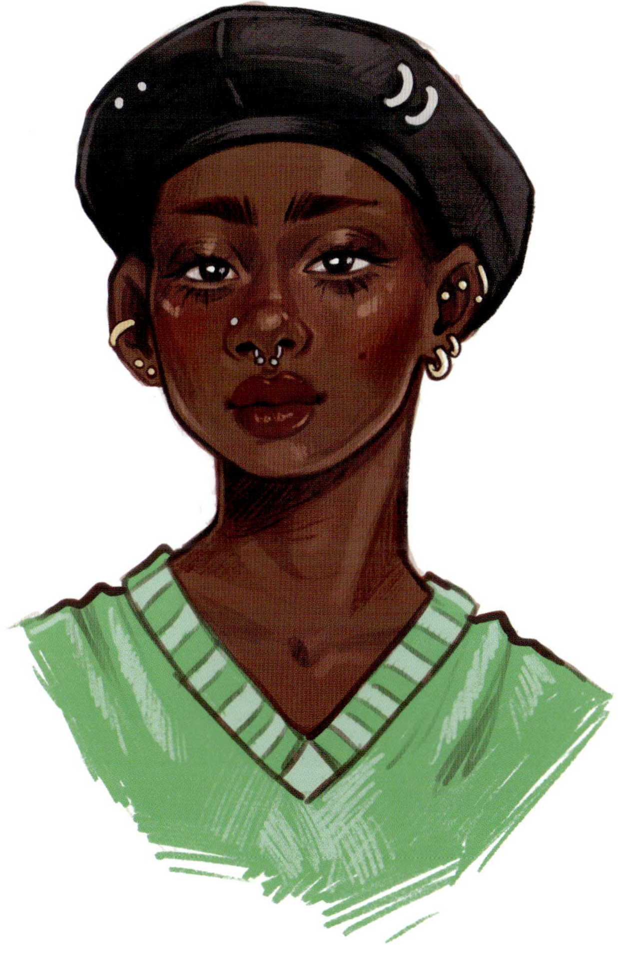

COLORED PENCIL PORTRAIT STEP BY STEP

Scan to watch a tutorial.

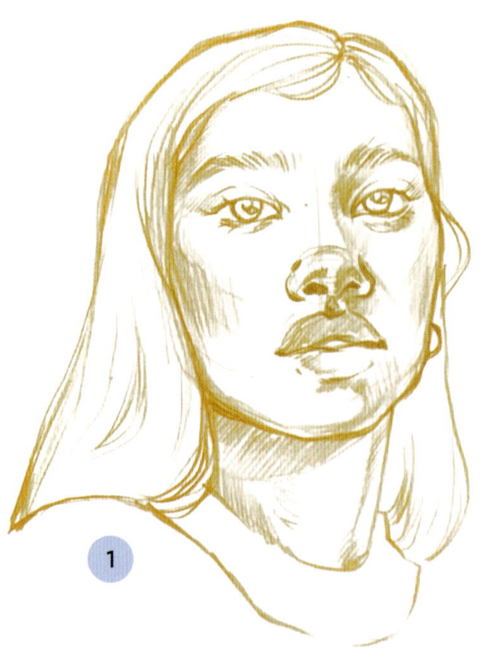

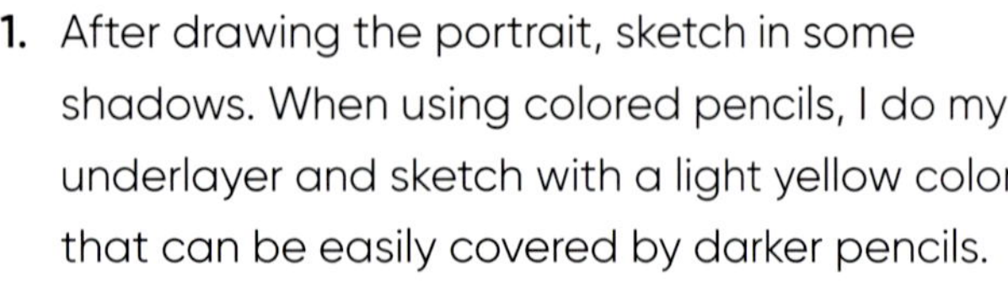

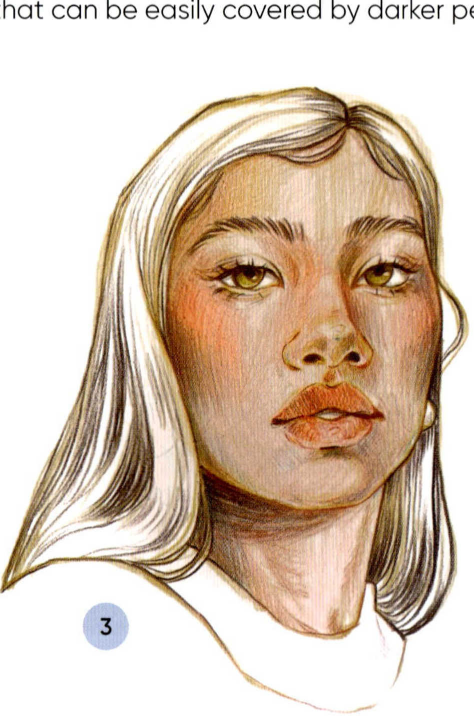

1. After drawing the portrait, sketch in some shadows. When using colored pencils, I do my underlayer and sketch with a light yellow color that can be easily covered by darker pencils.

2. Go in lightly with midtones and flat colors. I usually use a middle to light tone color of what I want the final complexion to be. I also add in the flat color for the lips and eyes, and even add in some light blushing with a red pencil on the cheeks and nose.

3. After adding in the flat colors, you can go slightly darker in skin tone color and start adding shadows. I use the shadows I sketched as a guide for where I want the shadows and highlights to go. I also start adding more contrast to the piece by slowly darkening the darkest areas of the face. I use some more orange and pink tones to layer over the blush areas from before to add some different hues to the skin.

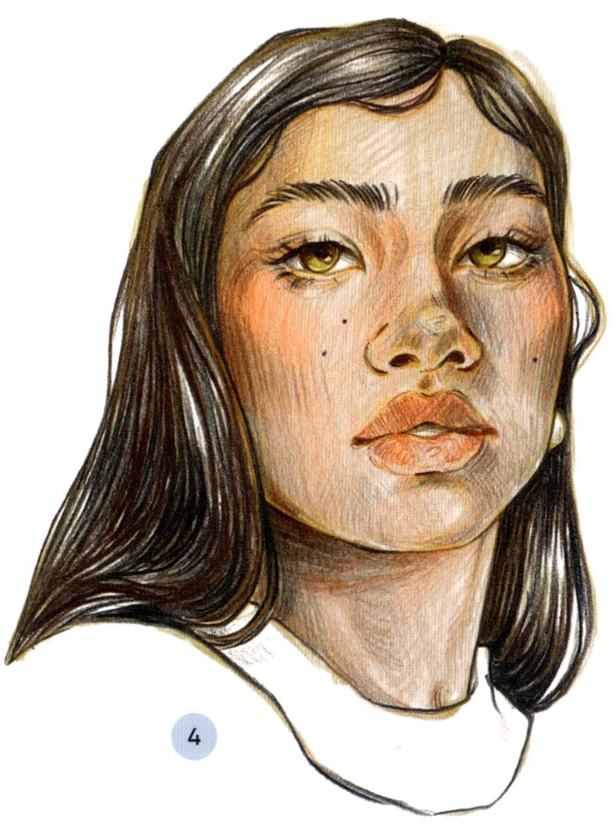

4. At this stage, all the areas of shadows and highlights are clear, so you can just keep using darker colors to lightly hatch in some deeper tones. Add in the details, such as the eyebrows, freckles, and eyelashes, with a very sharp pencil for maximum fine details.

At this point I also like to add in some cooler tones—usually a turquoise blue pencil—to the lower areas of the face. I go in with the light skin tone I used in step 2 to constantly go over every layer and lightly blend in all the colors. This step really adds a lot of seamless blending and realism to the portrait.

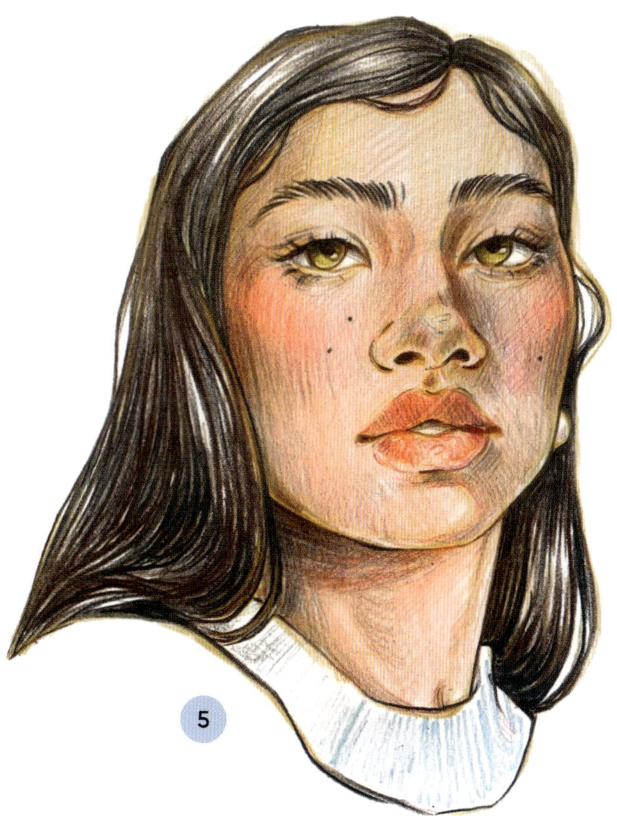

5. Finally, start adding in the final details, such as rendering the hair, the clothes, and any extra bits, such as jewelry.

At this point step back and look at the portrait from farther away. This allows you to look at the piece as a whole so you can assess the values and contrast of the piece all together.

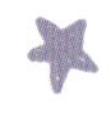

GOUACHE PORTRAIT
STEP BY STEP

Scan to watch
a tutorial.

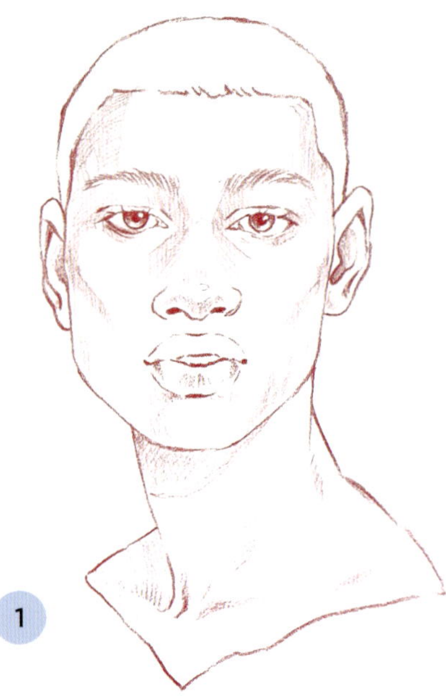

1

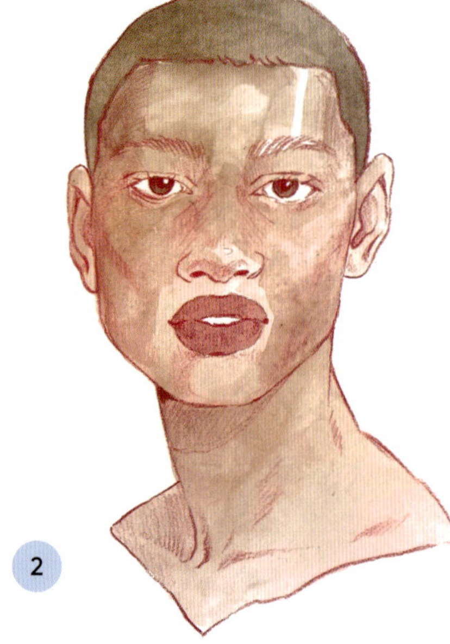

2

1. To start off any painting, I like to do an underlying sketch with a magenta/red pencil. I like using this color, as it gives the final piece a reddish/brownish undertone in some areas, which I think looks lovely on portraits. I also pencil in some shadows at this stage for reference.

2. Start going in with the paint. I like to keep my first few layers of gouache quite watery. This allows me to create sheer, flat washes for the midtone flat colors of the face. I keep these first few passes nice and smooth.

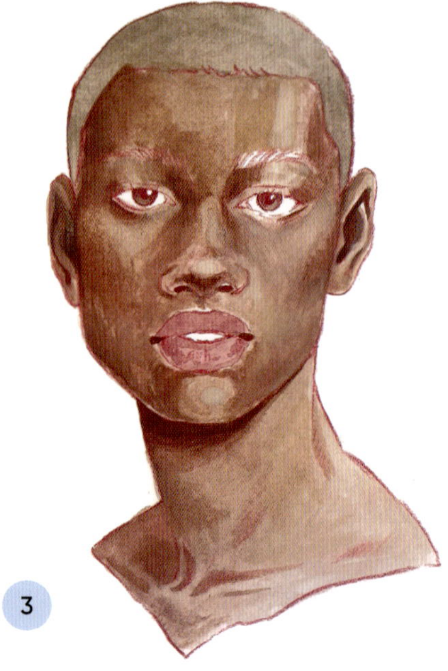

3

3. Once you've added the first base coats to the portrait, go in with more opaque paint to darken the colors in certain areas. Adding less water will make the color more opaque and darker, so I can keep using the same color and just change the amount of water.

   I will also start painting the iris of the eyes and blush the lips and cheeks with a watery layer of dark reddish-pink.

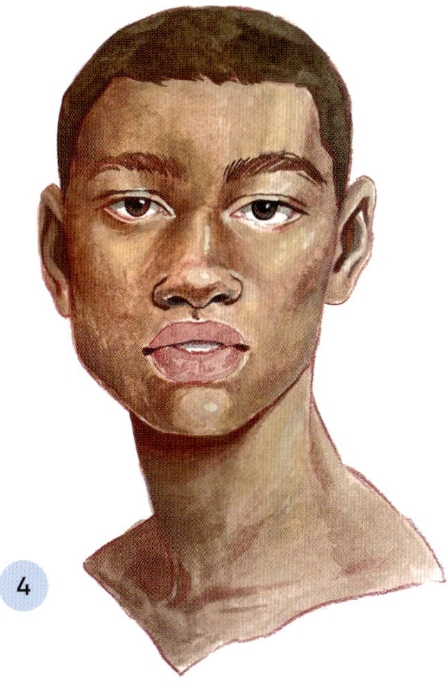

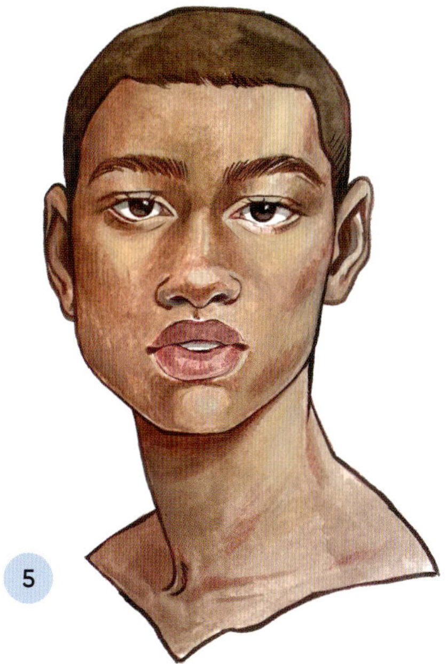

4. Once you're happy with the placements of the shadows, much like with pencils, keep darkening the shadows with each layer of paint. With gouache you can let the paint fully dry and still go back in with a wet paintbrush to reactivate the paint and blend colors together. It's why I love using this medium so much!

5. At this point you can switch to a smaller and thinner round paintbrush to start adding in smaller details, such as the eyebrow hairs, the creases around the eyes, etc. I also start darkening the lips and adding shadows to the inside of the eyes, as well as adding some very light yellow paint to the highlighted areas.

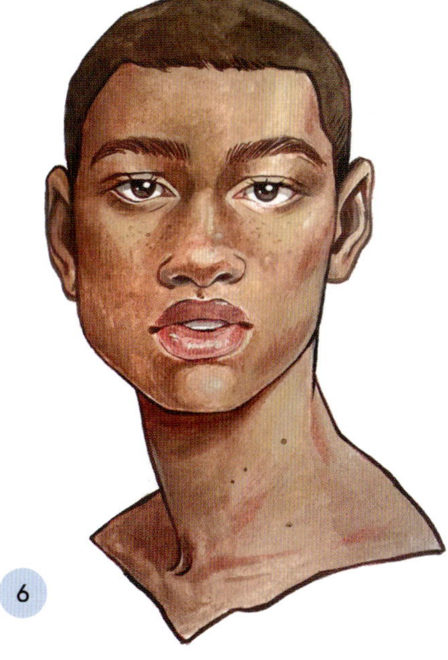

6. After each layer of paint is dry, take a step back and look at the piece, making a note of what you want to alter or add to the next layer.

   Close to the end of the painting, add in some finishing touches, such as some small spots of white to the eyes, the tip of the nose, and the lips.

   I also like to add in details like freckles and lashes right at the end, once I'm sure the painting is fully dry.

   The great thing about gouache is that you can keep painting layers over each other and completely cover what's underneath. I find this takes a lot of pressure off, as you know you can always fix your mistakes!

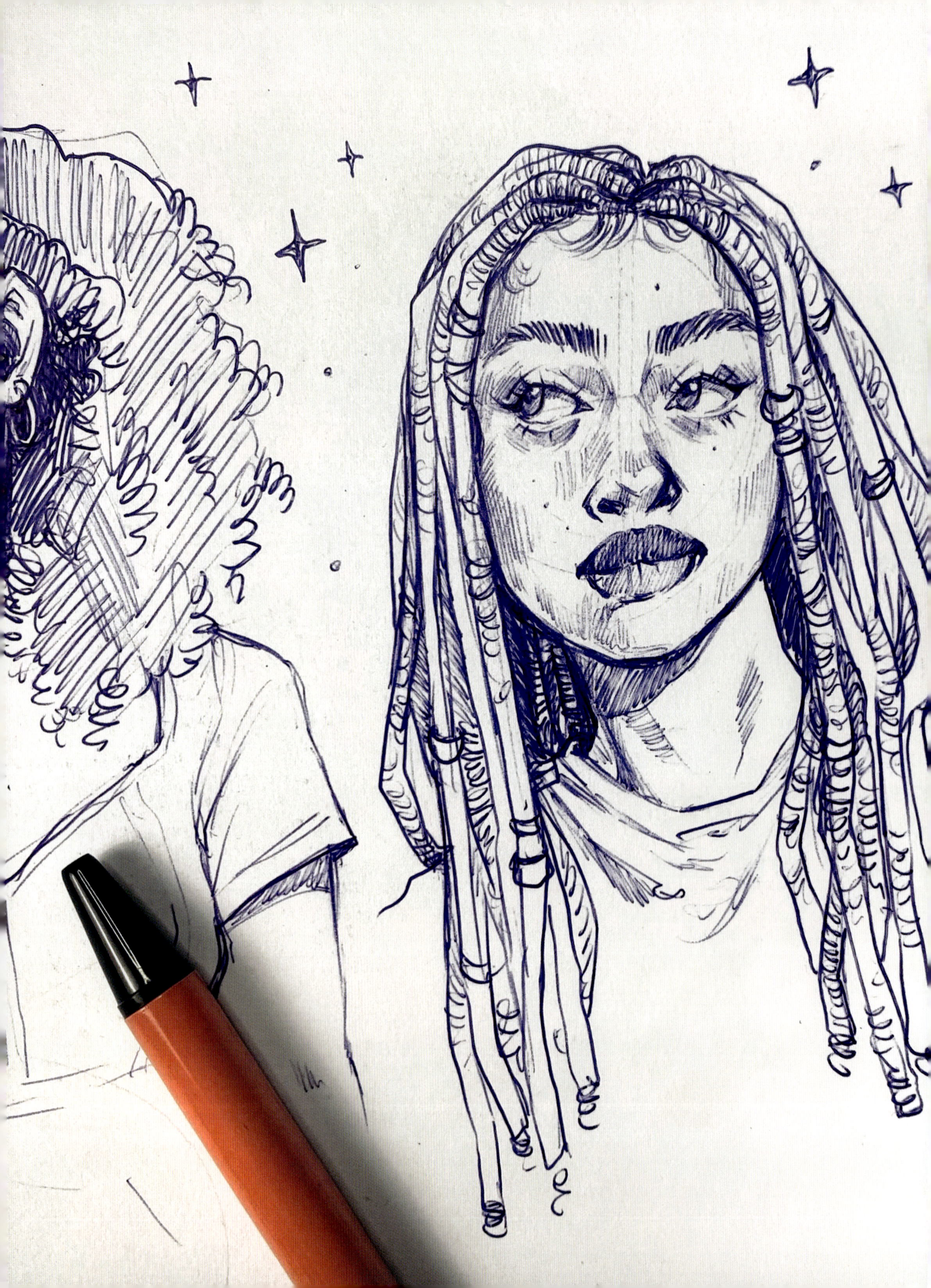

11

FURTHER PRACTICE

My biggest advice for improving your art skills is practice. It might not always be the advice everyone wants to hear, but it is truly the best thing anyone can do to get better at their craft. With every single drawing you make, you get better by a small percentage. With every drawing—good or bad—you learn something new, even if you don't realize it. But even so, practice is still a very general bit of advice. So let's have a look at some more specific exercises and ideas to keep your practice going.

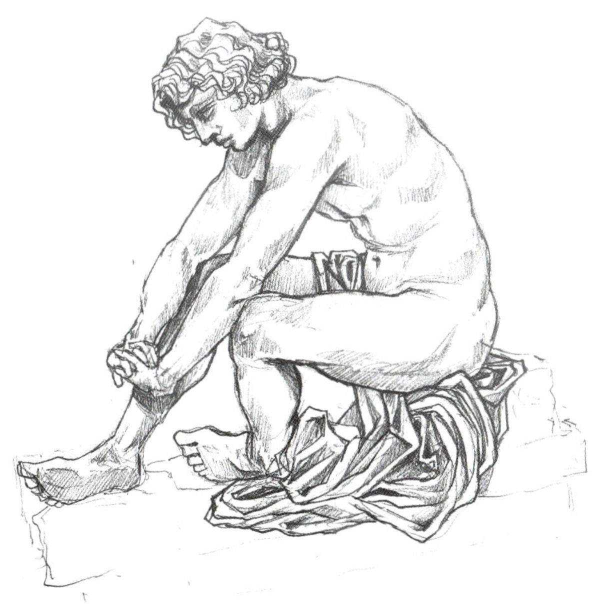

PLAYING WITH STYLES

One of the things I was taught early on in my art journey was that art rules should be learned well so that you can then break those rules to your liking. Doing this will allow you to develop your own personal art style. There are so many different art styles, and it does not just come down to how you draw certain facial features—more realistic, more cartoonish, more simplistic, a mixture of all the above, etc.

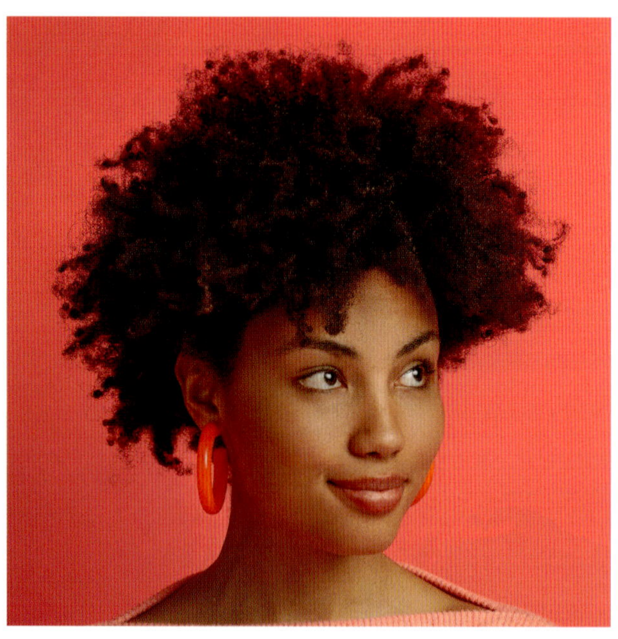

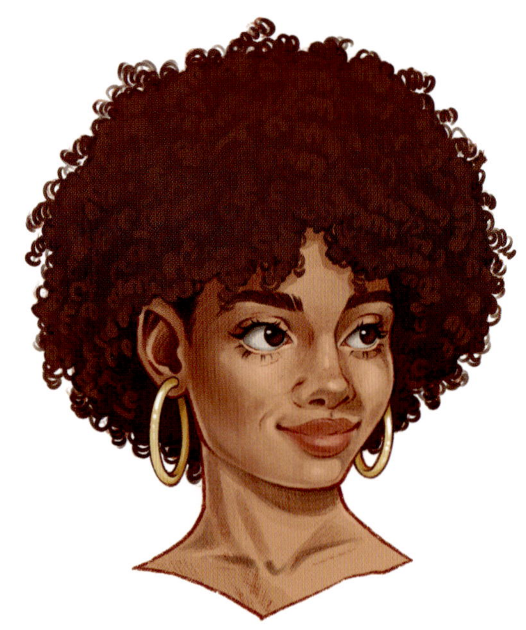

Here are just a few examples of different ways to draw eyes, noses, and mouths in different styles.

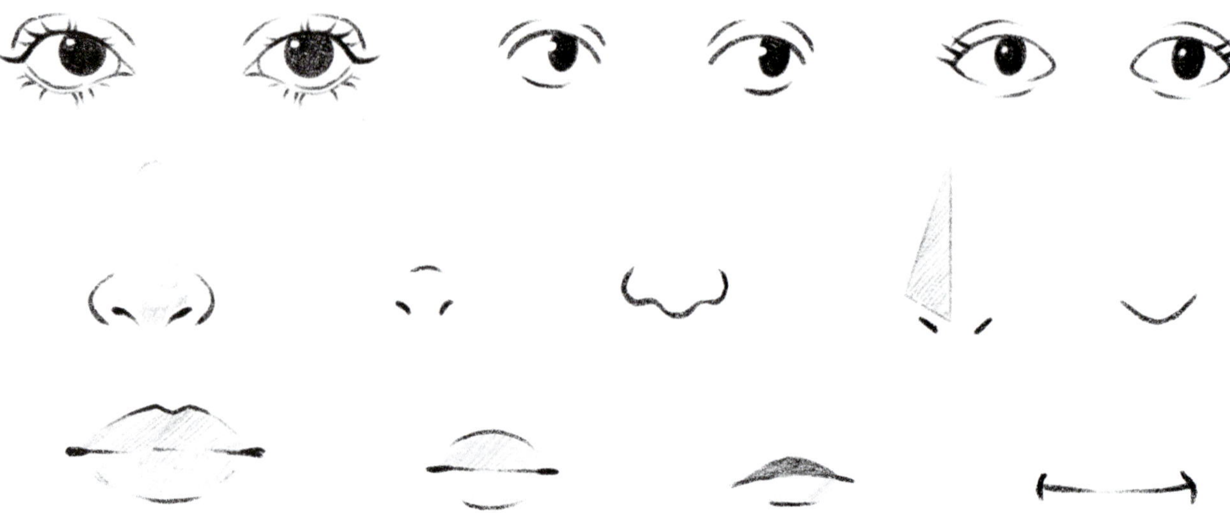

You can start picking out your favorite ways to draw characters by experimenting with different looks and shapes. Developing an art style is not done overnight—it can take a long time until you find your own niche or your favorite way to draw things. And even then, artists are constantly evolving, improving, and changing their art styles.

Art styles are a mixture of rendering techniques, color usage, composition, lighting, and so much more. Your own art style, if you choose to find one, will be a culmination of all the things you do to achieve your final drawings, both consciously and subconsciously! Don't resist your natural art style that starts to develop; instead, you should work toward it. Everyone's art style is unique to them and should be something to treasure.

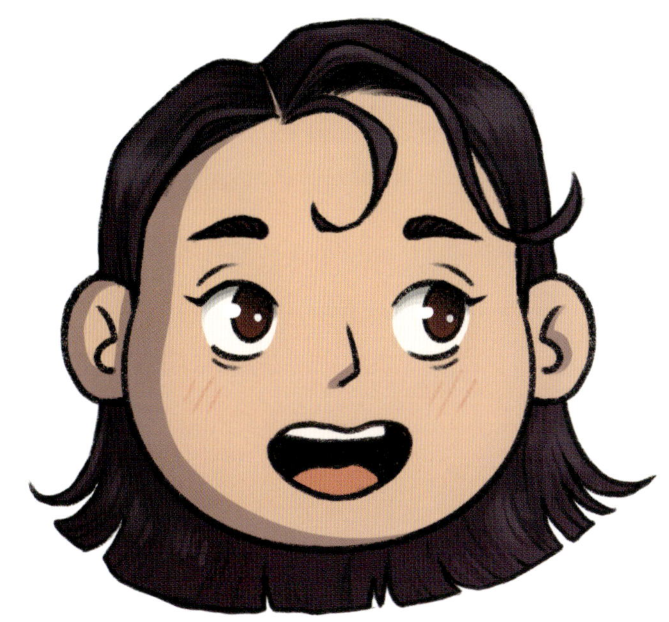

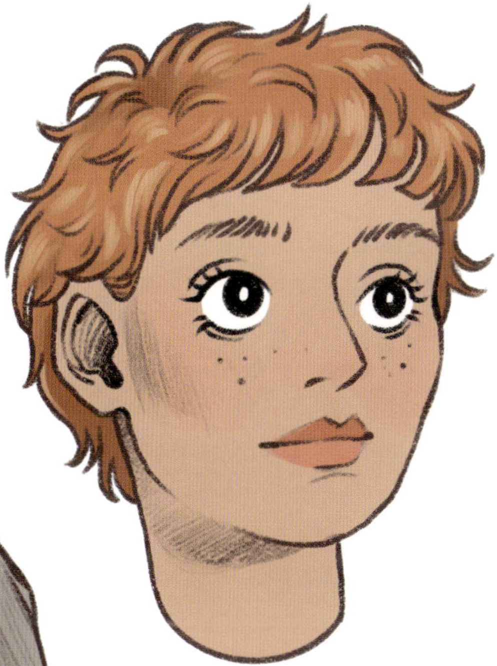

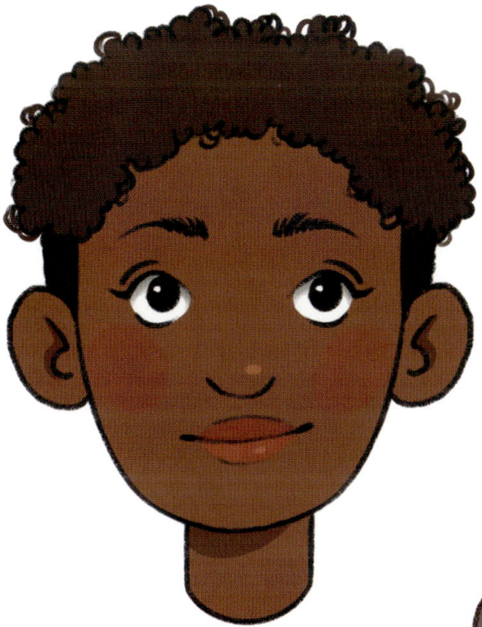

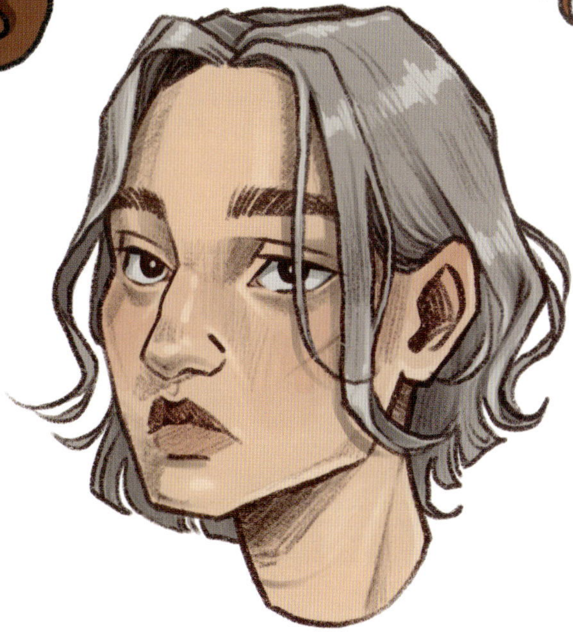

When studying portraiture, I always recommend using references for studies. You can ask your friends and family to pose for you, either for drawing or for a picture you can study later. You can also even use yourself as reference.

You can use a mirror and do some timed self-portraits from life, or you can take pictures of yourself like I did here, and use the building blocks of your face and then change the facial features, hair, etc. to suit whatever character you're drawing.

When I am lacking inspiration or need to draw a very intricate expression I have not drawn before, I turn to pages like Pinterest or Shutterstock and search for what I need. I then practice by using reference and building up my mental library of expressions.

There is no shame in using references! So don't be afraid to use images to help you learn and to keep up your practice. After all, I've been drawing for more than fourteen years, and I still use reference images for practice all the time.

Shown are some examples of how I take a reference image of a portrait and replicate it in my style for portrait sketching.

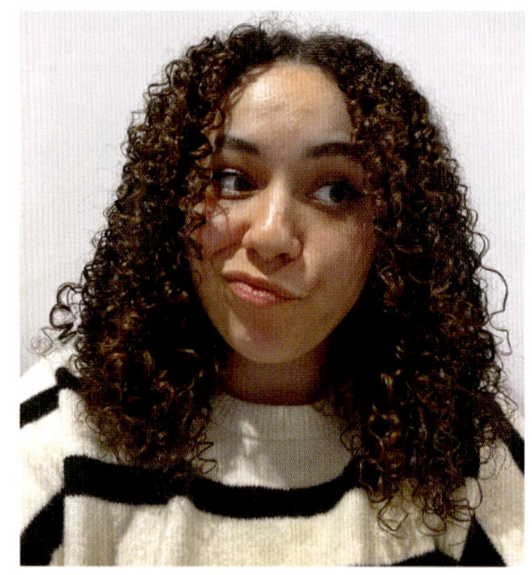
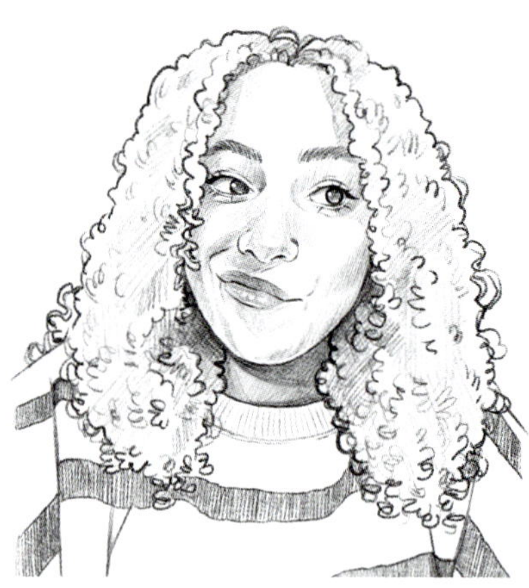
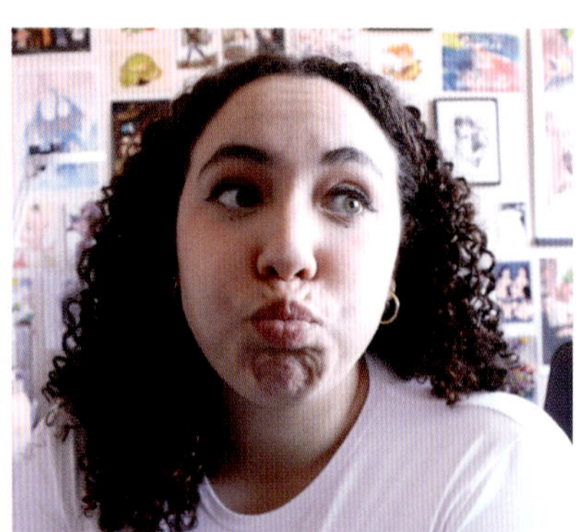
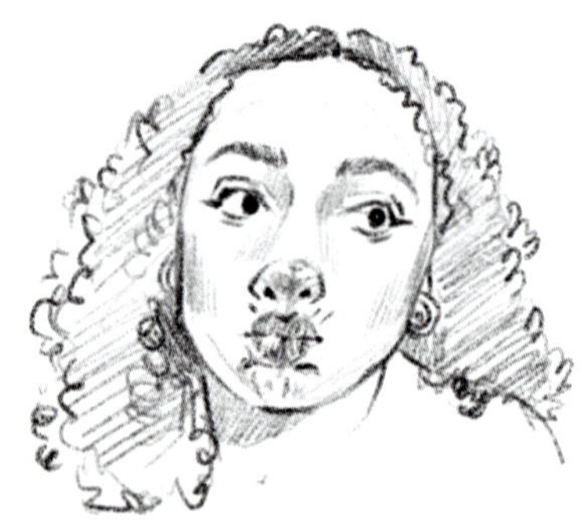
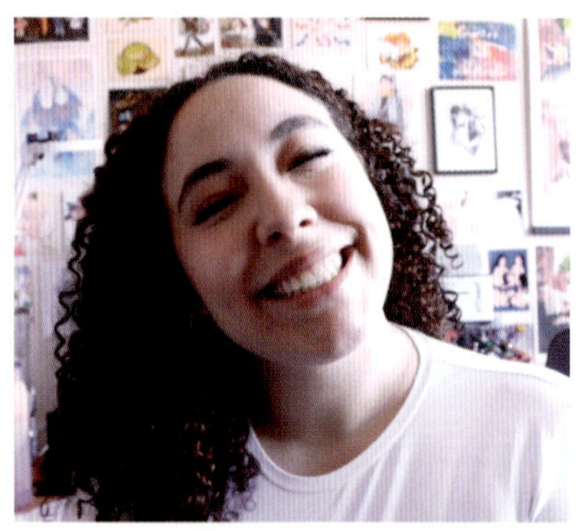
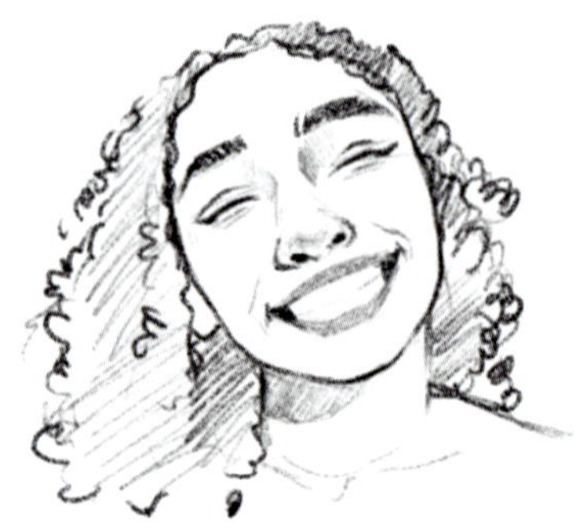
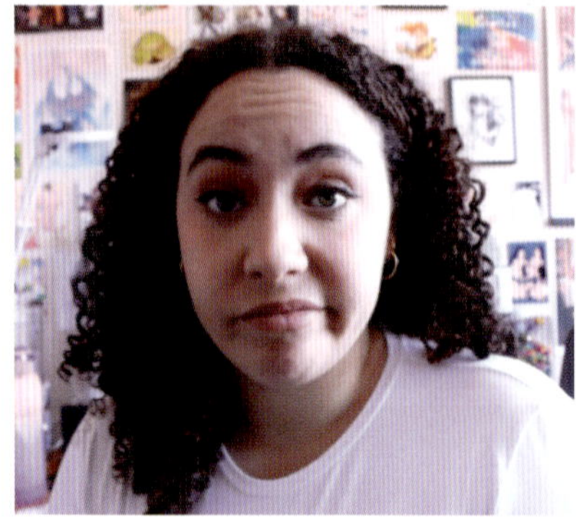
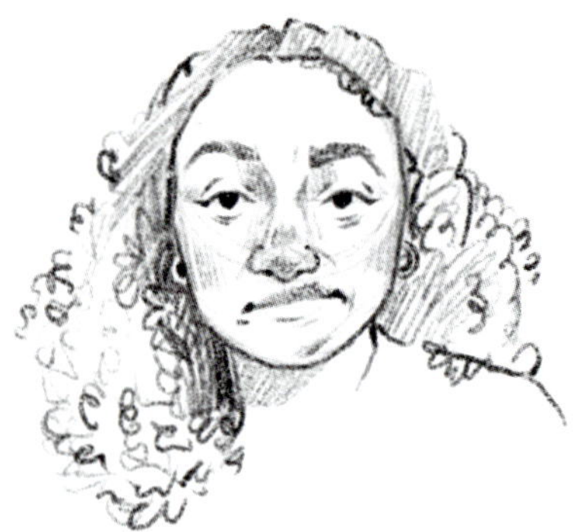

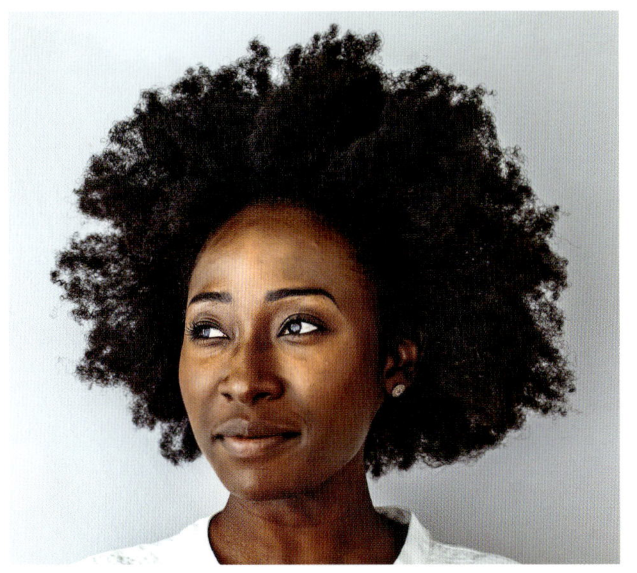

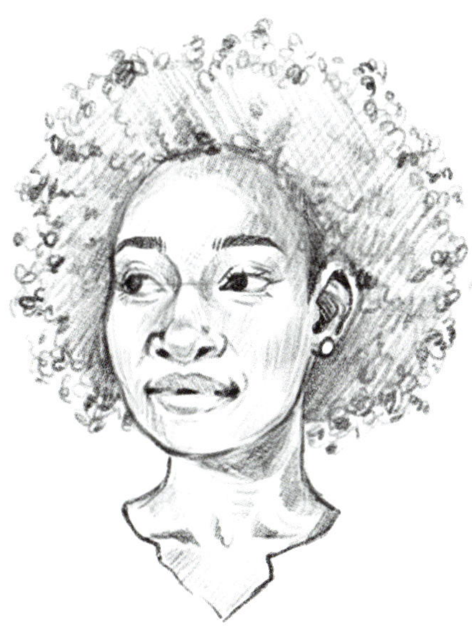

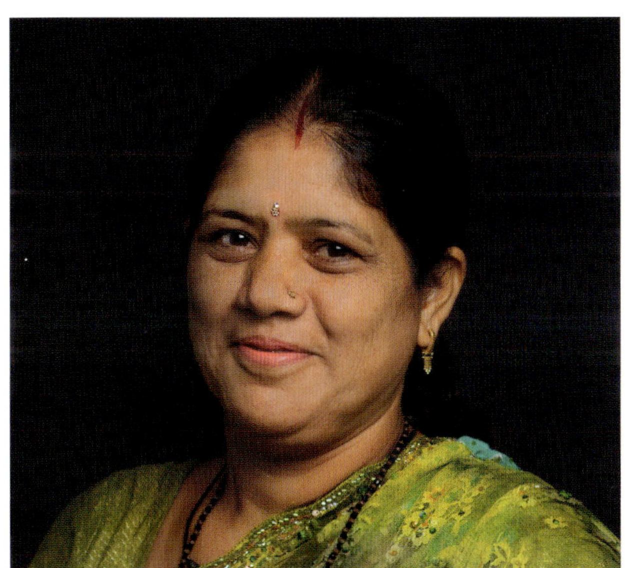

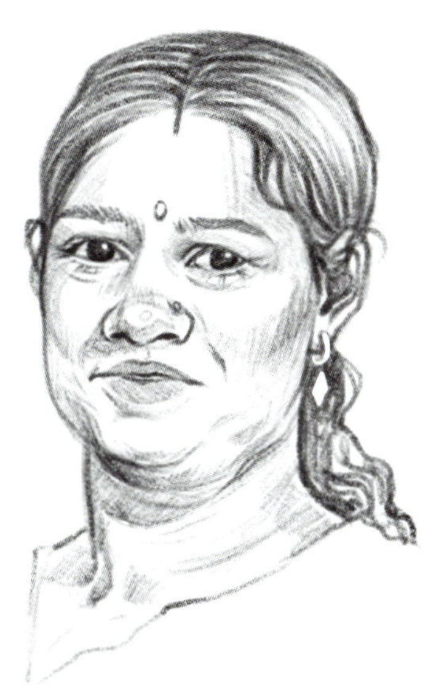

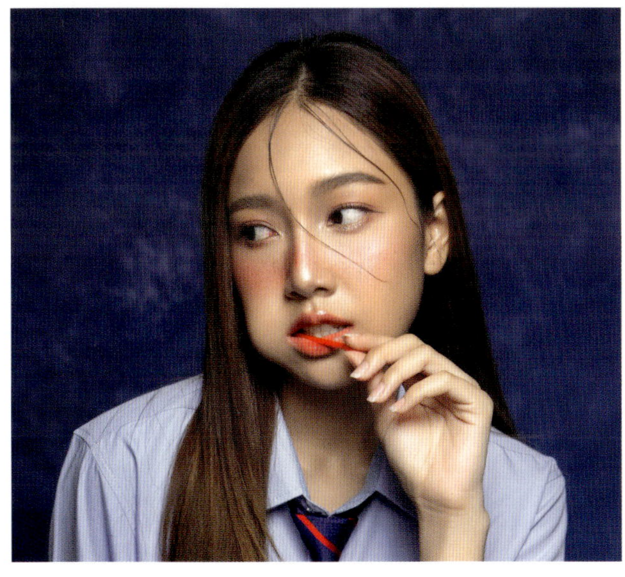

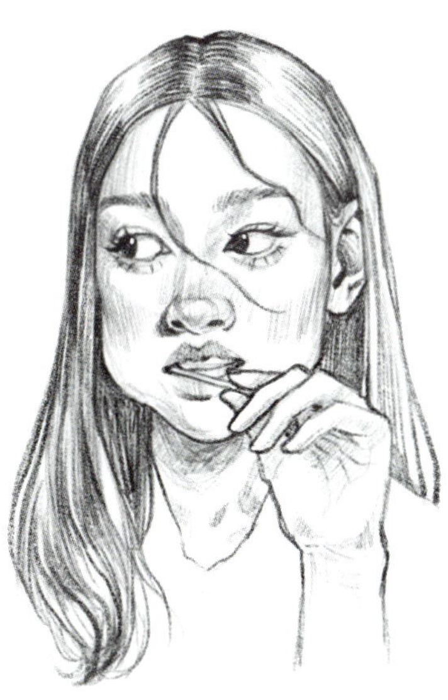

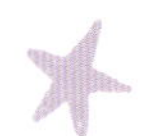

DRAWING FROM LIFE

I have developed a love for drawing in public places over the years. Usually I tend to go to coffee shops or parks. It's a whole new challenge drawing real-life people who are moving constantly—but it's an excellent exercise for a few reasons. First, you get a huge pool of subjects and models to draw from. Second, you have to be quick on your feet and try to jot down the subject onto paper before they move from their current position—and you never know when that might be! It's a great way to improve your life drawing skills, even if the drawings don't come out very polished.

Try doing some quick warm-up sketches of one to two minutes first, and check to see what things you might have missed or wished you'd jotted down, and then take that into your next sketches of five to ten minutes each.

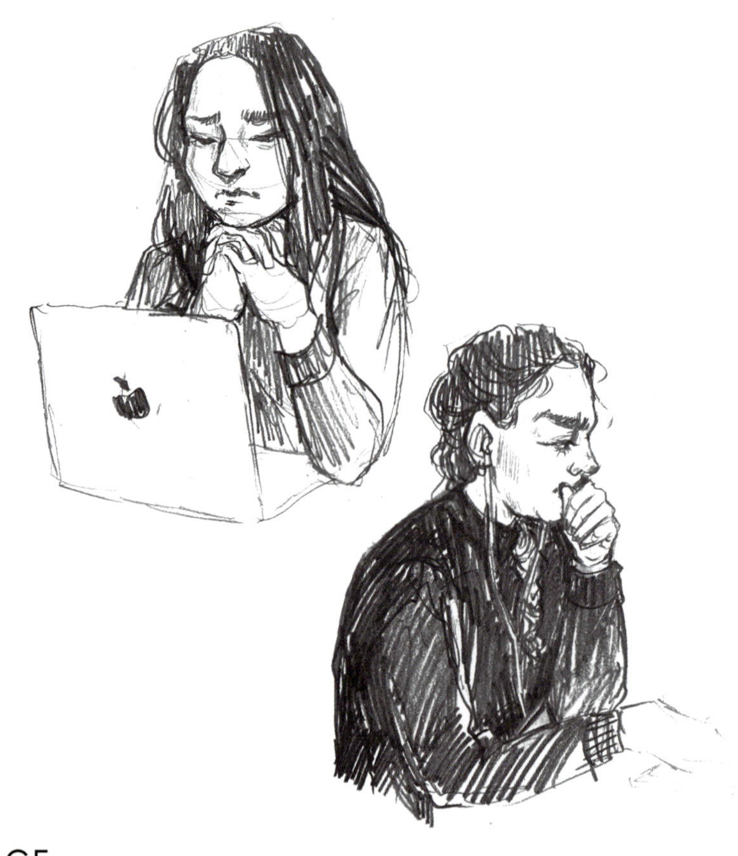

GESTURE DRAWING & SHAPE LANGUAGE

The great benefit of doing fast sketches of moving subjects is that you learn how to identify and draw out the important shape language of what you're seeing. Gesture drawing refers to the quick, messy sketching that primarily intends to depict the movement and fluidity of the subject. This is used mostly in drawings of the whole body and human anatomy studies, where you identify the line of action of the pose and draw out the basic shapes that the body is making to create that pose. The outcome is never intended to be perfect. It's purely for training.

This technique can be used for portraiture too. When looking at your subject, try to identify the general shapes of what you're seeing (much like we've done for most of this book at the beginning of every chapter) and then use those shapes to flesh out the pose and portrait.

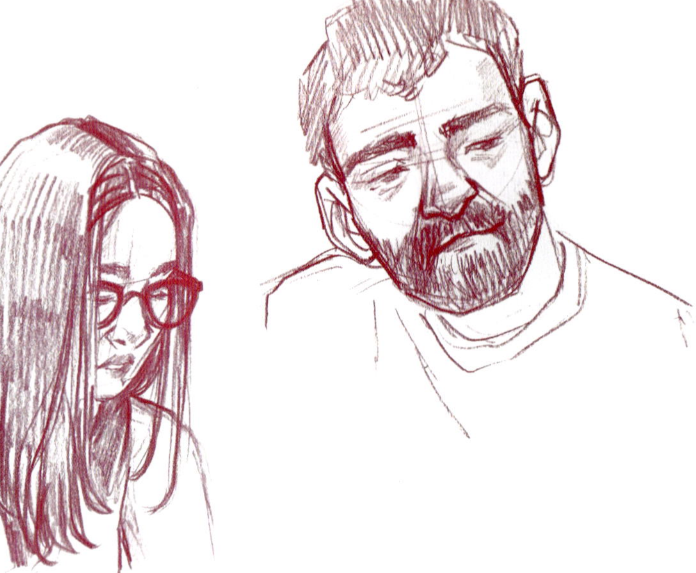

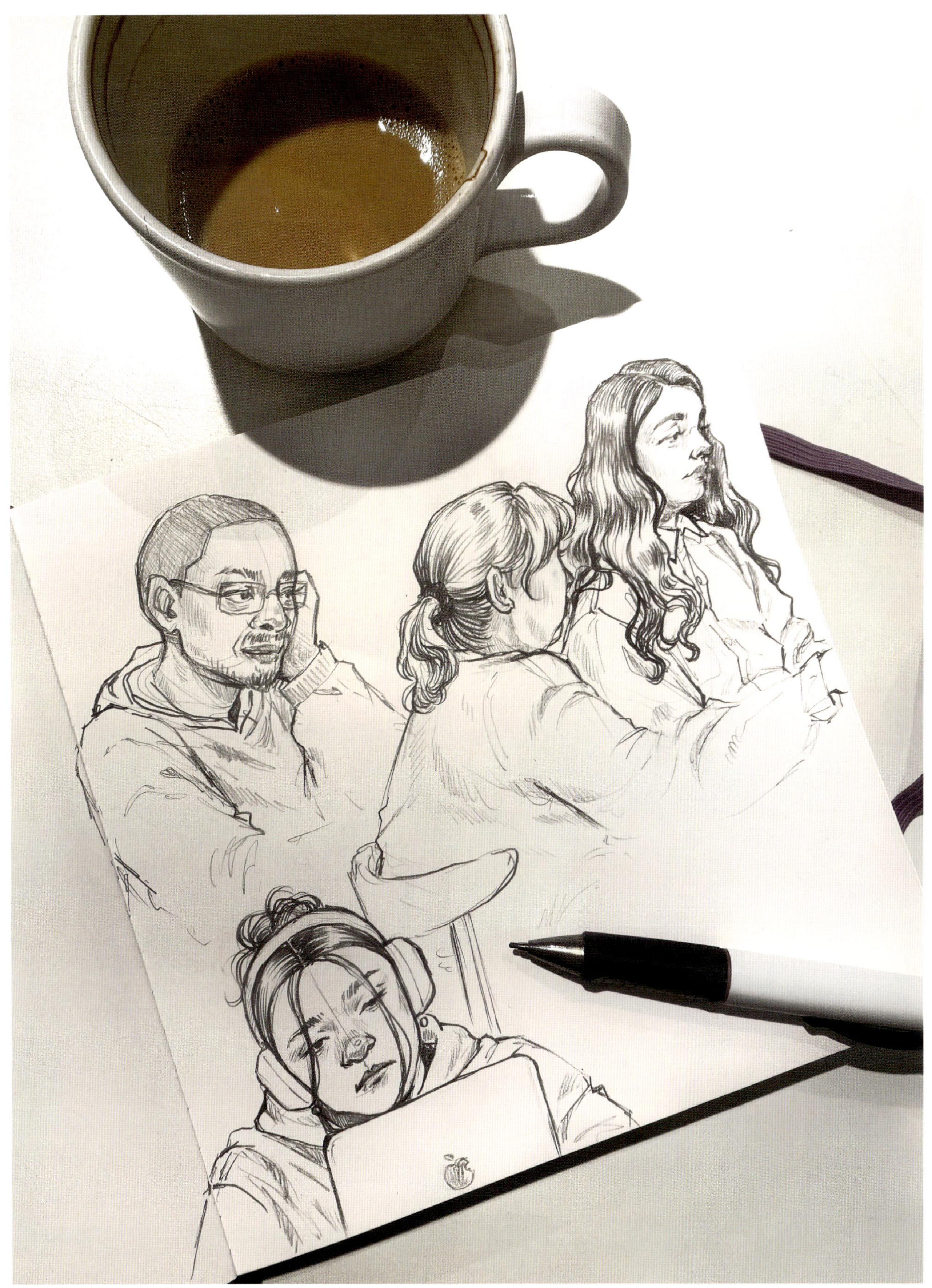

If you are a little shy, you can always try practicing drawing from life at a museum. Drawing at museums is one of my favorite things to do, as I'm surrounded by inspiration from incredible artists.

The great thing about sketching at museums is that you get to draw from references from some of the greatest artists in history, and you can draw sculptures from many different angles, meaning you have a full 360° reference for a portrait or the human figure. You also have access to tons of different styles of art from different periods to experiment with and see if any of them spark some inspiration.

You can try practicing with light and shadows, drawing specific parts or angles in the anatomy of the face, or even studying color palettes and rendering techniques used by different painters.

If you have access to a museum nearby or can travel to one, definitely make sure to use it to your advantage!

At right are examples of some drawings I made at the Louvre in Paris a few years back, and below are paintings made from references at Rijksmuseum in Amsterdam.

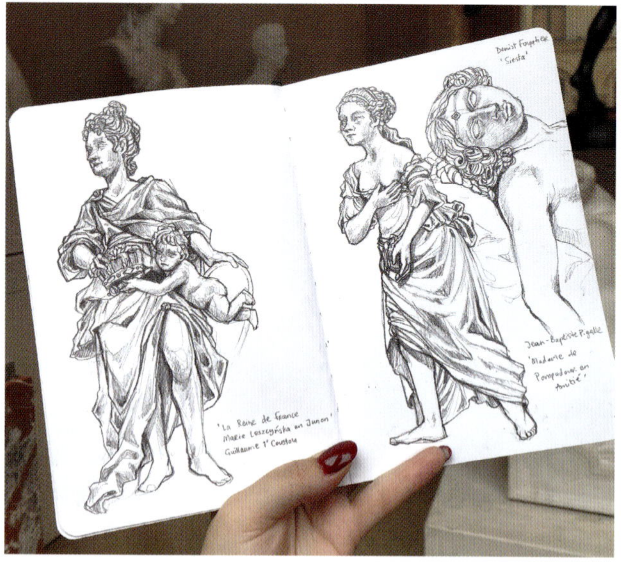

📍 The Louvre, Paris

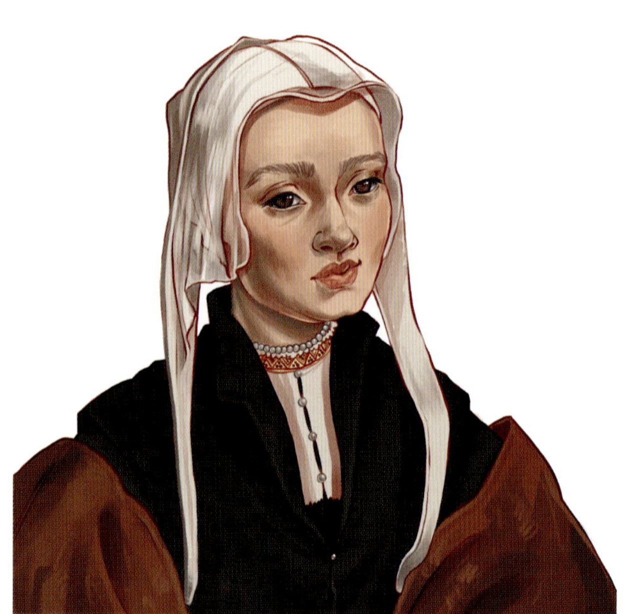

📍 Rijksmuseum, Amsterdam

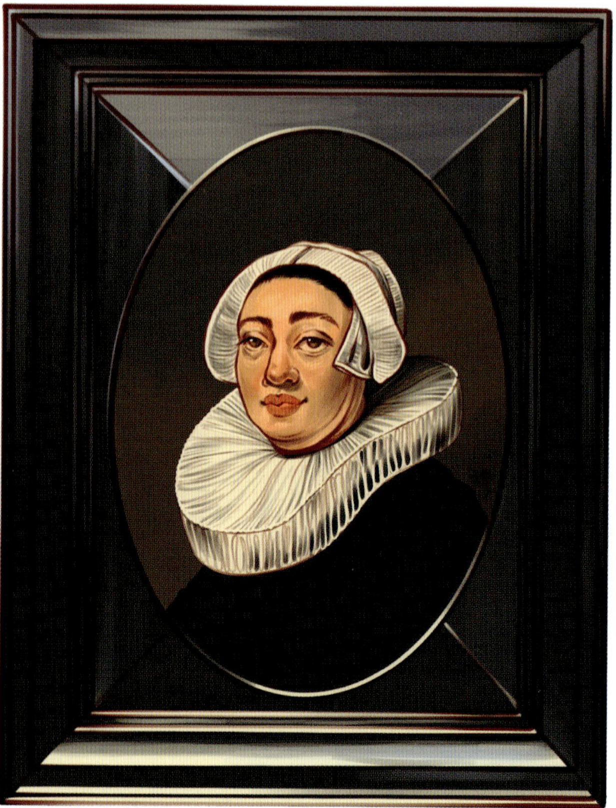

📍 Rijksmuseum, Amsterdam

DRAWING OBJECTS

You don't even need to venture out to a museum for practice or reference. One thing I did a lot when I started my art journey was draw random objects at different angles. It's a great exercise for practicing perspective and depth.

We all know what an apple looks like in theory, but it's important to have the apple in front of you to study how it might look different at different angles. Objects can look slightly skewed, and even weird, when viewed from a specific angle. So drawing objects in front of you will force you to draw exactly what you see, and not what you think the object looks like.

You can even draw the same object with different light sources to help you with your depth and shading techniques.

Drawing glass can very scary, but it's a great exercise to practice your skills of observation. Carefully study what you're seeing and try to capture the way light and shadows work through glass!

Set yourself timers when doing exercises such as these. Small five- to ten-minute sketches are enough for you to study an image and jot down the most important structures onto the paper, while keeping you motivated!

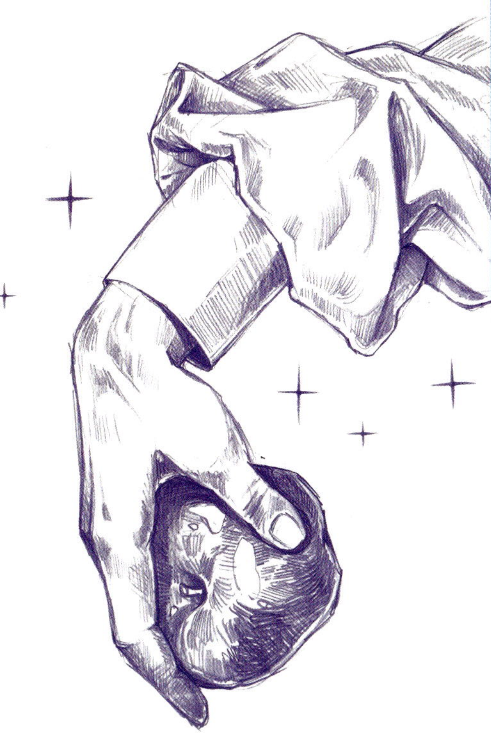

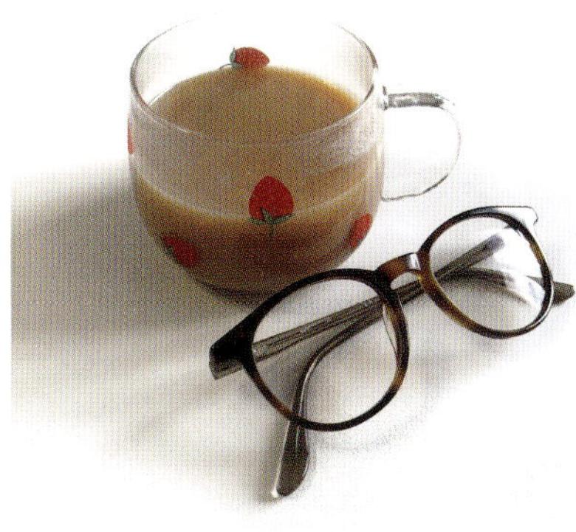

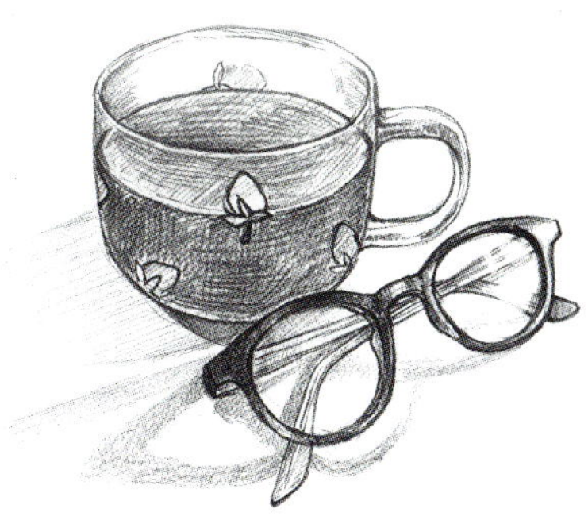

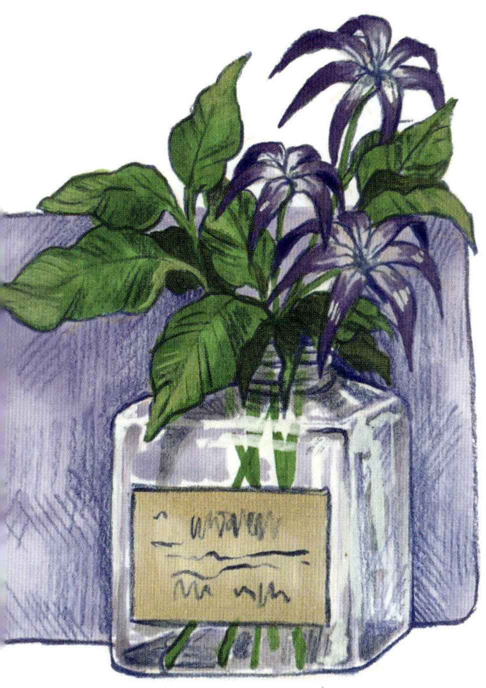

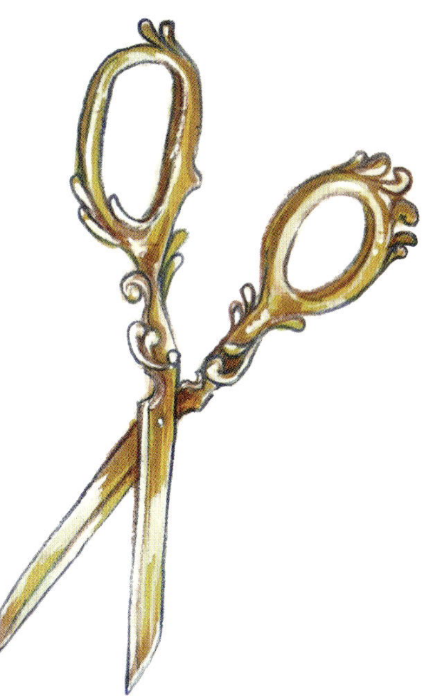

LIFE DRAWING SESSIONS

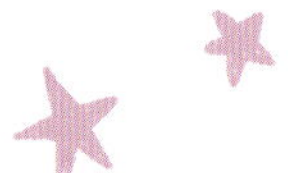

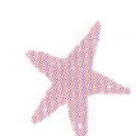

The next step after drawing people in public is taking some life drawing classes. Not only is it an incredible way to improve your skills, but you will most definitely make some friends who share something in common with you!

See if there are any places near you that host life drawing sessions (which can be nude or clothed, whatever suits you). Sessions like these usually have a model who poses for the group in different time increments. You will probably have some quicker warm-up poses of one to five minutes, and then poses up to one hour.

If this sounds too scary for you, or you don't particularly enjoy big groups of people (neither do I most days!), you can find resources online that do life drawing sessions, such as classes over Zoom. You can also use the amazing website **line-of-action.com**. On this website you can pick what kind of subjects/models you want to draw (animals, hands, feet, humans, faces, etc.) and for how long you want each pose to be up for. Essentially, you can create your own life drawing class from the comfort of your own home and take as long as you need for each drawing without the fear that someone is seeing your sketches!

Shown here you can see multiple examples of drawings I have done at life drawing sessions over the years (both in person and online).

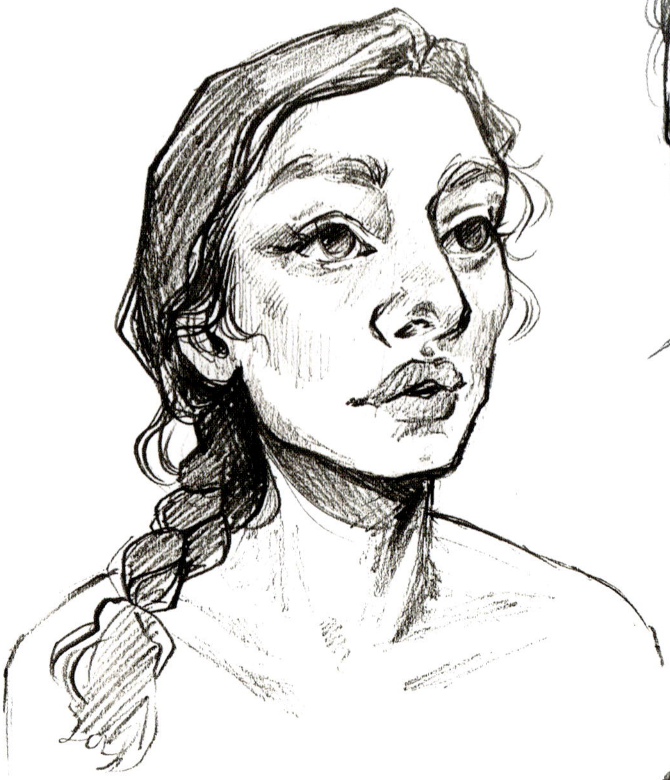

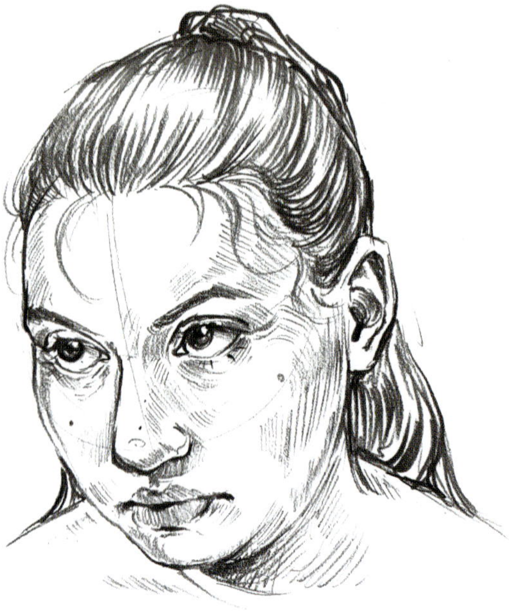

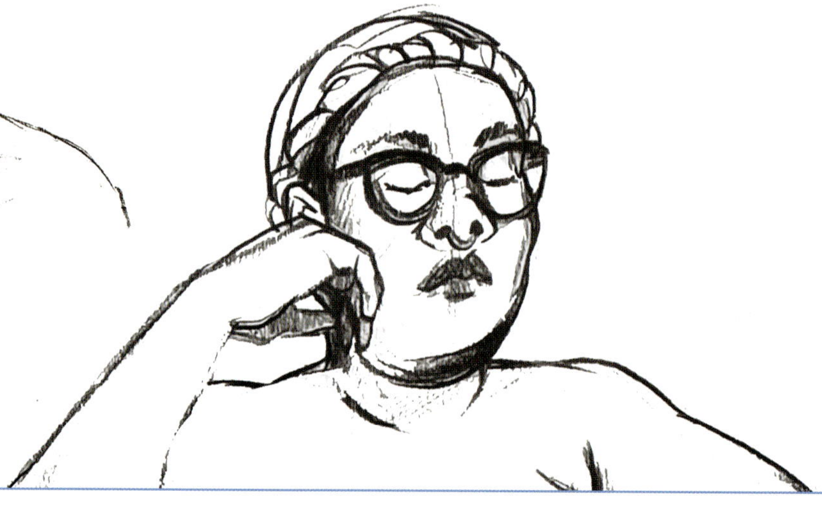

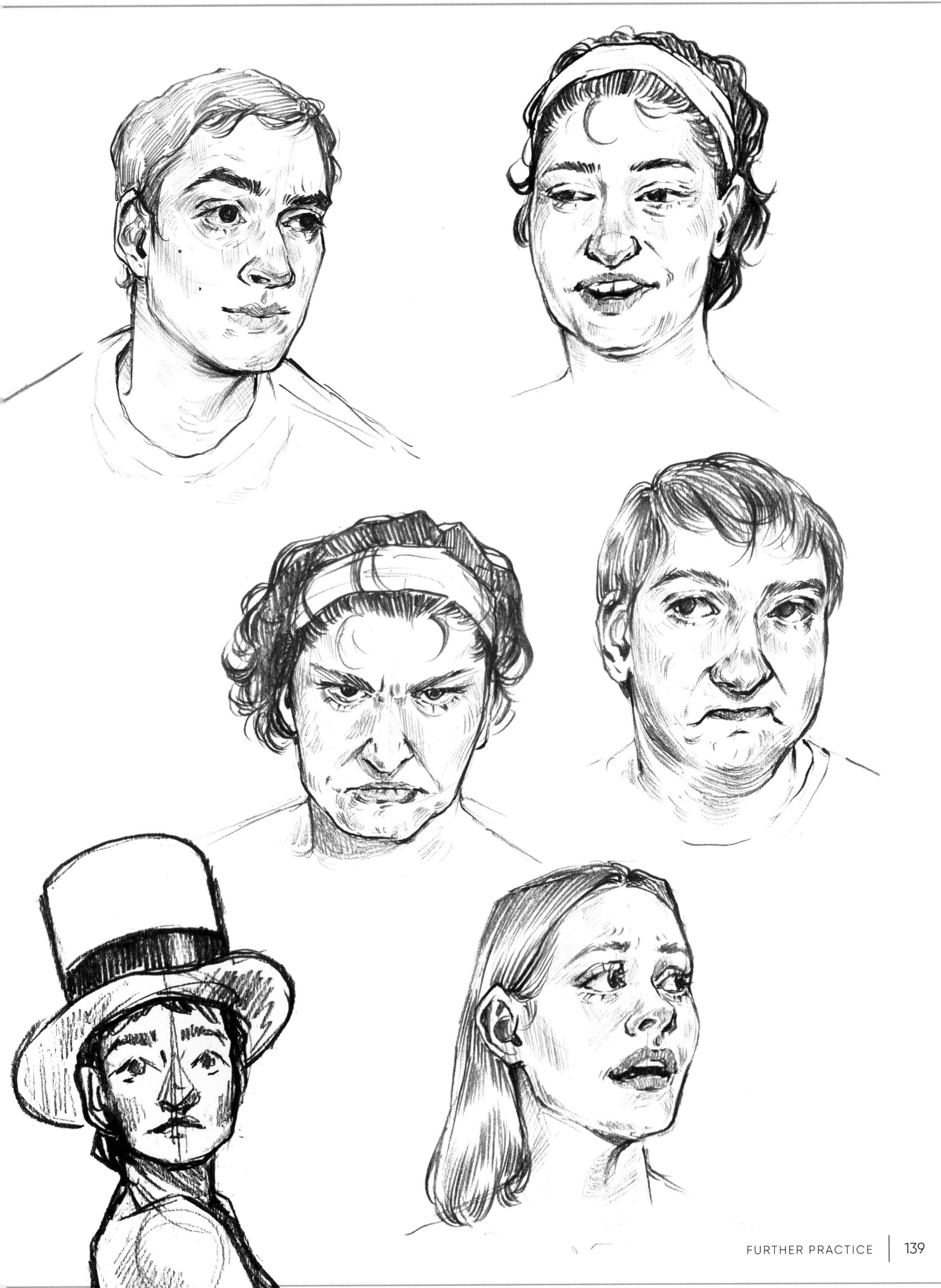

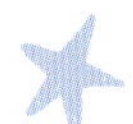

PARTING WORDS

We've reached the conclusion of this book, but I hope that you have only reached the beginning of your creative journey. This book has been a labor of love, a passion project, a love letter to portraiture and art. Hopefully you will have absorbed some of that love into your own practice and allow yourself to enjoy every step in your artistic path—even in moments when you might feel slightly discouraged or unmotivated.

I would like to leave you with some advice that I wish I had been given early in my creative journey:

- Remember that everyone who climbs a ladder must begin on the first step. Some people might be a few steps ahead of you, but they were still where you were at one point. In moments when you might feel discouraged by your art and find yourself comparing your work to that of others, remind yourself that everyone has had to go through a learning stage to get where they are now.

- Please keep reminding yourself of the reason why you picked up a pencil (or this book) for the first time. Remember the way you felt when you would draw without any care or agenda as a child, and allow yourself to create like that again from time to time.

- Don't get rid of those old drawings and paintings. If you ever find yourself feeling like you're stuck in your journey or like you haven't improved as you'd hoped, look back on those older drawings. See how much you have improved over time and think of how proud your younger self would be of where you are now.

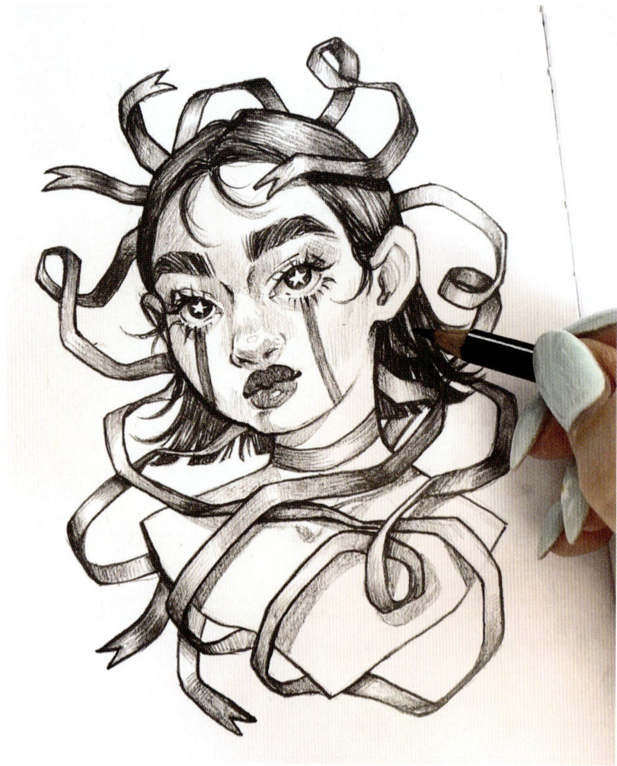

- Finally, trust the process. This is applicable to both your creative journey and any piece of art you make. Never give up and you will get you there. And even if you don't get where you expected, revel in the fact that you did something creative and lovely for yourself.

I hope this book has helped give you a comfortable starting point from which you can take your practice into your own hands. A life without art and color would be boring and gray. So, add a splash of joy into your life whenever you can.

RESONANCES

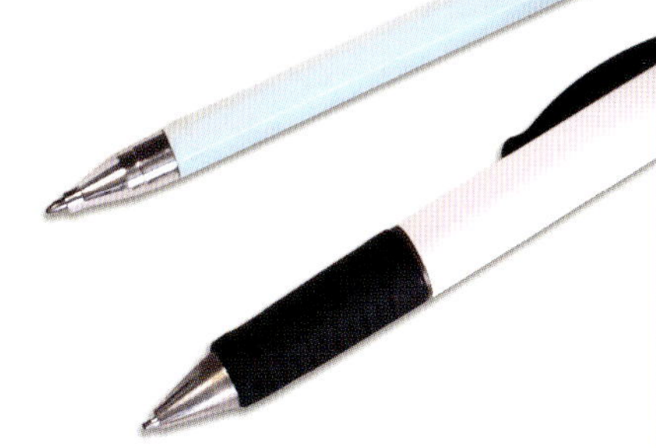

RESOURCES

ART SUPPLIES

Here is a list of art supplies I recommend:

- Graphite pencil set that contains pencils from 2H or HB up to 6B or 8B. I recommend the Derwent or Faber-Castell sets. They are affordable and high-quality.

- The best kneaded eraser I have found is from Faber-Castell. I have used the same one for years, and it still serves me wonderfully.

- A good set of colored pencils does not have to be extensive in color range (or in price). I always recommend the Arteza Expert colored pencils for anyone, but if you'd like to spend a little more, the Faber-Castell Polychromo pencils are super high-quality and a set for life.

- Gouache is very accessible to find, as it's used a lot in schools and marketed for young artists. I am a big fan of the HIMI Miya jelly gouache paints but also love to use some tubed gouache from Holbein when I feel a little more fancy.

- If you are in the market for a nice sketchbook, might I recommend anything from Seawhite of Brighton, Talens Art Creations, or Cass Art? These brands all make incredibly affordable and high-quality sketchbooks with thick paper that you can experiment with different materials on. I also sell my own sketchbook in my online shop, which has an illustrated cover by yours truly.

ONLINE LIFE DRAWING

The website **line-of-action.com** is an incredible free resource for reference and timed drawing classes. You can choose what kind of reference you want to draw, how many poses, and for how long you'd like to be shown each pose. You can basically curate your own life drawing session just for yourself.

FURTHER TUTORIALS & CONTENT FROM ME

If you'd like to see more content like this book from me, you can find me on YouTube under "Pypah's Art," where you'll find a huge library of video content from over the years.

You can also find me online on Patreon and most social platforms **@pypahs_art**, where I also post short-form content and share my own creative journey and life as a small-business owner.

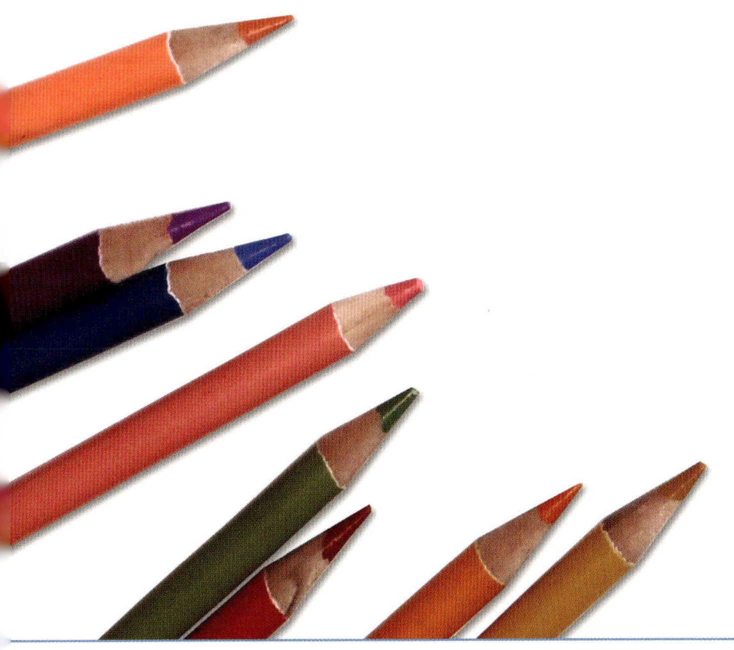

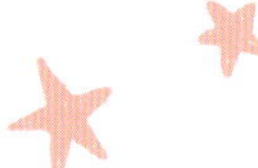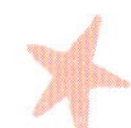

ABOUT THE AUTHOR

Filipa "Pypah" Santos is a Portuguese freelance illustrator, animator, and art content creator. She was born and raised in Porto, Portugal, and went on to continue her studies in illustration and animation in the UK, where she got her degree in animation. She now works from her studio in Manchester, UK, creating content online about her art and small business, running her online shop, Patreon, and doing freelance work.

Since she was young, Pypah has shown an interest in drawing and art more than other children around her, which inspired her parents to put her in drawing, painting, and sculpting lessons under the tutelage of a local artist, João Pedro Rodrigues. Alongside his teachings and her constant practice throughout her teen years, Pypah learned all the traditional techniques and mediums of art, which allowed her to broaden her creativity into various pathways.

Pypah loves to create illustrations that are colorful, dreamy, vibrant, and essentially portrait-based. She has always enjoyed drawing faces and continues to draw characters as the subjects of her artworks. Using both traditional and digital mediums alike, Pypah works as an artist full-time—sharing her work online and teaching others how to draw as well, guiding them through their artistic journeys.

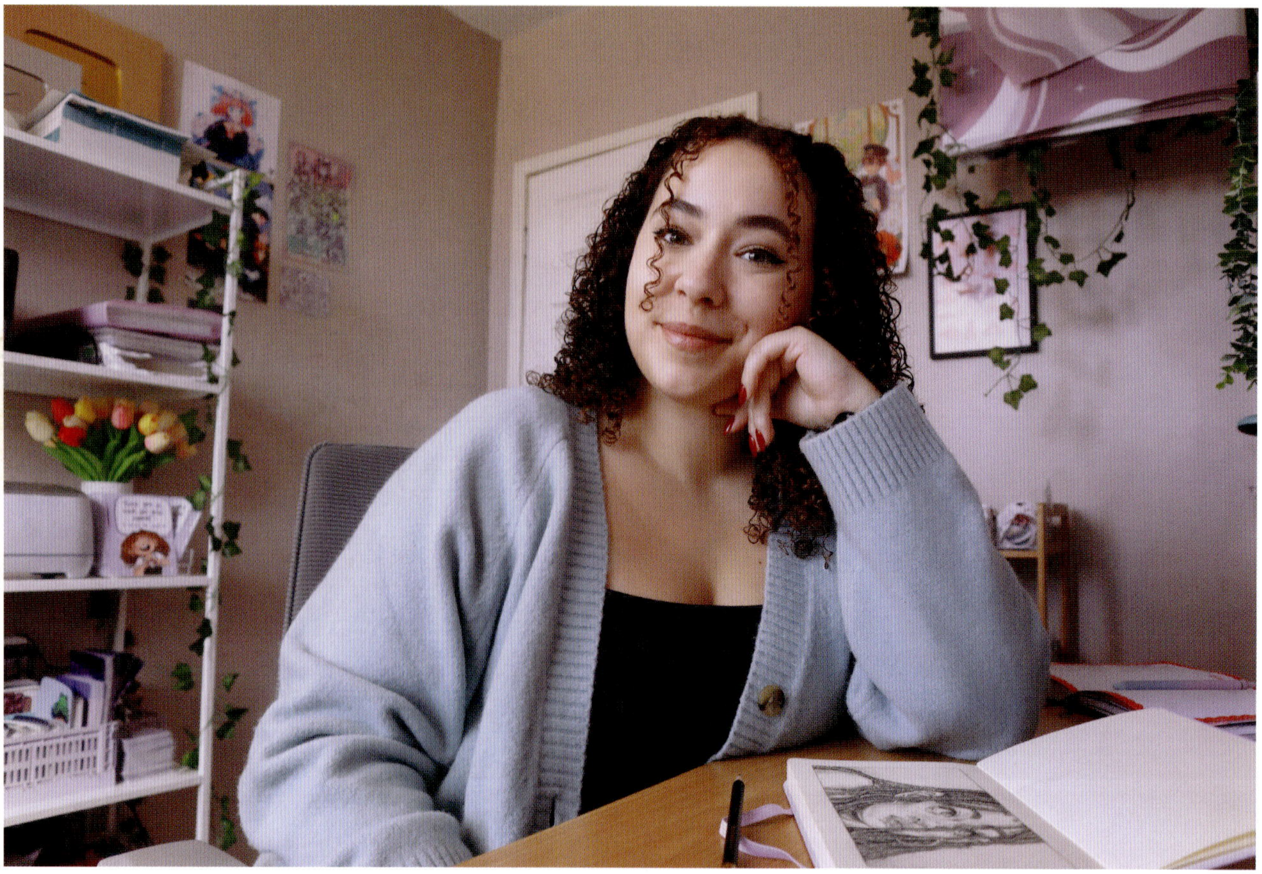

INDEX

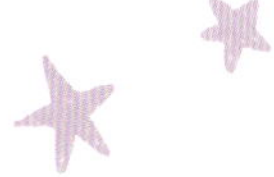

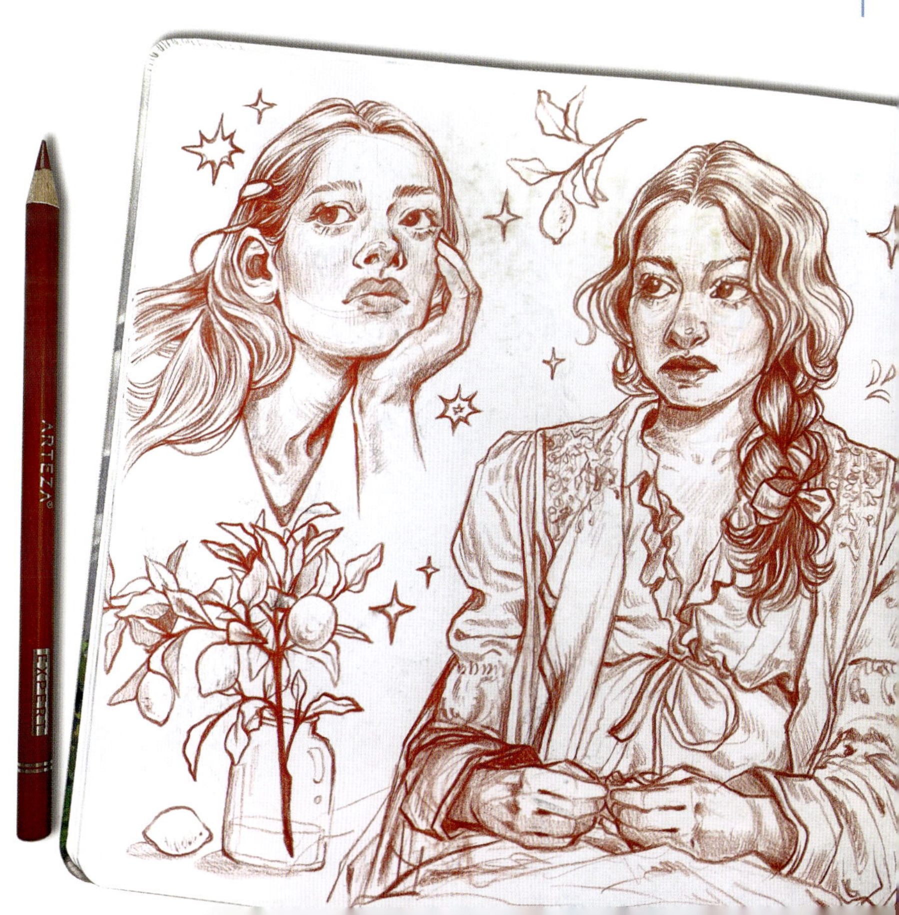